ACROSS CRETE

About the transliteration

It is impossible to transliterate Greek words into English in a completely satisfying way. Here we have chosen a system which fits in well with classical
Greek, the Greek which educated 18th- and 19th-century travellers would have
been familiar with before leaving for abroad. The accents indicate where the
stress lies in Modern Greek. In the quotations the transliteration used by the
authors is maintained.

The compiler

Johan de Bakker, who compiled this book, specialized on the Middle East and
North Africa and has published on Moroccan history, but lost his heart to Crete
thirty years ago. He travelled extensively on the island and studied its history in
the early Modern Age. With this book and its two sequels a full account of
Crete's discovery in the 18th and 19th centuries is provided.

The Apokórona

Across Crete

PART ONE

FROM KHANIÁ TO HERÁKLEION

Compiled by JOHAN DE BAKKER

World Discovery Guide Books

First edition, 2001

Published by
Logos Tekstproducties
P.O. Box 3342
1001 AC Amsterdam
The Netherlands

Translations by Susan Strickler, Amsterdam, The Netherlands
Cover design and layout by Brigitte Slangen, Nijmegen, The Netherlands
Maps by UvA-Kaartenmakers, Amsterdam, The Netherlands
Typeset in Janson mt and Scala sans; printed on Muncken Book paper
Printed and bound in Belgium by Snoeck Ducaju & Zoon

Notice: this book is compiled to provide *divertissement* and so has no scholarly preten-
sions. Of course, its editor has sought for accuracy and soundness, but nevertheless
flaws and misinterpretations may occur. The reader is kindly requested to be indulgent
in this matter and to inform the publisher of any inaccuracies. In following editions
these can then be corrected.

ISBN 90 806150 1 3

Contents

About this series

Modern travellers are hardly able to find pristine lands these days. So-called western civilization has penetrated everywhere and the wonders of the unknown have had to make room for the attractions of tourism.

But not long ago travellers could find regions where people lived who had hardly ever seen any foreigners other than tax gatherers, plunderers or military men, all invaders from an alien world. Only the occasional peddlar would have been a familiar figure from the outside.

This series attempts to show the wonders of the world as they were first seen by visitors who laid down their experiences for later generations. By following their travels the modern visitor can get a sense of the impression which the then forbidden and dangerous world must have made, only a short time ago. And the modern traveller can feel the drive and curiosity of those first adventurers who, without planes or cars, without the comforts of modern civilization, and often without maps, dared to enter unknown worlds.

Just why did they do it? Some wanted to preach the gospel to the heathens. Others were in the service of empires and were preparing colonial enterprises. Still others did it in the name of science or as part of their education. Some were just curious or restless. And in most cases it was a mixture of all of these.

Many of them wrote down their experiences. And when they did, the civilized reading public in Europe and America was thrilled and captivated. This is what this series wants to achieve: that you, in your armchair or on your comfortable beach bed, feel as if you were an adventurer, too.

Each book in this series contains a collection of travel descriptions dating from before the advent of mass tourism. The descriptions are organized as stages of a tour across a region. Each stage is preceded by a description of the modern setting of the region and its past.

Moreover, each book contains a selection of legends, stories, poems, press cuttings etc., all forming part of our common memory or imposing themselves on its editor as inevitable.

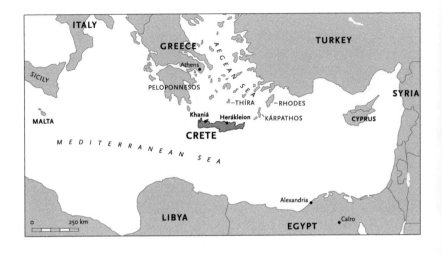

Historical overview

The history of Crete is determined to an important extent by its location: between Europe, Asia and Africa, at a strategic junction of sea routes through which commodities, cultural influences, and conquerors moved. Here we give an overview which is necessarily terse and, Crete's history still being the object of much debate, full of personal interpretation. In the different chapters of this book the past of each region is described more in detail.

Until 1898 (the beginning of autonomy), the following periods can be distinguished:

6500 – 3000 B.C.: Neolithic Period

Shipping using reed rafts and hollowed-out tree trunks developed in the Aegean Sea, and a first wave of immigration appears to have reached Crete from Asia Minor around 6500 B.C. The immigrants were agriculturalists and they brought their cultivation crops and domesticated animals with them. They lived in huts of mud bricks clustered in villages, or in caves. They spun and wove wool, and made crude earthenware pottery. Obsidian was also used for making all kinds of objects (it was imported from the island of Mílos). A mother goddess was worshipped and some caves served a cultic function. The dead were buried in caves and chasms.

3000 – 1900 B.C.: Prepalatial Period

A new wave of immigration from Asia Minor brought with it the arts of copper and bronze forging. Cities developed and the exchange of commodities by sea increased. The vessels used were paddled longships (canoe-like). Wine and olive oil were produced, as well as woven fabrics. The dead were buried not only in caves but also in beehive tombs. There was much ritual connected with burials. Cultic buildings were built at Knossós.

1900 – 1700 B.C.: Minoan Period: Protopalatial

The use of sailing vessels developed. The routes of exchange reached mainland Greece, the Greek islands, Egypt, Asia Minor, Syria, and Italy. The two metals of which bronze is composed, copper and tin, were imported from overseas. Gold, silver, perfumes and ivory were also imported. Items that were exported included bronze objects, wine, olive oil, wood, and woolen fabrics. The cities grew larger during this time. Cultic centers came into being, which had an administrative and economic function as well: the so-called 'first palaces' of Knossós, Faistós, Mállia and Káto Zákros. Peak sanctuaries also had a cultic function. Writing developed during this period, in the form of hieroglyphics which have not yet been deciphered. The potter's wheel was introduced.

1700 – 1500 B.C.: Minoan Period: Neopalatial

Around 1700 B.C. an earthquake and the resulting fires destroyed the palaces of the Protopalatial Period. They were rebuilt, even larger this time. 'Villas' blossomed: cultic centers with economic and administrative functions, like the palaces but on a smaller scale. Among these were the villa's of Ayía Triádha, Vathýpetro, Týlissos, Zóminthos and Sklavókambos. Contacts remained with the Greek mainland, the Greek islands, Egypt, Asia Minor, Syria and Italy. But contacts now also stretched as far as the Baltics, Britain, and Scandinavia, although probably through middlemen. Knossós was the main cultic and economic center. A mother goddess was still worshipped, and there was a bull cult. The peak sanctuaries also remained important during this time. The Linear A script, not yet deciphered, was used.

1500 – 1100 B.C.: Mycenaean Period: Postpalatial

Around 1500 B.C. the volcano of Thíra, an island north of Crete, erupted and partly collapsed, and a tidal wave struck the northern coast of Crete. The island was covered with a layer of ash and lava. The palaces were again destroyed. The Akhaians, Greek-speaking pirates from the Peloponnesos, grabbed their chance and occupied Crete. A number of the Minoan palaces were rebuilt by the Akhaians, but on a smaller scale. Knossós and Kydonía were probably the most important cities at this time. The Akhaians had a culture which was influenced by the Minoan civilization and which is commonly called Mycenaean after their most prominent city, Mycene, on the Peloponnesos. Their culture was, however, noticeably more warlike than the Minoan and their most important gods were male rather than female. At this time the dead were buried in sarcophagi in chamber tombs as well as in beehive tombs. Their ships, in addition to sails, had rows of rowers on top of each other, making them usable as war ships. Their Greek language was written in Linear B, a derivative of Linear A (Linear B has been deciphered).

1100 – 650 B.C.: The Dark Ages: Geometric and Orientalizing Periods

Around 1100 B.C. the Mycenaean civilization disappeared, on the Greek mainland as well as on Crete, and with it went the presence of the Akhaians. Prosperity also disappeared. According to some historians there was a destructive invasion of Dorians, relations of the Akhaians. They were pastoralists using iron and speaking Greek, although a different dialect from the Akhaians. Whatever the role of these invaders, after 1100 B.C. iron replaceed bronze as the preferred metal for weapons and tools, and city life in Crete withdrew to practically inaccessible settlements far from the coast, the so-called 'refuge settlements'. Cremation came into fashion. The pottery of this period was decorated with geometric patterns.

After 850 B.C. there was a cultural and economic revival, and pottery decoration showed influences from the Near East. City-states, politically and culturally analogous to the Dorian cities on the Peloponnesos, came into existence all over Crete. Aggressive aristocracies governed these city-states and war characterized inter-city relations. The Greek pantheon, such as Homer and Hesiod canonized it, was henceforth worshipped. Remnants of the Minoan beliefs, however, remained.

650 – 67 B.C.: Archaic, Classical and Hellenistic Periods

The conservative Dorian warrior culture continued to dominate, and Crete did not take part in the cultural prosperity evident elsewhere in Greece, particularly in Athens. The city-states in Crete fought against each other regularly and the surplus of warriors became an important export commodity. Varying alliances formed between the cities. Piracy emerged in the harbour cities. The Greek script as we know it was introduced, as were coins. In the Hellenistic Period (323-69 B.C) the Cretan cities were often allied to rivalling foreign powers such as Egypt, Rhodes and Pergamum.

67 B.C. – 395 A.D.: Roman Period

In 69 B.C. a Roman army invaded Crete, under the leadership of Quintus Metellus. Most of the cities offered powerful resistance, but Metellus was able to conquer the island in three years. Together with Cyrenaica in

Libya, Crete became a Roman province, with Górtyn on the Messará plain as its capital. The Messará plain formed one of Rome's major granaries. There was political stability and prosperity. Cities flourished: roads, bridges and aqueducts were built, as were temples, theaters and villas. Around 50 A.D. St. Paul and St. Titus brought Christianity to Crete. Under the emperor Decius (c. 250 A.D.) there was persecution of Christians, but in the 4th century Christianity became the state religion in the Roman Empire, and so also in Crete.

395 – 824: First Byzantine Period

In 395 the Roman Empire was split. Crete belonged to the eastern part which was governed from Constantinople (also known as Byzantium). Civilization was still mainly urban in aspect, and many basilicas were built in the cities. Crete suffered, however, from a series of large earthquakes and a severe plague epidemic. After 731, Crete formed part of the Patriarchate of Constantinople.

824 – 961: Muslim Period

In 824 a Muslim force from Alexandria conquered Crete for the Abbasids (the ruling caliphs in Baghdad). Al-Khandaq (Herákleion) became the seat of administration. From al-Khandaq marauding expeditions were made to the Byzantine coast. Part of the Cretan population became Muslim. City life in general deteriorated.

961 – 1204: Second Byzantine Period

In 961 the Byzantine general Nikifóros Fokás recaptured Crete from Muslim domination. All the Muslims in Crete were massacred and all traces of their presence were destroyed. Al-Khandaq (called Khandakas by the Byzantines) remained the capital. There was an influx of colonists from the home country, and a process of feudalization took place. There was a revival of Orthodox Christianity, led by Níkon the Repenter (who was active in Crete right after the recapture) and Ioánnis Xénos (970 1028). Crete remained Orthodox, also after the Great Schism of 1054.

1204 – 1669: Venetian Period

In 1204 Crete was given to the leader of the Fourth Crusade, Boniface of Montferrat, as a feudal estate by a Byzantine pretender to the throne. In the same year Boniface sold the island to Venice. Initially the archrivals of Venice, the Genoans, occupied large sections of the island, but they were driven away after about ten years. Venice occupied the island then as a colony and encouraged colonists to come from the home city. The island was heavily exploited and produced wine, olive oil, timber, and grain. The Catholic Venetian elite governed the island in a feudal manner. Candia (Herákleion), La Canea (Khaniá) and Rettimo (Réthymnon) were the most important cities. A large number of Orthodox churches, around 1000 of them, were constructed outside of the larger cities, often decorated with beautiful frescos in Byzantine style. Initially the Orthodox Church was suppressed, but when the Ottoman threat increased in the 16th century the emergence of Orthodox monasteries was encouraged by the Venetian administration, in order to win over the Cretans.

1669 – 1898: Ottoman Period

In 1645 an Ottoman army invaded the island (in this book we use the term Ottoman rather than Turkish, because ethnicity never played a major role in the pluralistic Ottoman state) and in 1648 the whole island was conquered, except for Herákleion. A siege of this city began, which would last until 1669. In that year the city was captured. From that time on Crete was an Ottoman province with Herákleion as its capital. During this period many inhabitants became Muslim. Mosques were built, or Catholic churches were turned into mosques by adding a minaret and a *mihrab*, a prayer niche facing Mecca. Under Ottoman dominion, the Orthodox Church enjoyed more freedom than in the time of the Venetians.

With the worsening economic situation at the end of the 18th century and increasing nationalism, a series of rebellions began which led to autonomy in 1898. The first big uprising took place in 1770, supported by Russia. In 1821 a new uprising began, triggered by the War of Independence that had broken out on mainland Greece. However, Crete was not permitted to join the independent Greece which was established in 1832. In 1866 another large rebellion took place, which was suppressed after three years. In 1878, 1889, and 1895 new uprisings took place.

A final uprising, in 1897, led to Crete's long-awaited autonomy. In this year a military force, sent by the Greek government, landed in Crete to provide support for the Cretan rebels. In order to stop the resulting war between Greece and the Ottoman Empire, the Great Powers (England, France, Russia and Italy) brought Crete under their own control: eastern Crete under French control, Herákleion and its surroundings under British control, Réthymnon and its surroundings under Russian control, and western Crete under Italian control. Khaniá was under joint control of the four Powers. Moreover, the Ottoman troops were to leave Crete and the island would be governed by a High Commissioner on behalf of the Great Powers, albeit under Ottoman suzerainty. On November 2nd, 1898 the last Ottoman troops left the island and on December 9th the Greek Prince George (second son of the Greek King George I) landed in Soúdha Bay by Khaniá, and assumed the position of High Commissioner. In 1913 Crete finally joined up with Greece, thanks to the efforts of the great Cretan statesman Elefthérios Venizélos.

Introduction

Crete is rugged countryside. There are uncompromising mountains split with harsh chasms, bare in the east, wooded in the west. Olive trees grow everywhere. The people are also tough, having spent centuries resisting the numerous oppressors who have tried to dominate Crete. And, of course, there is the sea: it is always close by. It is an inviting azure blue, but at the same time is frequently ravaged by storms. And Crete is also the land of gracious Minoan culture and of countless churches adorned with lovely frescos. And of cities with an oriental flavour, and archetypal mountain villages. It is also a land with miles of beaches.

You can read about the charms of present-day Crete in countless travel guides. But this book does not concentrate on the Crete of today. It is about the 'discovery' of Crete in the 18th and 19th centuries, before the Minoan civilization had been unearthed. And in a time before the sea and the beaches had been discovered as places of amusement. The explorers whose descriptions we encounter in this book were not concerned with amusement, but with the expansion of knowledge: knowledge in particular about classical antiquity, the cradle of European civilization.

In this first volume of three we start our discovery tour across Crete in Khaniá and travel from there to the east, to Herákleion. In the next two volumes of this series, the eastern part and the western part of Crete will be 'discovered'. In this volume, dealing as it is with Knossós, some of the ancient stories around Minos and Theseus and their 'contemporaries' can be found, translated from the original languages. You will also find the story of Atlantis, Crete being one of the candidates for the location of this mysterious lost continent.

Let's get in the mood for our tour with a quotation from the works of the British traveller Richard Pococke, who visited Crete in 1739. In the quotation Pococke gives a description of the 'natural history, people, customs, and the military and ecclesiastical state' of Crete.

The island of Candia [the contemporary European name for Crete, as well as for Herákleion] is for the most part hilly and mountainous, resembling Wales, or the territory of Genoua. The mountains are mostly either of free stone, or of marble, which is either grey or white. The hills are nearest to the south side of the island, and consequently the northern parts of it are the most pleasant, and best inhabited.

It abounds much in springs and fountains, which they find even close by the sea side, if they dig wells down but a few feet deep. Most of the rivers are dry in summer, but in winter many of them are very dangerous torrents. I do not find that they have any fresh water fish except eels. The most remarkable sea fish here are the scarus, and the red shelled oyster shaped like a scollop. The island does not produce any minerals, and very few natural curiosities of any sort, except in the vegetable kind. There are a great variety of trees in it, both of the Asiatic and European growth.

As to wild beasts, I could not be informed that they have any other except the goat and the hare. They have the red large partridge, which they call coturno, and a particular bird of the size of a black bird, and of a blewish grey, which, when kept in a cage, sings finely, and is called petro cockifo, or the bird of the rocks, which it frequents, and by the English the solitary sparrow. They have also another bird called potamida, because it is mostly about the rivers, and sings very finely. It is reported that there are no venomous animals in this island. They say, they have two sorts of snakes, one called ophis, which is spotted black and white, much of the colour of the adder. The other is the ochedra, which is smaller, and, as some pretend, is the sort of viper which fastened to saint Paul's hand in Malta, and, as they say, was afterwards harmless. They have an animal like a lizard called Jakoniè, which the people apprehend to be exceedingly venomous in its bite, and some say by a sting in its tail. But having some of them caught, I saw they were the very same as the sinco or stinc marin of Aegypt, which are harmless there, and are sent dried to Europe from Aegypt, without dismembring them, and go into the composition of the Theriaca. They have also the lizard, and a sort of spider called Phalangium, which is very venomous, especially in hot weather, and it is said that music and dancing helps towards the cure, as in the bite of the Tarantula. They have a strong rough middle sized breed of horses, used mostly in the towns. In the country they have generally mules and asses.

The former are used by the Christian ladies, who ride after the English manner. But the Turkish females, who veil their faces, ride like the men. The roads being very stony, and in many places narrow, there are no wheel carriages in the island.

They do not compute above three hundred thousand souls in the whole island, and reckon the number of Christians to be more than double the number of Turks. The inhabitants consist partly of the antient people of the island, who may be supposed to be very few, and partly of the descendants of the twelve noble Cretan families already mentioned [wealthy immigrants from Constantinople who settled in Crete in the 12th century], partly of Saracens [the Muslims who ruled Crete in the 9th century], who conquered the island, of whom it is probable there are not many; and some Venetians settled here during their government, who are now all of the Greek church, except some few of Suda and Spina Longa, who remained on the island when those places were taken, and have come under French protection; or lastly they are Turkish Mahometans brought from Constantinople, and other parts to this island, either as soldiery, or as colonies to forfeited lands.

The people of the island do by no means want parts, however defective they may be in the improvement of them. For they are sharp and sagacious, which they discover in their countenances. The young people are very fair and handsome, and have fine eyes. It said the Turkish women, who veil, are more beautiful than the Christians. They answer their antient character as to invention, and taking pleasure in spreading falsehoods, and they seem also to be credulous, and fond of believing strange things. They are civil and hospitable to one another and to the Franks, but with great reason avoid opportunities of being burthened by the Turks, who command every thing as a debt due to them, and make use of their monasteries, and the houses of their parish priests as inns. These are indeed the places for entertainment of strangers, but Christians who have any hounour always bestow some gratuity, that, at least, they may not be sufferers by their civility.

The dress of the men here is the same as that of Cyprus. Those of a middling condition and children wear only a small red cap, without any sash round it. The boors wear a black cap close to their heads, with a black silk tossel hanging down at each ear, and in summer are always clothed in white, which is a general custom among all the people in the

Turkish empire for all the habits, except the outer garment, imagining that white is a cool dress. The country people wear about their necks a long towel, with which they cover their heads when they are in the sun. The children here plait their hair round from their foreheads, and bring it down so as to hang in a plait behind, and the females have often two or three such plaits, which are very becoming. The Greek women do not cover their faces, but wear a muslin veil upon their heads, and bind up the hair in ribbands, and roll it round their heads, so as to make it a high dress. They tye their petticoats and aprons near as high as their armpits; and when in high dress, they wear a sort of short stays, adorned before with gold lace. The women never sit down to eat with men that are not of the house, and though they are not so strict as the Turks, yet they rarely come into the room where any strangers are.

All people here have such a property in their lands, that only the seventh of the produce belongs to the grand signor [the Ottoman sultan], and when they die, the lands, according to the law, are equally divided between the children, which has reduced all the Christian families to poverty. Nor can the father leave the lands in any other manner.

All along the north coast of Candia small watch towers are built to observe the coast, particularly by night, and to give the alarm by making fires, in case of any descent. The Christians are obliged to keep this watch. And to shew they are on the guard, every tower is obliged to have a fire as soon as it is dark, and at break of day. The pashas have often taken money to excuse the attendance of the watch, and in three or four months after sent an order to keep it again, and then they come to a new agreement to be excused. But there having been some descents made of late by the Maltese, the guard is strictly kept, and a company of soldiers go out every night from the garrisoned towns to watch the coast.

The caia, or prime minister of the pasha, gives an account of all duties to be levied, to the Christian secretary of the pasha, who sends it to the castel caia, or high constable, and he goes round to the capitaneo of each village, who levies the sum laid on the village from every house. The harach, or poll tax on the male Christians above sixteen years old is five dollars [the currency of account around the Mediterranean in the 18th century] and ten medins a head, which is about thirteen shillings sterling, and is collected by a Turkish officer sent to every castellate, who goes round and receives it. There are twenty five thousand Christians who pay harach, not including those who are in the three great cities.

There are in the garrisoned towns seven military bodies. First the janizaries, of which there are in each a certain number of different companies, or chambers called odas. But besides these there are a greater number of janizaries called jamalukes, who belong to chambers which are in other parts of the empire, and are settled here as merchants or tradesmen, and yet receive their pay as janizaries. And if any one of the companies are ordered away, those only go who please, and they make up their number as they can, and then the persons who refuse to go belong no more to that company, but they frequently go to Constantinople to be put into another company, and return to Candia, with a patent to receive their pay. As there are many janizaries about the country on their little estates, they are governed by a sardar in every castellate, and are subject only to their own body. These odas or chambers like the Roman legions are called by their respective numbers, there being a hundred and sixty of them in the empire. Each company has from one hundred to five hundred men, which is their compleat number in time of war; in peace they generally consist of about a hundred men. The second body are the jarleys. The tisdarlees are another body of foot, who cannot be sent out of the place. The fourth are topgis or canoneers. The fifth jebegis, who have the care of the ammunition. The sixth spahis, who are the cavalry, and are supposed to have horses, and when the pasha goes out they furnish him with half the number of horses he wants, the town furnishing the rest. All the Turks belong to some military body. The harach and customs pay all the soldiers, except the janizaries, whose money is brought from abroad.

The grand signor sells the seventh part of the lands of Candia for one life, and no proprietor can be dispossessed. But the purchasers can lawfully receive out of them only a seventh of the produce, which of corn, flax and cotton, is taken in kind. As to the oyl of their olivetrees, it is exorbitantly estimated. And for their vineyards, they pay a certain sum according to the quantity of land. And silk pays a medin or three farthings an ounce. The person who buys the seventh part of any village, is lord and master of it, leaves his soubashee or steward to collect his rents, who has all the power, and the business of the capitaneo, which is to collect all occasional impositions raised on the village by the pasha. He has the number of Christian families registered, and the tax is equally divided among them, the Turks paying nothing. And even sometimes a Christian family by great interest may be struck out of the list.

The archbishop is put in by the patriarch of Constantinople, and the metropolitan makes the bishops, who put in the parish priests. The archbishop besides the revenues of his own diocese, receives a yearly sum from all the bishops; and as he pays a yearly tribute to the grand signor, every bishop is impowered to levy five medins for that purpose on every house, and pays a certain sum on that account to the metropolitan. The bishop's revenue is a certain measure of corn, wine and oyl, besides the voluntary contributions of the people. He has also fees on marriages, and they generally go round their dioceses in the three Lents, in March, August, and November.

If a Christian woman marries a Turk, she is not admitted to the sacrament, till she is at the point of death, and must then renounce her husband. But she goes to church, which they cannot hinder. And many of those who live in the villages are perverted by the Turks.

When Candia was taken, the Christians had generally two bells to every church, which they were ordered to bring into the cities. Many of them hid the bells; and it is delivered down from father to son where they are. This is known by the Turks, so that the pasha, if he would raise money on a rich family, the master is accused as having the bells hid somewhere in his land, he is carried to prison, and there remains until he pays a sum of money for his deliverance.

Though many of the villages are inhabited by Turks, yet there are some villages where the inhabitants, who were formerly Christians, are almost entirely become Mahometans. Some to avoid punishment, or to be revenged on a Turk, whom a Christian cannot strike. Others are encouraged by the thriving of the renegadoes, who pay no taxes. So the Christians grow poor, the Mahometans rich, and purchase their lands; and thus the Christian religion daily loses ground in all parts of Turkey.

1. Khaniá

Our journey across Crete begins in the harbour city of Khaniá. With its 60,000 inhabitants it is the second largest city in Crete, and is an extraordinarily attractive place.

Unspoiled by tourism, Khaniá calls up memories of its Venetian and Ottoman past. It is beautifully situated at the foot of the high Lefká Óri (the White Mountains, also called the Madhára Voúna). The city stretches out around the inner and outer harbours, where old Venetian houses are reminiscent of the past.

The Kastélli Hill is in the center of the town. This is where the oldest settlement was located. It is also where the highest governmental and military authority of the region was established, both in antiquity and in Venetian and Ottoman times. In the 16th century a strong wall with five bastions and a wide moat surrounded the city. The ruins of the wall can still be seen between the San Salvatore bastion in the northwest, close to the Firkás sea fort, and the Siavo bastion in the southwest.

To the south of the inner harbour stretches the Splantzia district, the old residential center of the city. On the central square here, the Plateía 1821, is the 14th century Áyios Nikólaos church. At the foot of the Kastél-

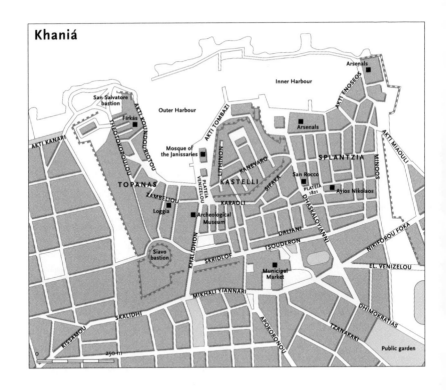

Khaniá

Arsenals

Inner Harbour

AKTI ENOSEOS

San Salvatore
bastion

Firkás

Outer Harbour

AKTI TOMBAZI

Arsenals

AKTI MIAOULI

AKTI KANARI

THEOTOKOPOULOU

AKTI KOUNDOURIOTOU

Mosque of
the Janissaries

KANONION

KANEVARO

SPLANTZIA

MINOOS

TOPANAS

PLATEIA
VENIZELOU

KASTELLI

SIFAKA

San Rocco

ZAMBELIOU

KARAOLI

PLATEIA
1821

Ayios Nikolaos

Loggia

Archeological
Museum

DHASKALOYIANNI

NIKIFOROU FOKA

Siavo
bastion

KHALIDHON

SKRIDLOF

DALIANI

ISOUDERON

EL. VENIZELOU

Municipal
Market

MIKHALI YIANNARI

DHIMOKRATIAS

SKALIDHI

APOKORONOU

TZANAKAKI

KISSAMOU

0   250 m

Public garden

li Hill, on the eastern side of the outer harbour, rises the sturdy Mosque of the Janissaries. To the west of the outer harbour, in the Topánas district, were the palaces of the well to do Venetians. To the south, in the direction of the Siavo bastion, lay the Loggia in Venetian times. This is where the Khaniote nobility amused themselves. Here is also where the San Francesco is located, the cloister church of the Franciscan monastery in Khaniá. It now houses the Archeological Museum.

After Khaniá became the capital of Crete in 1841 (this lasted until 1971, when Heráklion took on that role), the village of Khalépa, now a suburb in the eastern part of the city, became the preferred residential quarter of the European diplomats and merchants. The harbour also shifted at this time. The Venetian and Ottoman harbour was too shallow and small for 19th century ships, so the nearby Bay of Soúdha took over the role of harbour. After Crete's independence the city of Khaniá quickly expanded beyond the city walls. An early example of the city's modernization was the building of the Municipal Market in 1911, on top of debris filling up the moat around the Venetian wall (the wall itself was demolished here and the debris caused by this demolition was used to fill the moat).

Khaniá, especially the Kastélli Hill, suffered greatly during the Battle of Crete in 1941, as the area around Khaniá was the central target of German attacks. But the Venetian-Ottoman past can still be seen and experienced fully.

THE PAST

The city's history goes back to Minoan times, as witnessed by excavations on the Kastélli Hill (research shows that perhaps a palace, such as that at Knossós, stood here). But it was mainly after the Greek-speaking Akhaians had conquered Crete that the city gained distinction. The ancient name for the city, Kydonía, 'quince,' is already mentioned in Linear B tablets (as ku-do-ni-ya).

After the Akhaians disappeared the city lost its significance for several centuries. Only in the 6th century B.C., when colonists from Sámos established a settlement here, did Kydonía become important again. In 69 B.C. the city was captured by the Romans under the leadership of Metellus.

Kydonía remained significant, however. After the arrival of Christianity it became the seat of the bishopric and a basilica was built on the Kastélli Hill. But after this, during Muslim dominion over Crete (824-961) and the Second Byzantine Period, little was heard of the city. The

Kastélli Hill was fortified with walls by the Byzantines, but as everywhere else on the island, the demographic and economic focal point shifted from the ancient city to the countryside. A characteristic example of this is that the bishopric of Kydonía henceforth had its seat in Ayiá, south of Kydonía.

Then came the Venetians. But only in 1252, 40 years after they had definitely taken control of Crete, did they settle on the site of the old Kydonía and build a city which they called La Canea (changed to the Greek Khaniá).

The city remained in the shadow of the administrative and economic center of the island, Candia (Herákleion), but it was the most important regional center. The outer harbour was the commercial port, while the inner harbour was for the war galleys. The Arsenals (shipyards) at the inner harbour recall this function. At the end of the mole a lighthouse was built.

In the 14th century both Franciscan and Dominican orders were present in Khaniá: the Franciscan monastery church now houses the Archeological Museum, and the San Nicolo (now Áyios Nikólaos) in Splantzia was the church of the Dominican monastery. On the Kastélli Hill stood the governor's palace and – on the site of the early Christian basilica – the Catholic cathedral, the Santa Maria.

In the beginning of the 16th century Crete became a pawn in the power struggle for supremacy in the Mediterranean between the Ottoman Empire on the one side and the Habsburg Empire and Venice on the other. In 1533 the great corsair Khayr al-Din Barbarossa took up service with the Ottoman sultan Suleyman the Magnificent (1520-1566). As admiral of the Ottoman fleet he attacked Spanish and Venetian possessions in the Mediterranean Sea. In 1537 he attacked Corfu, but was not able to conquer it. He subsequently moved along the Venetian islands in the Aegean Sea, plundering as he went, and in 1538 he raided the coast of Crete and enslaved many inhabitants. In answer to the Ottoman threat Venice decided to make Crete into an impenetrable fort. The two most important cities, Herákleion and Khaniá, were fortified with a wall designed by Michele Sanmicheli, an engineer from Verona specialized in defence works (Réthymnon was also encircled with a wall, but it was not sufficiently reinforced). Each wall, with protruding bastions and a wide moat, satisfied all the requirements of modern siege warfare after the development of firearms had revolutionized the military arts.

The stronghold of Crete would remain in Venetian hands for another century. But in 1645 the Ottomans came again, this time to stay. In June of that year 50,000 Ottoman troops landed at the monastery of Goniá, to the west of Khaniá. The initiator of the invasion was Yusuf Pasha (called Issouf Pasha in the cited text), admiral of the Ottoman fleet during the reign of sultan Ibrahim the Mad (1640-1648). It is doubtful whether there was any sound strategic plan behind the invasion. The sultan himself suffered from paranoia and was only interested in his harem (he was eventually assassinated by order of his grand vizier, in the interest of the state), and the empire at that time was governed by scheming courtiers, one of whom was Yusuf Pasha.

After a 54-day siege the Ottoman troops occupied Khaniá without much trouble. The city was defended by a garrison of only 800 mercenaries and a guard of 1000 Greeks. Venice offered no support to the beleaguered city. On August 22th, 1645 the city surrendered. The few remaining soldiers were allowed to leave the city. Yusuf Pasha, the successful commander, was executed half a year later, in January 1646, as a consequence of jealous intrigues at court. In the next two years the Ottoman troops would conquer all of Crete except for Herákleion, which only surrendered in 1669.

After the whole island had come under Ottoman rule the city, now called Khaniya, remained the center of administration of western Crete. Catholic churches were changed into mosques by adding a *mihrab* (the prayer niche facing Mecca) and a minaret. The San Nicolo in Splantzia is an example: it was changed into the Hunkar Mosque, the main mosque of the city (it is now the Orthodox Áyios Nikólaos, still retaining both a bell tower and a minaret). Another example is the Santa Maria on the Kastélli Hill, which was changed into the Musa Pasha Mosque (after the Ottomans had left it was changed again, this time into a warehouse; it was destroyed during the Battle of Crete in 1941). The palace of the Venetian governor on the Kastélli Hill was taken over by the Ottoman *pasha* of Khaniá.

On June 14th, 1821 there was a revolt against the Ottoman authority in Crete, following the outbreak of the War of Independence in mainland Greece on March 25th of that year. The bloody uprising would last ten years and cost the lives of nearly half the Cretan population – the population went from 213,000 to 130,000 during this time. Because Pashley, the traveller whose journey we are concentrating on in this book, visited the island shortly after the end of the rebellion, we will discuss the revolt quite extensively.

After the outbreak of the rebellion on June 14th, Khaniá was the center of Ottoman retaliations. These were initially met with little success, however. On June 15th Latif Pasha of Khaniá, with his army of 5000 men, was completely destroyed at Lákki, to the south of Khaniá. He had to retreat to Khaniá, leaving his weapons behind. The weapons were subsequently used gratefully by the rebels. The Ottomans were also defeated around Réthymnon. On June 19th, however, the bishop of Kíssamos, Melkhisédek Dhespotákis, was hung in the central square of Splantzia, which was later renamed Plateía 1821 in memory of the events. The execution of the bishop was modelled after the hanging of the Orthodox patriarch in Istanbul on Easter Sunday in 1821 (since he was held responsible for the rebellion of his religious followers in Greece). At this time, moreover, the bishop of Kydonía was imprisoned and several hundred Christian inhabitants of Khaniá were killed during the subsequent rioting. All over the island, bishops and abbots were imprisoned and sometimes executed, monasteries and churches were plundered, nuns were raped and monks and priests were murdered.

In the following months the Ottomans had successes against the rebels in other parts of Crete, but in early 1822 an impasse was finally reached. The sultan in Istanbul, Mahmud IV, then asked for assistance from his viceroy (*khedive*) in Egypt, Mehmed Ali. In May this former troop commander from Kavalla in Macedonia sent a fleet of 30 warships and 84 transport ships to the Bay of Soúdha, where the Egyptian troops landed (these were mainly Arnauts, i.e. warriors from Albanian stock, like Mehmed Ali himself). As discussed later in this book, these troops smothered the Cretan uprising in two years.

In 1827 the Great Powers (England, France and Russia) forced an independent Greece out of the hands of the Ottomans, an independence which was implemented in 1832. Initially the Cretan rebels tried to affiliate themselves with the newly-formed Greek kingdom, but they were not successful. In 1830 it was clear that England would not permit Crete to be part of an independent Greece, but rather wanted Crete to be ruled by the *khedive*, Mehmed Ali. Indeed, Crete remained under Egyptian rule until 1840, with Mustafa Pasha, who had already acted as Egyptian commander-in-chief during the rebellion, as its governor.

Egyptian rule, harsh though it was, also brought modernization. In Khaniá a large number of public works were carried out. One example of this is the lighthouse at the entrance to the harbour, which was rebuilt on its Venetian base in the form of a minaret.

The Outer Harbour of Khaniá and the Lefká Óri

In 1840 Crete was again placed under the rule of the sultan in Istanbul under pressure from the Great Powers, who feared the increasing power of Mehmed Ali. Mustafa Pasha remained governor of the island until 1850, when he became grand vizier in Istanbul. In 1841 Khaniá, with its Bay of Soúdha a better harbour for the large 19th century ships, became the capital of Crete in place of Herákleion. Four years later, in 1845, a new government building, the Konaki, was constructed next to the Venetian palace which had served as the seat of administration until then. It was totally made of wood, though, and was burned down under mysterious circumstances in 1897.

In December 1898 the time had come for the Ottomans to leave. The Great Powers (now including Italy) had decided that Crete would become an autonomous protectorate. The second son of the Greek King George I, also named George, would become High Commissioner on behalf of the protecting Powers. He landed in the Bay of Soúdha on December 9th. The Great Powers each took a part of Crete under their protection: the Italians took western Crete, the Russians took Réthymnon and surroundings, the British took Herákleion and its surroundings, and the French took eastern Crete. Khaniá, remaining capital of the island, came under joint control. Crete remained a protectorate until 1913, with Prince George its initial High Commissioner. In 1908 the Cretan assembly declared unilateral *énosis* (affiliation) to Greece. This was done under the influence of the great statesman Elefthérios Venizélos, born in Mourniés by Khaniá. Finally, on December 1st 1913 Crete was formally united with Greece, and the Greek flag was raised symbolically on the Firkás sea fort.

THE TRAVEL DESCRIPTIONS

Pashley, the explorer whose adventures form the major part of this book, first set foot in Crete in Khaniá on February 8th, 1834. This Cambridge scholar had left England at the end of 1832 on a one and a half year journey which would bring him to the Ionian islands (under British control since 1814), Albania, the Greek mainland, Asia Minor, Istanbul, Lesbos, Malta and Crete. He had spent the winter of 1833-34 in Malta. He was then taken to Khaniá on a British warship, the Hind, by order of the commander-in-chief of the British fleet, Sir Pulteney

Malcolm. He was accompanied on his entire journey by Antonio Schranz, a Spaniard who had lived on Malta for a long time and who created the lithographs and engravings in his book.

For the Muslims in Crete, February 1834 was the fasting month of Ramazan. That meant fasting during the day, and feasting after sundown. The Ramazan ended with the Bayram: the feast of the breaking of the fast.

Pashley, I, p. 1 – 4, 6 – 10

On entering the gulf of Khaniá I was struck with the grandeur and beauty of the White Mountains, which well deserve the name bestowed on them by both ancients and moderns, and attract the notice of every one who passes the southern promontories of Laconia, either on approaching or leaving the islands of the Egean.

The fame of the Cretan Ida is greater than that of these snow-clad summits, and I had some difficulty in persuading my companions [apart from Schranz, Pashley was also in the company of a certain Mr. Glasscott until Khaniá] that the majestic forms before us were not those of the loftiest and most celebrated mountain in the island.

At daybreak this morning, we could only just discern the distant outline of the Taenarian promontory: now, we rapidly approached the city of Khaniá; the minarets of which, towering above its buildings, and conspicuous from afar, where the first sensible object that reminded me of the wide difference between the social scenes which I had left, and those by which I should soon be surrounded.

As the boats of the Hind pulled into the harbour, to land me with my companions, we were asked, in a language the sounds of which I had not heard for several months, whether we had come from a Turkish port; and thus learnt that Mehmét-Alí has bestowed on Crete a sanitary establishment. Coming as we did from Malta, we landed immediately, as, in all likelihood, we should have done, even if we had been from Constantinople [Pashley adds in a footnote: 'In Crete a slight quarantine is now imposed on ships of war, but only when from a place where the plague is actually raging']. I delivered to the British Consul, Signor Capo Grosso, a native of Spalatro who has resided more than half a century in the Levant, a letter of introduction from the Admiral Sir Pulteney Malcolm: and I was received by him with even greater demonstrations of hospitality than I could have wished; for he would not hear of my hiring apartments in the city, but insisted on my becoming his own guest.

At sunset a salute was fired from the guns of the fortress, and the minarets of the different mosques in the city were illuminated with numberless lamps.

> Just at this season Ramazani's fast
> Through the long day its penance did maintain;
> But, when the lingering twilight hour was past,
> Revel and feast asumed the rule again.

Similar nightly festivity and revelry were likewise indulged in, during the first days of my stay in Khaniá, by the families of all the Consuls. This year the Carnival of the Catholics, and the Ramazan of the Mohammedans, happen at the same time.

The uniform tranquility, which now reigns within the walls of this fortified city, is very different from the habitual violence, in which the Mohammedan Khaniótes used to indulge before the Greek revolution [the uprising of 1821]. The population is nearly six thousand souls, of whom the Christians and Jews amount to about the seventh part.

The Venetian city dates from A.D. 1252, when a colony was sent to occupy it. The object of the foundation was to keep down the Greeks, who had been in arms, and at open war with their Italian lords, almost without intermission, from the day when the Venetians first set foor on their shores...

The bronze guns which had been allowed, ever since the Turks acquired possession of the island, to remain on the ramparts both of this city and of the Kástron [Herákleion], have most of them been removed by Mehmét-Alí-pashá, and taken to Alexandria; where doubtless they have already been melted and converted into money.

The several Consulates look on the port, and are distinguished by the flags of their respective countries, which each Consul hoists on Sundays, and whenever a vessel of his own nation arrives or leaves the harbour...

At daybreak on the 11th of February the guns of the fortress announced the welcome arrival of the long expected Bairám. Another great religious festival, called by the same name, and which will take place in April, is annually celebrated in remembrance of the sacrifice offered by Abraham [Büyük Bayram, the sacrificial feast].

During my stay at Khaniá I became acquainted with most of its European inhabitants. French is the general language of social intercourse in use among them. The only person, however, out of the whole Frank population of the city, whose life had not been almost entirely spent in the Levant, was Monsieur Fabreguette, the French consul. From this gentleman, and his amiable consort, I received every attention, and with them I spent most of my time. The records of the Consulate throw much light on the history of the Turkish domination; and the facts which they disclose, would alone suffice to justify the revolt of the Christian population of Crete, at the outbreaking of the Greek revolution.

Mustafá-pashá, the Governor General of Crete, resides chiefly at Megálo-Kástron [Herákleion], the principal city of the island. It was celebrated throughout Europe, about a century and a half ago, under its Italian name of Candia, for the heroic resistance which the Venetians made, within its walls, to the then all-powerful and all-conquering arms of the Turks.

The day after the commencement of the Bairám I visited Ismaél-bey, the present Governor of Khaniá, accompanied by the interpreter of the English Consul. The Bey is a nephew of the Viceroy of Egypt [Mehmed Ali]. I found him, of course, on his divan. He rose to receive me, and was extremely civil. While we were smoking pipes and taking coffee, the conversation turned, as is usual on such occasions, on various unimportant topics. He has lived chiefly at Alexandria, and once began to learn French, with which many Egyptian Turks are somewhat acquainted; but the number of his employments compelled him to abandon it. While I was with him, a most corpulent man, of very lofty stature, Alí-agá-Suftá-Zadé, one of the old Cretan Turks of distinction, came in and walked up to the divan. The Bey rose and saluted him on the right cheek. The Cretan gentleman presented the Governor with a rose, a rarity here, as I am told, at this season, though it is very common in Malta. This Cretan speaks Greek, as is done by all the inhabitants of the island, both Mohammedans and Christians...

It is not difficult to account for this universal prevalence of the Greek language in Crete. Nearly all the rural population of the island may be said to have a common descent from the Christian Cretans of the middle ages. The worldly advantages, which used to result from embracing Islamism, have induced whole districts to abandon the faith of their forefathers. This effect of the Turkish rule was sensibly felt even by the end of the seventeenth century; and was complained of, by the Archbishop of Gortyna, when Chevalier visited the island. Thus a mere change of religious faith was naturally unaccompanied by any change of language.

The same historical fact serves also to account for another peculiarity in the manners of the Cretan Mohammedans, namely, that they all drink wine without the least scruple. The Cretan Greek used to have plenty of excellent wine, at a very slight cost; and had always been in the habit of drinking it before his *conversion*: thus, after he became one of the faithful, he neglected to comply with the practice of the Mohammedans. His children followed him, in this disregard of an unpleasant observance of their adopted religion; and, even to the present day, a Cretan Mohammedan drinks his wine, as unscrupulously as any Christian in the country.

It is probable that other characteristics of the social relations between the Mohammedans and Christians of Crete, have been owing to the same cause. It was far from unusual, before the Greek revolution [the uprising of 1821], for a Mohammedan to stand as godfather to the child of his Christian friend. I may instance two persons, whose names were both celebrated in the history of the war in this island, the Mohammedan Agriolídhes, of Dibáki [Timbáki] in the plain of Messará, and the Christian Captain Rússos, of Askýfo in Sfakiá, who were thus connected

This is all the information Pashley gives about the city. The remainder of his chapter on Khaniá is spent on a discussion about the identification of Khaniá with the ancient Kydonía. A century earlier, in 1739, 70 years after the Ottoman conquest, the English scholar and traveller Richard Pococke also visited Crete. He made a trip around the Levant, and visited Crete on the way from Alexandria to Istanbul. Pashley knew Pococke's account and commented on it frequently in his own book. The following is Pococke's description of Khaniá.

Pococke, p. 242, 243

The city of Canea, capital of the western province of Candia, is situated at the east corner of a bay about fifteen miles wide, which is between cape Melecca, antiently called Ciamum to the east, and cape Spada, the old promontory Psacum to the west. It has been commonly thought to be on the spot of the antient Cydonia, but the chief reason is, because the bishop of Canea is called in Greek the bishop of Cydonia. About the middle of the north side of the town there is an old castle within the fortifications, which is about half a mile in circumference. This possibly might be called in Turkish a chane, or public place for strangers, and from this the name of Canea might be derived. The city is of an oblong figure, about two miles in compass, fortified towards the land after the modern way by the Venetians, with four bastions, and a ravelin at the north east corner. On the north side of the town is the port, well defended by a wall, built on the north side on the rocks. There is a light-house at the end of it, and a castle in the middle, which serves as a cistern. The entrance to the harbour is narrow, and there is a very fine arsenal for laying up gallies, which was built by the Venetians. This city was taken by the Turks under the conduct of Issouf captain pasha, in one thousand six hundred and forty six [this is a mistake, the city was taken in 1645], after a brave defence for fifty seven days. It is a neat town, the buildings being almost all Venetian. Most of the mosques are old churches, of which together with the chapels, there were twenty-five. One particularly belonged to a large convent of Franciscans, and that on an advanced ground within the castle seems to have been the cathedral called saint Mary's. All the Turks who are inhabitants of the city, belong to one or other of the bodies of the soldiery, and those fit to bear arms are about three thousand. There are three hundred Greek families in the town, and only four or five Armenians, and about fifty families of Jews. The pasha of the province of Canea resides here, who is the head of the famous family of the Cuperlis, whose grandfather took the city of Candia [Köprülüzade Fazil Ahmed Pasha]. This pasha is the general that retook Nissa. And some say, that the cause of his disgrace was his cutting off so many Greek villages in the neighbourhood of that city, by which the lands were left uncultivated. But that he alledged in his defence, that he acted according to his orders.

The people of this city are very much inclined to arms, and had fitted out this summer two galleotes, each manned with sixty persons, to cruise for Neapolitans, or any other enemies. They were attacked, as they say, by the Venetians; one of them was taken, and all the men cut to pieces. It is thought that the Venetians meeting them beyond a certain place, which, by a late treaty of peace between Ottoman Port and that Republick, they ought not have passed, was the reason of their falling on them. However, it caused a tumult in Canea, particularly against the French, who had given them certificates of their being Caneotes. So that many of that nation fled to Retimo. Some took shelter in the English consul's house, and none of them dared to appear for some time.

The consuls general both of the English and French reside here, though the latter have a consul both at Candia and Retimo, but the English have only a droggerman [dragoman, interpreter] at those places, who does the office of a consul. The English having very little trade this way, the consul's is the only English house on the island, but the French merchants are numerous; the chief trade consists in sending oyl of olives to France to make soap, and for working their cloths. They export also a small quantity of silk, wax and honey, into the Archipelago, and wine to all parts of the Levant, which is very strong and cheap. It is sent mostly from the city of Candia. The common sort is red; but about Retimo they make a fine Muscadine wine. They export raisins, figs, and almonds to many parts. English ships sometimes carry oyl from Candia both to Hamburg and to London. The capuchins of the mission [Franciscans] have a small convent here, and are chaplains to the French nation.

Twenty years after Pashley's visit the city was visited by another explorer who we will often come across in these pages: Captain, and later Admiral, T.A.B. Spratt. Spratt visited the city in 1853. This was during a survey of the island ordered by the British government which had taken him earlier through central and eastern Crete, and later would take him to the western part of the island. He was always accompanied by his personal attendant Spíro, and frequently by one or more officers, particularly the lieutenants Mansell and Wilkinson and the ship's doctors Dr. Smart and Dr. Wilcox. It was his intention to add to the work of Pashley. He arrived in Khaniá from Réthymnon.

Spratt, II, p. 137, 138, 141 – 143, 146 – 148

Khania, the second city of Crete at the time of the Venetians, is now its capital, although occupying only half the superficial area of Candia.

The fortifications surrounding it, which were entirely built by the Venetians, are still in a good state, as also are the greater part of their fine gallery-arches, which formed their arsenal. It is an over-crowded town, as it was in the time of the Venetians, from the narrowness of the streets, the height of some of the houses, and the confined limits of its original plan. It is said to contain 12,000 inhabitants at present, and is in consequence not so healthy as Candia. Two streets of shops or bazaars run through its centre, from the port gate to the land gate, and thus separate the town into nearly equal divisions on either side, one of which is exclusively inhabited by Turks, and the other by Greeks. The citadel or keep enclosed an eminence immediately over a rocky point, separating the eastern part of the port, or arsenal, from the western or commercial port...

The population of Khania and the trade to its port have greatly increased since it became the seat of government and the official location of the European consuls; some of the consuls, merchants, and tradesmen, however, reside at the pretty little village of Khalepa, on the rising ground towards the Akrotiri, about a mile to the east of the town.

A large Arab village of between 2000 and 3000 souls has recently risen on the sandy shore just outside of the fortress on that side, the inhabitants of which have, for the most part, come from Egypt and the Cyrenaïca since Khania became the capital. They are chiefly boatmen, porters, and servants; and it may be said to be the only Arab settlement in Europe where their habits of life and habitations are fully retained in every respect as in a pure Arab village; and the most arid and sandy part of the shore is selected, apparently as most resembling their own African coast and its associated desert. It is a perfect little African community and village in all its features, having also a sprinkling of Bedouin tents adjacent, in which dwell families of the purest Bedouin race and colour, most of whom fled from the Cyrenaïca during some recent famine...

The fosse or ditch which surrounds Khania is wide and deep, and has become its chief vegetable-garden, chosen from its bottom being a dead level, and from its having several wells of water, and a filthy stream, formed for the most part of the town-drainage, running through it; for in Crete, as in the Levant generally, irrigation is so necessary to all annual vegetation, to enable it to endure the summer heats, that it requires to be planted by the side of a furrow or trench into which the water can be made to flow once or twice a day during this hot season of the year...

Hence certain forms of trenching for irrigation became general; and no doubt it was from the plan of the ancient gardeners' trench that the simplest and earliest pattern for architectural mouldings and bordering was taken – which is now known as the meander pattern, from its supposed origin being that of the meanderings of a river, but which every oriental gardener at the present day still gives to the channels which convey the water to the plants that require daily irrigation,– first making the two long exterior parallel trenches or canals in the soil he has levelled and prepared, and then at intervals along them, on alternate sides, opening inwards as many rectangular spiral trenches as there is room to carry out, so as to admit water to every part. When irrigation is proceeding, each spiral trench is closed again, as soon as filled, with the earth temporarily removed from the side of the long canal, that the water admitted into each spiral may be all retained and absorbed around the roots of the plants within it; and thus each, in succession, is sufficiently supplied.

On April 10th, 1864 another Englishman arrived at Crete. He was the well-known nonsense poet and water colourist Edward Lear. Lear had made it his habit to winter in Corfu, which had been under English control since 1814. After Corfu had become a part of Greece at the beginning of 1864, Lear, who was by then 51 years old, went searching for another picturesque area. He hoped to find that in Crete, but was disappointed. His journal, from which the quotations in this section come, is full of melancholy grumbling and complaining. He left the island again at the end of May. Lear knew Pashley's book, but not Spratt's. Just as Pashley had done, Lear first set foot on Cretan soil in Khaniá. On April 9th he arrived, from Athens, on the island of Sýros – junction of the shipping trade – where he had to await the arrival of a ship from Smyrna (now Izmir). He was in the company of his servant George Kokális, from Súli in Epirus, who had been in his employment since Corfu.

Lear, p. 26 – 28

Evil fortune! 350 or 400 pilgrims returning from the Madonna of Tinos are to embark; half the upper deck is already full of them. Great row in separating men from women: one man and wife dismissed: Ἑῖμαι ἐλεύθερος – Ἕλληνας.' ['I'm free – and a Greek.'] The *greco-orientale* from Smyrna is not yet in sight – 3.30 – and that is expected before the *celere*, so apparently we may be here till midnight. The second steamer came in about 5-5.30, but independent of delay in shipping freight and many more passengers, there was an awful row, four men having drawn knives, and one man was seized by the Captains and kept below till police came. Screams of the man's wife etc. etc. etc. were like a drama, and once or twice I thought worse would come of it. About nine the man was got off by policemen after great resistance, and later three other men were taken. At 10.30 we started. Went to bed, and the night being quiet – slept. Morning fine; but wind increasing. Called by George at seven, up by eight, but could not stay on deck till after ten, when I lay down, only rising now and then all through the day. Crete in sight, but at 1 p.m. it is horridly rough, and a great sea on, with wind dead against us. It grew worse and worse and blew hard, though the *Persia* pitched only and rolled but little, and so on, till at five we entered the port of Haniá. But the beautiful approach to the Island of course I did not see, as it was hidden in cloud and, latterly, heavy rain. The 160 or 200 women and children all vomiting and wet through were a sight to see! Port is very picturesque, Pasha's Palace, etc. etc. but the boats! and crowd! At last the καφιγί [doorman] having recommended a black man, George and I and the eleven objects got on shore. No trouble with luggage etc. But the *Hotel* ('Constantinople') – *what* a place! A most filthy and wretched hole, and impossible to stay in. But the Pasha was away and the Consul lives some miles off; so all I could do was to send off my letter to him, and hope. Presently a young merchant, Guarracino (Dutch Consul), called and became a good Samaritan by offering me his house, a bachelor's room only, which I gladly accepted. The English Vice-Consul (Mr Boone) also called, and I sent out my letter to Mr Hay [the English consul]: also Elizabeth of Crete's brother called. So I then set out with my new friend, and was soon at a tiny little house, where I was cordially welcomed, and installed in a room – my host's sitting room – many carpets etc. around. Soon came George with the *roba* [baggage] and, Mr Guarracino going out, I washed and George put up the camp bed. At eight came dinner: good macaroni, fish, and veal, olives and good cheese and wine. A Frenchman, Dr Baume, came who had known Pashley: Maniás (Pashley's guide) is dead. These people say I can go *anywhere* in safety. 10.15, bed; George has, I fear, rough quarters. So goes on my beginnings in Crete.

Rose at 6.30, having slept tolerably. George put up my bed, and we got out the 'Coliseum' (a sack so called) in hopes to draw: but it soon clouded and threatened rain. At 8.30 Mr Guarracino walked with me to the ramparts, I hoping to get a view from the walls, but it began to rain hard and nothing could be done. I see, however, that the Port is immensely picturesque. After the rain stopped and Mr Guarracino left me, George and I went through the bazaars – picturesque and crowdy – and 'out of the town'. Being shut up in high walls it is very invisible, but there must be some good views from the ramparts. We went out to a little height, and saw the village of Halépa, and the great White Mountains, half hidden in mist. Then towards a cemetery, where cypress and pine gleamed against far snow hills: and later, towards the west, but it rained hard, and we had to stand up, and at last came on to the city by 9.30, and, Petros (Mr Guarracino's servant) being out. we had to wait opposite the house till 10.30. The Cretans are vastly picturesque: great number of blacks, male and female.

4.30. I waited ready until twelve, when Mr Guarracino's breakfast took place: not very good, but heartily given. At one, he went out with George and me, taking us round the harbour by the lower gate and the great galley arches of the Venetians, and then George and I went on, as the rain had cleared off, by the shore towards Halépa, a village massed on the hill slopes two miles east of Haniá: and very like parts of Beirut, as to yellow or white flat-roofed houses, gardens, etc. etc. On the way are several fine views of Haniá, rocky and broad; and the queer village of the blacks, with houses in a cluster, was pretty. At Halépa I went to Mr Dendrino's with Paramythiótti's letter: a large house with many kavasses and much pomp. I fought off dinner tomorrow, and went next to Drummond Hay's, who is a very nice fellow, losing, I fear, one eye by ophthalmia. His little girl and lovely Spanish wife were beautiful and interesting, and he also offered me a room. Looked at the country 'box' of Mr Guarracino, brought away some curry powder, and went up the hill some way, and then back by the shore; but it was far too windy to draw, so we walked by the cemetery and beheld the plain of Riza and its villages, and also the Sphakian mountains; though their tops are hidden, still a noble sight. Returned by six: how cold! Dinner not till eight: curry and hare, and one Petritini (nephew of Marcoran's, cousin of Padovan) sitting a long while – a bore – a greater his flea-full dog. The dogs are all timid, amicable and curly-tailed here. Bed – bored – by 9.45.

2. Between Khaniá and Yeoryioúpoli

The next stage of our tour takes us from Khaniá to the east, to the Apokórona: the fertile plain which stretches out between the snow-capped Lefká Óri in the west and south, the sea in the north, and the Dhrápano hills with the sea behind them in the east. This is the basin of two large rivers: the Kiliáris flowing to the north, which is fed by the Yeráni and the Dhíktanos with its beautiful gorge; and to the south, from west to east, flows the Almyró. Up in the Kiliáris basin lie villages such as Kiriakosélia with its splendid Áyios Nikólaos church, and Rámni, with Stýlos and Neokhório farther downstream. In the Almyró basin lie such attractive villages as Pemónia, Frés, Níppos, Vrýsses (more a town than a village, an important crossroads), Embrosnéros and Alíkambos. And at the mouth of the river is the beach resort of Yeoryioúpoli, named after Prince George, the High Commissioner of Crete from 1898 to 1906, who had his country house here. Before that the site was called Almyró or Armyró. On the northern coast is Kalýves a major area of attraction, with beaches stretching past Almirídha. At the watershed which runs through the middle of the plain, between the Almyró in the south and the coastal plain in the north, Vámos is the most prominent village. On the northern

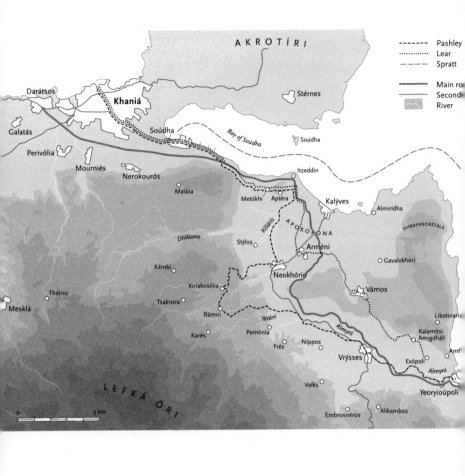

AKROTÍRI

Stérnes

Darátsos
Khaniá

Galatás

Soúdha
Bay of Soúdha
Soúdha

Perivólia

Mourniés
Nerokourós
Itzeddin

Maláxa
Metókhi
Aptéra
Kalýves
Almirídha

Dhíktano
Stýlos
APOKORONA
DHRAPANOKÉFALA

Kámbi
Arméni
Gavalokhóri

Kiriakosélia
Neokhório
Vámos

Thériso
Likotinaria

Tsakistra
Kalamítsi
Amigdháli

Mesklá
Rámni
Yeráni
Almyró
Amf

Karés
Pemónia
Nippos
Exópoli

Frés
Vrýsses
Almyró

LEFKÁ ÓRI
Vafés
Yeoryioúpoli

0   5 km
Embrosnéros
Alíkambos

side of the watershed Gavalokhóri is a picturesque village with many reminders of Venetian and Ottoman times, a center of local silkworm breeding. A nice walking tour in this area goes from Yeoryioúpoli via Likotinariá past Kalamítsi Amigdháli, and back to Yeoryioúpoli.

The Apokórona is cut off from the rest of Crete by the foothills of the Lefká Óri. In the west there is a narrow passageway between Aptéra and the sea to Khaniá, along the Bay of Soúdha, and in the east there is only a passageway at Yeoryioúpoli. At Embrosnéros and Alíkambos in the south one of the only passes to the area of the Sfakians, the inhabitants of the Lefká Óri, begins.

THE PAST

The area was already inhabited in Minoan and Mycenaean times, as can be seen from traces of an early-Minoan settlement above Stýlos and a monumental beehive tomb from Mycenaean times between Stýlos and Aptéra. But it is mainly the impressive ruins of the ancient city of Aptéra, magnificently situated on a 250-meter high foothill of the Lefká Óri above the mouth of the Kiliáris, which capture the imagination. This city, with its strategic location, dominated the Apokórona and the area to the west along the Bay of Soúdha for 1400 years, from the 7th century B.C. until the destruction of the city by an earthquake in 700 A.D. Many ruins recollect the prime of the ancient Aptéra. Contemporaries of Aptéra were Almirídha on the northern coast (with not only attractive beaches but also a lovely mosaic floor in a 5th or 6th century basilica) and Amfímalla by present Yeoryioúpoli, at the mouth of the Almyró.

In the Second Byzantine Period the area around Stýlos (including Aptéra) was ceded to the monastery of St. John at Patmos by the Byzantine emperor. After this the monks of the monastery established a *metókhi*, a dependency, in Aptéra (now partly restored). A dependency was also established at Stýlos in 1088, of which only a church, the Panayía Serviótissa, remains. This imposing church is one of the oldest still remaining in Crete. Close by, lonely and magnificent in a valley by Kiriakosélia, lies another church from this time: the Áyios Nikólaos. It is not only because of its age (c. 1100) that it is one of the treasures of Crete, but also because of its very old and beautiful frescos, which date back to 1230.

In the Venetian Period this area was an important agricultural region. This can be seen, for instance, in the Venetian mansion where the folklore museum of Gavalokhóri is now housed. As so often in Crete, it is

View from Aptéra over the Bay of Soúdha

especially the beautiful frescos in the Orthodox village churches which were painted in the Venetian time – in Byzantine style – which call to mind this period. At Alíkambos the church of the Panayía is one of the most beautifully frescoed churches in Crete, with frescos painted by Ioánnis Pagoménos in 1315, among others. Frés also has a church with lovely frescos, the Áyios Yeóryios.

The fortified mansion of Embrosnéros and especially the impregnable fortifications on the island of Soúdha recall the military occupation by the Venetians. The island was fortified in 1579 in answer to the renewed Ottoman threat at the end of the 16th century. Indeed, the son and successor of Suleyman the Magnificent, Selim II (better known in Europe as 'The Sot' because of his excessive consumption of alcohol) had set forth his father's political expansion in the Mediterranean Sea. In 1566 the Venetian Cyclades as well as Genoan Chios were conquered by the Ottoman admiral Piyale Pasha and in August 1571 Cyprus fell (until then it had been a Venetian possession). In October 1571 a confrontation took place between the Ottomans and the Catholic nations: the Battle of Lepanto, between the Ottoman fleet on one side and the united fleet of Venice and Spain on the other. In order to have enough galley slaves the Ottoman fleet swept through all the Venetian-occupied territories in the summer of that year. Corfu suffered greatly, as well as Crete: the island of Soúdha was attacked, as was the city of Réthymnon, and the coast of Mylopótamos was plundered in the search for galley slaves. The outcome of the Battle of Lepanto was that the Ottoman fleet was defeated. It was quickly restored, however. In 1574 the Venetian proveditore Foscarini made a survey of Crete and partially because of his critical report Venice took up the reinforcement of Crete. The island of Soúdha was reinforced, together with Réthymnon (where the Fortétsa was built) and the small islands of Spína Lónga, near Áyios Nikólaos, and Gramvoússa, in the far northwest.

But in 1645 the Ottomans succeeded in invading the island. In that year Khaniá was occupied, followed by the occupation of the surrounding area. The Apokórona also came under Ottoman rule in that year. By 1669 the whole island was in Ottoman hands. However, the island of Soúdha remained Venetian for a time, as did Spína Lónga and Gramvoússa. Gramvoússa was lost in 1692, and Soúdha and Spína Lónga in 1715.

In the Ottoman Period we hear of the area again in the 19th century, after the uprising of 1821. Soon after the official proclamation of the rebellion on June 14th, 1821 the Ottoman armies passed through the region to 'pacify' it. As can be seen from the map, control of the Apokórona was essential for the route between Khaniá and the eastern cities of Réthymnon and Herákleion. Moreover, one of the passes to the region of the Sfakians was located here. In the summer of 1821 Ottoman troops wreaked havoc in the region. There were 3000 civilian casualties. At the end of that year the revolutionaries succeeded in driving out the Ottomans, and Arméni became a center for the rebels' temporary government.

But the Albanian troops of Mehmed Ali who were called on to help in 1822 by the sultan in Istanbul brought the region back into Ottoman control, under the consecutive commanders Hassan Pasha and Huseyn Bey, both brothers-in-law of Mehmed Ali. In May of 1824 the revolution temporarily failed.

Then, in order to subdue the rebellious Greeks, Mehmed Ali sent his Albanian troops to the mainland. In 1824/1825 the Bay of Soúdha became the assembly point for the troops, who under Mehmed Ali's son Ibrahim Pasha would recapture the Peloponnesos in 1825 from the Greek rebels. In Crete Huseyn Bey was replaced by Mustafa Pasha, Hassan Pasha's nephew. He would be governor of Crete until 1850. In 1830 it was clear that England would not accept Crete being separated from the Ottoman Empire. Under English instigation, the island became a province under the Egyptian *khedive* Mehmed Ali (albeit under suzerainty of the Ottoman sultan). In 1840 Crete came under direct Ottoman rule again.

Later, the Apokórona played an important role during other uprisings against the Ottomans, such as those of 1866-1869, 1878 and 1895. But because our travellers had no knowledge of these uprisings, we will not go into them any further. One thing to mention, however, is that after the revolution of 1866-1869 the Ottoman rulers built the fort Firkás, with the lower bulwark Itzeddin, at the ruins of Aptéra.

This is the region where Pashley began his exploration of Crete on February 16th, 1834. He was accompanied by his regular draughtsman Antonio Schranz and by a Turkish guide who, it was soon apparent, hardly knew the territory. Western visitors to Crete moved from monastery to monastery as much as possible, to spend their nights there. When a monastery was not available they usually found shelter with the head of the village (the *proestós* or the *kapetán*).

Pashley, I, p. 28 – 35

We started from Khaniá about noon, and traversed the plain by which the city is surrounded, and the greater part of which, in the direction of Súdha, was stript of its olives when Ibrahím-pashá landed here with his troops in January 1825, on his way from Egypt to the Moréa [the Peloponnesos]. Half a mile before we arrive at the Salt-pans, which have changed their Italian name Saline into the Turkish Túzla, the ground becomes a marsh, and would be impassable but for the aid afforded us by portions of an old paved road, doubtless the work of the Venetians. The marsh is about three miles in circumference, and is said to abound in snipes. After passing the head of the bay we wound along the north-western acclivity of Mount Maláxa, and again found considerable remains of the Venetian paved way, which was in fact our only road for nearly two miles; no labour seems to ever to have been bestowed on it since the Turks obtained the island, so that it is, in general, a far worse road than an unpaved path would be.

The rock of Súdha [the island of Soúdha], which is a conspicuous object during most of the ride, is said to have served as a constant receptacle for corsairs, during the sixteenth century; and was also used as a landing place in 1571, by Turkish troops, some of whom ravaged the territory of Khaniá, while others sacked and burnt the town of Rhíthymnos [Réthymnon]. The Venetians therefore prudently determined to fortify the islet; and, in consequence, retained it, with Spina Longa and the almost impregnable castle of Grabúsa [Gramvoússa], during many years after the whole island of Crete had been acquired by the Turks.

The events which were caused by this hostile descent on the district of Khaniá and the town of Rhíthymnos, serve to throw light on the Venetian government of the island.

The Greek peasants of the neighbourhood of Rhíthymnos supposed, at that time, that certain nobles were preparing to take signal vengeance on them for the violent death of a Cavaliere, which had just happened: and, on this account, they sent a deputation to the Turks at Súdha, whom they hailed as their deliverers from the cruel tyranny of their Venetian lords.

Another Venetian writer assigns these practices of the Greeks with the Turks at Súdha, simply to their general oppression by the Cavalieri, and to the extreme despair to which it reduced them. Their dealings with the Turks seem to have produced at least one good effect, in awakening the Venetian senate, not perhaps to a sense of justice, but, at all events, to one of policy; for the Proveditor Foscarini was soon afterwards dispatched from Venice, to enquire into the real condition of the Cretan people. His extremely interesting Report is still in existence, and presents a melancholy picture of systematic oppression and legalized iniquity, on the part of both the privileged order of nobles and the local government...

At length we began to leave the bay of Súdha, and to pass the ridge: as soon as we reached its summit, we saw the plain of Apokórona spread before us. It is bounded on the south by the eastern half of the White Mountains, the outline of which is very bold and beautiful: they are entirely covered with snow. Immediately on commencing the descent, towards the plain of Apokórona, we turned to our left, in conformity with directions obtained from some peasants whom we had met, and soon saw two ancient tombs; sure indications of our approach to the Palaeókastro, to which I was endeavouring to find my way. They were hewn out of the rock, which is soft and calcareous, and, like the stone of Malta, is full of embedded shells. One of them was a chamber containing resting-places for three occupants, the other had served for four. Scarcely had we passed these tombs before we met a kalógheros, whose Greek shewed at once that he was not a Cretan; and from whom I learnt that we should find a lodging for the night in a monastery or rather metókhi, belonging to the great convent of Hághios Ioánnes the Theologian, at Patmos. The kalógheros was sent here, about a year ago, along with a patéras, to superintend the management of the land and olives possessed by that society in Crete, and which had been entirely abandoned and uncultivated during the whole war [this refers to the uprising of 1821- 1830].

We soon arrived at considerable remains of the walls of an ancient city, and I partially examined them; but sunset put a stop to my researches, and I was glad to hasten to find out the patéras at the metókhi. On approaching it my ears were saluted by the loud barkings of several dogs: they continued to shew their dislike for strangers, who wore dresses which they were so little used to, for some time after we were settled among them. These Cretan dogs are not so ferocious as those of Albania, where the ancient Molossian breed seems to be preserved, in all its purity, to the great discomfort of European travellers. The Cretan animals are all of one race, and are peculiar to the island. Tournefort calls them 'des lévriers bâtards.' They are smaller than the greyhound, and have a longer and rougher coat of hair: their head is somewhat like that of the wolf: they follow their game by scent, and are very sagacious animals, resembling, in every respect, the lurcher rather than the greyhound. I feel no doubt that these dogs are the undebased descendants of those mentioned by ancient authors.

The celebrated dog of Cephalus, to which those of Molossis and Chaonia were proud to trace their pedigree, was supposed to have been obtained, by Procris from Minos, the mythical king of this island: a fact which alone shews how celebrated the Cretan breed must have been in times of remote antiquity.

I had every reason to be pleased with the kindness and hospitality of my reverend host, although his means of displaying his excellent disposition towards us were very limited. The furniture of his room consisted of a bed, a table, and two rude chairs: but my travels in Albania had taught me to consider even beds, tables, and chairs, as the peculiar possessions of those who are surrounded by the other comforts of civilized life; and as ordinarily unattainable by the traveller, while he is exploring the most interesting countries of antiquity.

The venerable priest thought it very odd that I should speak Greek fluently; and had great difficulty in understanding, what he seemed very anxious to learn, how I could leave 'Lóndhra', which is commonly used both by Turks and Greeks of all parts, as synonymous with England, to travel in these districts.

On my enquiring for coins the peasants gave me such as they possessed: they had found them in tilling the ground about the monastery: more than half of those which I obtained were of Aptera. The prices asked by coin-finders in most parts of Greece is so high as to cause considerable difficulty to those who wish to purchase them. Here the peasants would not even name a price, but told me to give them what I thought the things were worth, since I knew their value better than they did. One of them possessed a small marble hand which he also gave me. It was not difficult to find out that I was among a very different people from those with whom travellers become acquainted in following the commonly frequented routes in Greece and Asia Minor; and I began to suspect that, whatever the ancient Cretans may have been, from the time of Polybius to that of St Paul, the present race can hardly deserve the bad character bestowed on their ancestors [this refers to the Roman historical writer Polybius, who described the conquering of Crete by Metellus, and to St. Paul, who describes the Cretans' lying and laziness in his letter to St. Titus].

A boy of about ten years of age, a nephew of the old priest, tells me that the Cretan labyrinth was one of the seven wonders of the world, in the time of the ancient Hellenes, and that these seven wonders correspond to the seven sacraments of the Christian church. Our fare this evening, after I had had a long chat with the priest, consisted of ricemilk, Sfakian cheese, a few onions, some barley bread, and as much water as we wished.

Pashley spent the night in the monastery and continued his story the next day.

Pashley, I, p. 36 – 39

Early this morning [February 17th] I recommenced my examination of the ancient remains. The monastery is in the midst of them, and is not far from the centre of the ancient city. A little distance to the south and south-west, I saw traces of two public buildings where several fragments of shafts of columns, one of which was fluted, were lying near the foundations of walls. To the north-east of the monastery like vestiges of another ancient edifice are noticed: and a little to the eastward similar fragments of columns indicate the sites of three or four other buildings. Not far from these remains I found, on a subsequent visit to the spot, a theatre, which, not having been cut out of the living rock, as most of the Greek theatres are, had lost, as it seemed to me, about two-thirds of its original size, by the degradation of the soil above and around it: sufficient however remained to shew plainly that it was the theatre of the ancient city. To the north of the monastery, and at some little distance from it, near the edge of the descent towards the gulf, are several pieces of columns, one of marble, and two fragments of a bas-relief. Of the outer walls, on the southern and western sides of the city, I saw something last night. From an ancient entrance, which I then passed, on my way to the monastery, they extend about 600 paces towards the gulf, to the north-western point of the city: and, since they are on the brow of the hill, all the ground within their circuit is tolerably level...

To the north-east and north of the metókhi is an extensive brick building consisting of numerous arches, some above ground and others below. Any vaulted building is called a *thólos* by the Greeks, and they took me to one, under ground, which was plainly once a cistern: its width is 13 feet 8 inches, the present height to the spring of the arch 10 feet, and its length 36 feet. In the arch I observe an aperture, as is usual in buildings of this kind. I also notice near the entrance an earthen pipe, and, near the farther extremity, the mouth of a small aqueduct which is eighteen inches wide and almost as high. The walls are covered with a very hard cement: where they have lost this covering, we see the regular brickwork. I have no doubt, from the appearance of the ground outside about this cistern, that it formed one of several, which must have been necessary to ensure a supply of water to so considerable a city, through the long drought of a Grecian summer.

Pashley continues with an elaborate story about earlier visitors to the ruins and about the identification of the city with Aptéra. Then he turns to more worldly matters:

Pashley, I, p. 60
While I was busied in examining some of the existing remains of Aptera, my companion made a sketch of the bay and islet of Súdha, taking it from the walls of the ancient city. On returning to the metókhi the old priest gave us for breakfast some meat fried in oil, and served up swimming in that favourite condiment of almost every Cretan dish. I made him a suitable recompense for the hospitality he had shewn us, preventing any difficulties, which might have arisen in the way of his receiving it, by suggesting, that the trifle which I gave was 'for the Church.'

Thirty years later, on May 3th, 1864, Lear also visited Aptéra and the monastery where Pashley had been welcomed so hospitably. He had left Khaniá that morning on his way to Réthymnon and from there to Herákleion. He was now not only accompanied by his servant George, but also by Zeriff, an armed guide who had been assigned to him by the Ottoman authorities.

Lear, p. 51 – 53
9.30 Set off down to Bay of Suda. Fine view of bay. 10.15 Low marshy plain – Tuzla: saltworks, a few cafés, warehouses, etc. 10.30 Bay of Suda; good wide road. Flat long lines of Akrotíri. Eleven: narrow bay, black arums – smell. 11.15 Ascend. Plane and rill. 11.30 Ascent – and leave road to Kalýves on left; second fountain and fig tree. 11.45 Great ascent: top, 11.50. Turn left: scattery village cum pigs; Apokórona below, and Sphakiá mountains – cloudy. 12.30 Near *metóhi*, having lost our way and returned. Monastery: courtyard, many men and women and pigs and children; priest's room, *rakí*, etc. *Hegoúmenos* – dull man. Lunch at two. Cloudier. Take man as

guide to walls. Nothing can be more mortifying after such trouble and expense than to find all thrown away; through cloud everywhere. Ida, Sphakiá, all invisible; not even Akrotíri nor Cape Dhrepanon discernible! Walls magnificent, but could do next to nothing for it began to rain. Walked round walls. Write this at four, having come in from the rain. Beastly noisy boy. Fooly *kalógheros*, blessing God for the English affection and benefits towards Greece. Zeriff says nothing. Red waistcoats of men, laced behind. Guide said, pointing to the walls and entrance of Aptera, "Εδῶ ἦτανε τό γκέττο, διά τούς Ἐβραίους' ['here was the ghetto, for the Jews']: a nook in the walls. At four it began to rain as we were near some finer, but less old, bits of wall, and then I came in to the *kalógheros's* room, when it rained hard. The *kalógheros* asks many questions about me and George. Zeriff says we can sleep at the Monastery of Karídhi tomorrow, at Episkopí on Thursday and Rethymnon on Friday.

When we set out to see the walls a quiet peasant accompanied me, and showed all very well. Some are very grand and fine, like Tiryns; others like Krani, though not nearly so good. Yet the views of Akrotíri and of Dhrepanon would have been quite splendid had it been fine, and the Sphakiá view glorious if any hills could be at all seen. To make the vexation worse, a beastly little boy made a continual row, till I sent him back, being irritated beyond all bounds. All was mist and rain.

From 4.30 to seven have gone as best it might in the *kalógheros's* room. Lord! how dirty it is! The rain, however, not ceasing and the wind increasing. Converse little. The *kalógheros* is dull; a very weary man of Patmos, to the monastery of which the land here belongs – St John the Theologian. He spoke of the Διάδοχος [the Prince of Wales] and General Bruce, having been at Patmos when they came. "Ω τί μεγάλη δυστυχία!' ['What a great misfortune!'] he continued to howl when I said General Bruce was dead. (Even Zeriff, who listens to all but says nothing, was half alarmed: and after a time, particularly when he began to talk of Turkey and of England's protection of Greece, I was obliged to tell him that the Sultan was a friend of my Queen, as well as the King of Greece.) He acts as steward here for five years. At seven food was brought: *dolmás* (rice and meat in vine leaves), and we had our own cold lamb and *baccalà* [dried salted fish], bread and cheese and a little wine – here there is none. The objectionable boy stood and stared, and the old women also. A most filthy napkin nearly made me sick, so unclean are these people. Good coffee after, and at 8.45 we cleared the room. Then good George made my bed on one side, and now I am in it. Zeriff on the farther sofa, and

George on the one nearer. George's quiet attendance is a very great blessing, but I really doubt if I can go through much more of this Cretan life. There are no signs of better weather tomorrow, and I can't decide what to do: go back, go on or wait. Meanwhile, vermin and *dreadful* sufferings. *Dreadful* sufferings. *No* sleep at all: vermin, blasts of wind, and snoring. So terrible a night it is long since I have passed, and it is only 1.30 a.m. now! A knowledge of Cretan Topography would be hardly gained thus, even if one could make drawings; but with such torture added to the entire throwing-away of time and money! Bah!

5.30 It is fine, thank God! We are packed, and George and I are going out. 7.45 I am back at the very nasty room, St John of Patmos staring, and Mrs St John fanning the coffee. I and George have been able to go all round the walls, and I to draw Ida and what-not; the Sphakian mountains being delightfully clear. Everywhere from the circuit of this ancient place there is a fine view, but the vast hollow of Apokórona plain, backed by the snowy range and seen between crags of a pale gray or nearly white, is magnificent. With the Roman remains I could do nothing; but the end of Akrotíri with Dhrepanon are fine. Well: so far one has to be thankful.

Spratt, travelling by ship from Réthymnon to Khaniá, passed Aptéra in 1853. He obviously enjoyed his visit more than Lear did.

Spratt, II, p.127 – 129, 132 – 134

This Peninsula [Akrotíri] forms one of the most important features in the contour of Crete; and under it is sheltered a deep gulf, the entrance to which is from the east, called the Gulf of Suda – a harbour which is one of the most capacious, safe, and easy of access in the Mediterranean.

The shores confining the entrance are wild and picturesque in the extreme, especially the north-west shore of the Akrotiri, where bold bare cliffs overhang it. Cape Drepano terminates it on the east, in a narrow cliffy point somewhat bent or curved like a reaping-hook (hence the name), alongside of which the largest ship could rub her sides without her keel touching the bottom.

The inner shore of the Akrotiri is rather forbidding, from the absence of cultivation or vegetation, as its chief cultivated part lies upon the high plateau rising abruptly from 500 to 1000 feet above the shore of the bay, upon which are ten villages and a monastery of some repute, the church of which is dedicated to Agia Triadha (the Holy Trinity). There is another, called Agia Katholica, in a picturesque gorge over the north coast. Both of these have been figured and described by Pashley [this region is described in Part 3 of this series], as also by Tournefort and previous travellers, from being so near the town of Khania.

The southern shore of the entrance to Suda bay, however, is well culti-vated and beautifully diversified by hill, and vale, and streamlet, olive-groves spreading over the retiring undulations within the Apokorona valley, from which the eye is carried up to the steeps of the Madara Vouna, or White Mountains, rising as a wall behind it.

It is said in classic fable, that it was here that the Muses and Sirens con-tested for the mastery in music and song, upon a hill over the point of the entrance to the Gulf of Suda, and that the Sirens being vanquished, and losing their plumes in consequence, threw themselves into the sea in front of it in despair.

A town afterwards rose upon the site of the contest, called Aptera, or the wingless, in consequence; and two white islands (according to some three, as there were three Sirens) rose from the sea to represent them: we now actually pass two, indeed three, whitish islets as we enter this fine gulf.

The largest is called Suda. It was well fortified by the Venetians, and was retained by them for some years after the loss of Crete, but at more cost to the republic than profit or advantage. It contains a small garrison of Turks now; but the fortress is crumbling to decay, and its few guns are useless, for a man's thumb or a good walking-stick can be introduced into most of their touch-holes…

Whoever has crossed the deeps of the Aegean Sea on a calm sunny day can never forget the intensity of its ultramarine blue, as it combines the azure reflected from the firmament above, with the blue hues arising from its own crystal-clear transparency and profundity beneath. And if he so crosses this land-locked bowl, this bath of the Sirens (as we may fairly call the deep pool in front of Aptera), and is reflective, imaginative, he might pass from an admiration of the scene around, and of the sub-marine tints below, to such a reverie as the voyagers of past times doubt-less did when slowly sailing over it with the fable in their minds, and at last might figure to himself the attempted flight of the Sirens at the moment of their defeat, and their plunge, with now plumeless pinions, into the clear blue waters – or perhaps even see them again, as mermaids, or nereids, returning to its surface for pastime, and scattering the pearl-drops from their tresses, as gems fall before the footsteps of a fairy. And if he had seen what I and many others saw in these very waters, in this very bay, as doubtless the ancient Cretans or the navigators to its shore often did, and had not modern science and experience to guide him and settle his judgment, he might have believed in mermaids and sea-nymphs too.

Early one calm summer's morning, when we were lying at anchor off the Tuzla Scala, at the head of Suda Bay, and the surface of the bay was like a mirror, the officers and men then on board were suddenly attracted by something unusual that was seen splashing and apparently sporting upon the surface of its waters at no great distance from them, and to naked eyes looked remarkably like a human head and neck, with long flowing tresses, which, from its action, the creature seemed to be occasionally throwing and tossing about from side to side, or beating upon the surface of the then calm bay, as if to free them from their entanglement, or from the matted weed they had caught up from the rocky recesses of the deep whence the strange creature had come. A mermaid, truly! might easily have been the exclamation and belief of many who saw it, had they lived a century or two earlier.

And what was this phenomenon? is the natural inquiry. Merely a common seal that was disappointing a Cretan gentleman of a delicacy of the deep; for it was breakfasting upon a huge Octopodia, or species of eight-armed sepia or cuttlefish, with which it had risen from the bottom and come to the surface to free itself from the long tenacious arms which the strong and muscular creature had entwined round the head, face, and shoulders of the amphibian; and as these arms are each provided with large cup-like suckers, the Octopodia's strength of hold is such that it could easily drown a man with two or three of them only, if the rest were firmly attached to a stone or rock at the bottom. Hence the seal's struggles and splashing to detach them.

When the seal had tired out by wounding, or half-drowned its victim in the air by remaining sufficiently long at the surface, it then leisurely and apparently playfully tossed and turned it over and over as a cat does a mouse; and thus represented to a distant observer all the fanciful attitudes of a mermaid in sport, or in the act of clearing her tresses from entanglements.

What more is wanting to explain the origin of mermaids, or perhaps even that of the fable of the Sirens of Aptera, over whose bath or pool we have been induced for a moment here to pause and to contemplate?

We now direct our attention to Pashley again, who after his visit to Aptéra on the morning of February 17th went searching for more ancient cities that same day.

Pashley, I, p. 61 – 67

On taking leave of the venerable priest, and of the site of Aptera, we descended the eastern slope of the hill into the plain of Apokórona, and, soon after reaching it, crossed a river [Kiliáris] which arises from several copious sources, near the village of Stýlo, seen a little to our right at the foot of the White Mountains. The water of these springs is said to be deliciously cold in the summer. They are mentioned by Buondelmonti [in the beginning of the 15th century the Florentine monk Buondelmonti wrote a description of Crete]. Hardly had we reached the plain before my ignorant and stupid guide lost the road, and in consequence we had to cross the river, which winds considerably in the plain, no less than three times, and, on the third occasion, the narrow stream was so rapid, that a dog, by which I had long been accompanied, was carried down it much more that a hundred yards, as he swam across. After traversing the greater part of the plain, we arrived at the village of Neokhório, situated on a gentle ascent. Near it is a lofty country house, which, I should suppose, must once have belonged to a Venetian cavaliere. I found the dhidháskalos Anagnóstes, and learnt from him that there are other very considerable remains, consisting of 'great stones and marbles, just as at the Palaeókastron near Súdha' at Hághios Mámas, on a hill about two miles to the west of Neokhório. I thought myself fortunate in obtaining this information, especially since I believed the word Apokórona to be a corruption of Hippocorona or Hippocoronion, the name of an ancient Cretan city…

Having obtained this gratifying information respecting the existence of ancient remains, similar to those examined yesterday and this morning, I pursued my journey towards and up the barren and unfrequented side of the mountain, and traversed a wild and dreary glen in the full hope of finding ere long some vestiges of another ancient city. At length I arrived at the hamlet of Kyriakusália, and one of its peasants offered to conduct me to the ancient walls. He took me to the cave of Hághios Mámas, and to a dripping source below it: thence, with no slight difficulty, I clambered up to the top of the hill, and found the supposed ancient remains to be walls of a middle-age fortress. The reward which I obtained was a fine view of the whole plain of Apokórona, and of the bay of Armyró with Cape Dhrépano on its west: unfortunately I had scarcely enjoyed it for a moment before it began to rain. The only vestiges of buildings which I found where those of a church. A single wall surrounded the whole summit: remains of it are seen in a great part of its extent.

Finding, on my return to Kyriakusália, that I had not time to reach Fré, the principal village of Apokórona, by sunset, I proceeded only to Rhamné, a little hamlet, situated on the lower ranges of the White Mountains, to which a Greek undertook to shew Our Highnesses the way from Kyriakusália. My stupid Turk knew neither the road nor any thing else. A very short ride, chiefly through groves of olives brought us to Rhamné. The Proestós of this village had such indifferent accommodation to offer, that he took us to the house of a friend, where however we certainly did not fare sumptuously, and had to sleep in the same room with our horses. The people were most anxious to do all they could for us: the Proestós spent some time himself in searching the village for eggs, which at last he found: the only addition to them consisted of olives, black barley-bread and plenty of excellent water. The evening meal of my host and his wife was a dish of wild herbs, on which the Cretans seem chiefly to live: they boil them, and then serve them up in oil; bread, olives, and sometimes cheese, completing the meal. On this occasion our accommodations were certainly most indifferent, and the people were fully aware of it. 'What a difference there must be, said they, between Lóndhra and this place.' They had never seen an European before. We found it cold in spite of our host's exertions to keep up a good fire: the snow was lying on the mountains down to within fifty or sixty feet of the level of the village.

The daughter of the Proestós of Rhamné was taken prisoner, by the Mohammedans, during the war, and was sold as a slave at Alexandria, where she remained twelve years. On obtaining her freedom, a few months ago, she immediately returned to her native village, speaking both Turkish and Arabic nearly as fluently as her mother-tongue.

The party of Mohammedans, which carried off this young woman from Rhamné, fell in with my host's father on the same occasion. In conformity with their general custom, they put him to death. At the same period of the struggle the Christians used invariably to slay even their female prisoners: this was done to avoid, what was regarded as a still deeper crime than murder, improper familiarity between their own warriors and any woman who had not received Christian baptism.

Thus also, in the tenth century, on the capture of the Mohammedan capital of the this then Mohammedan island, by the troops of Romanus II, we are told of the general massacre of the inhabitants, without distinction of age or sex; and the Christian poet, Theodosius Diaconus, praises the Emperor for his paternal solicitude to prevent the possible pollution of his Christian soldiers by familiarities with the unbaptized women of Crete.

The recent custom of the Christian insurgents in this island, repugnant as it is to *our* notions of religion and humanity, resembles the conduct which was sometimes enjoined on the ancient Israelites. Their too lenient treatment of the Midianite women, whom they took captives 'with their little ones,' slaying only all the males, is represented as having excited the indignation of Moses. Elsewhere the Greeks used to be more merciful to their female captives, than they were in Crete, during the early part of the struggle for independence: and an English missionary considers, that the great mischiefs, caused during the revolution by the captive women and the plunder, 'throw light on the command of utter extermination laid upon the Israelites.' I learn, from the same respectable authority, that 'Turkish women have been a snare, even to several of the Greek Bishops; and they have thereby occasioned not only incalcuble injury to these Ecclesiastes themselves, but have also brought infinite scandal on their profession.' These inconveniences the Cretan mode of warfare effectually prevented.

The following day Pashley travelled on to the east, to Almyró (now Yeoryioúpoli).

Pashley, I, p. 67 – 69

We descended into the plain by a stony mountain-path, and after passing a copious fountain, called White-Water, arrived at the Hellenic bridge [over the Almyró]. I found a number of Greeks sitting round a chafing dish in the little hut, called a coffee-house, just by the bridge: I drank a glass of wine with them, and was told that considerable Hellenic remains exist two miles inland at Alíkampo [Alíkambos, to the south]. One of the company was a Papás, who, supposing, like most of his fellow-countrymen, that my journey could have solely a political object, addressed me very warmly in behalf of his fellow Cretans of the Christian faith, expatiating on the injustice they had suffered, at the hands of Allied Powers, by being transferred to the dominion of Mehmét-Alí. He spoke of all that they had done, and of their present condition: 'We are mere slaves now, have pity on us, and set us free. We arose and took our arms, and slew the Mohammedans, for the sake of our religion and of our Christ: he dwells above his own kingdom, and will recompense our deliverers.'

On leaving this coffee-house to pursue our journey towards Rhíthymnos, we follow the eastern bank of the river which runs down from the White Mountains, and falls into the sea about a mile and a half from this bridge, near a hamlet called Armyró, where are seen the remains of a ruined castle. The valley is narrow here, and the modern fort was probably built both to defend the village from any attack of pirates, and to defend the gorge.

There was a good deal of fighting hereabouts at the beginning of the Greek revolution. On one occasion the Mohammedans effected their passage through the defile, and, on advancing into the district of Apokórona, fell in with more than a hundred Christians, who surrendered to them. These prisoners were all taken to a field near Kalýves, where most of them were put to death. Several were impaled, and the stake of one of the unhappy men who endured this cruel torture, fell with him during the succeeding night. On this he managed to crawl to a neighbouring fountain, assuaged his thirst with its water, and immediately expired. This event reminds us of the sacred narrative: 'When Jesus had received the vinegar, he said, It is finished: and he bowed his head, and gave up the ghost.' [Pashley adds a long, learned footnote to this incident, where he refers to the use of the stakes. Among other things, he says, 'I was often told that those who suffered these horrible and excruciating torments, which were frequently inflicted on the Christians of Crete during the war, used always to cry out, while on the stake, 'Water! Water!']

At no great distance from the coffee-house we saw in succession the villages of Kalamítzo and Xystópoli, on the hills which rise up a little to the west of the opposite bank of the river. At Armyró all is desolation: the castle was stormed and dismantled by the Greeks at the very commencement of their insurrection, and the village seems to have shared the castle's fate. A little to the east of it the salt spring, from which its name is derived, flows out of the bank: an acquaintance of mine once drank freely of its water, in the summer time, and quickly found out what potent virtues it possesses.

Spratt was also at Almyró, right before his visit to the Bay of Soúdha in 1853.

Spratt, II, p. 123, 124

The harbour and river alluded to by the anonymous 'Periplus' is no doubt the deep but brackish water-stream of the Armyro, in the corner of the bay, where numerous springs, gushing out of the base of a hill a mile from the sea, and near the ruins of a old khan and castle, unite with a rivulet and torrent-bed that issues through a gorge from the Apokorona valley.

The entrance to the river is, however, now barred by rocks and a sand-bank, over which there is never more than three feet of water at the present time; but the adjacent coast-cliff shows that there has been a rise of fully six feet of the littoral margin and sea-bed, a rise which, from evidences in other parts that will be hereafter noticed [see Part 3 of this series], I can affirm has resulted from successive small movements since the time of the authors who have written of these Cretan cities. Yet there is no record or local tradition of the fact, although elsewhere it has destroyed several old sea-ports, and thus tended in part to the desertion of the towns in connexion with some of them. This is an interesting physical fact that I shall have frequently to refer to in the concluding notice of the western part of Crete, and by which, until accident developed to me the late date of the movement, I was greatly puzzled in respect to many interesting points in the ancient geography of this part of the island.

Lear was also here, after his visit to Aptéra. He was grumbling, of course.

Lear, p. 53 - 55

Off, 8.30, I giving the silly *kalógheros* 20 piastres, who came some way with us. At nine, going down an odious stony descent and making for the plain; the landscape vast and imposing, though wanting in character as to detail. We are to go and halt at Arméni, and to sleep at Karýdhi. 9.15 Below Aptera. Magnificent green valley, and clear line of snow mountains. 9.30 I and George pass the river, on foot. It was *awfully* cold, and rapid, and up above my knees, and I funked cramp. We had to cross direct, and then zigzag, to avoid holes and currents, but Zeriff knew all well. The scene was green and delightful; dark green foliage and snow beyond. After which we went along green fertile fields, here and there by muddy paths or lanes, here and there by viler pavements, till we reached Arméni: an Ottoman village chiefly – mosque outside, and with wooden bazaars and water channels reminding me of Macedonia. At 10.30 we unload at a 'General Shop' and eat: cold lamb, *baccalà* – the shop like most in Akrídha and elsewhere. It is odd enough to hear Mussulmen and Christians all speaking Greek. Blues predominate in dress, but there are red broad belts and caps and waistcoats – or the latter are black. Nasty wine, but a polite Greek in sober dress brought me some good (but not even this act determined the religion of the donor, as it would in other Moslem places, for here the Mussulmen as well as the Christian Greeks all drink wine). Men and women all very large and fine. Boughs on a rough wooden trellis make a shade, and swallows flit thereunder. Gleams in cool greens a plane tree: beyond I see the Sphakian snow. *Nargilehs* are the mode. The river we crossed was the Sphakoryáko; Kiliáris [is the name of] river next Kalýves, which names a Greek tells me, and an *Othomanós*, who take me to see great springs of water and planes in a nearby garden. Returning, at 11.30, we prepare to go. No-one will take any money for anything – I – and another Greek, Manouélis Ierakákis, gives me an ornamented Easter-circular-egg-bedecked bread; the wine-giver was Iannákis Papalákis. Arméni is called in Turkish Tistiklí. Off at twelve, up stony hill. Snake – dead – at 12.15. Akrotíri seems all one with the land; the Aptera a flat and level height, and all the rest becomes very ugly.

A hideous stony undulating ascent succeeds, shutting out all, and at 12.45 we are at the top: anything uglier one cannot imagine. 1 We come to a wide stony Cerigo-like tract – long ugly lines: Vamos and all the end of Dhrepanon visible, but with no hope of beauty. Vamos, 1.30: stop for water. 2 After *horrid* roads, we come in sight of Karýdhi: a broad low valley below great hills and the snow range. Arrive at two; apparently at a village, but really a cluster of *metóhia*. Surprising to relate, a sturdy blue-clad *kalógheros* said, 'Μέ δυσκολία ἔχεις νά κοιμηθῆς ἐδῶ' ['it'll be difficult for you to sleep here']; and an older fellow said 'Δέν ἔχομε καθαρό σπίτι' ['we haven't got a clean house']; 'the *Hegoúmenos* was away', etc. etc. In fact they would not take us in, and Zeriff oddly did not seem to like to press them. We got a glass of superexcellent wine, and prepare to go in disgust. Descend, and rise again, by very pleasing olive parky ground. 3 p.m. always broad olives and corn, and long mountain lines, but *nothing* novel. Horrid, but very picturesque, roads and some fine deep dells. At 3.45 arrive at [Exópolis] and wait at a filthy pothouse outside the ruinous village, while the *Proestós* [village president] is sent to. If I am to suffer again tonight I shall make straight for Rethymnon tomorrow and travel here no more. Torture, and nothing gained by it, is a bore. [Exópolis] is a most miserable place; no decent house can be found, and we must abide in this pothouse. No wine either. Meanwhile, things grow more odious in that pothouse: several drunken Greeks were there, and some sober but angry Turx (both parties being armed it seems likely some row will ensue, and it does not require much travelling in Crete to perceive that its elements are extremely volcanic). In vain we tried two houses or rooms: more filthy still, and the *Proestós* was out. And it was too late to return to Karýdhi and too far to go to Episkopí. (The journey from Haniá to Rethymnon is either performed by steamer or in a single day by horsemen, so that there are no places of any kind used as dwellings by travellers between the two towns.) So I made up my mind to stay with the disgusting drunkards and beggars and filthy people.

Later however the *Proestós*, Harálambi, came and we got an upper empty room, where at seven I write this. At 7.45 asparagus salad, lamb and *baccalà* and good wine. Three Cretans sit and stare. The little owl doth cry; the fleas do bite. Also the Cretans stare at my going to bed. George and Zeriff sleep in the same room.

3. Between Yeoryioúpoli and Réthymnon

To the east of the passageway between the Lefká Óri and the Gulf of Almyró is a coastal plain which stretches between the Lefká Óri in the west, the west-east spine running across the island in the south, and the ridge between the Níppi and the Vrýssinas in the east. This is the basin of two abundant rivers. In the west flows the Moussélas which originates on the Lefká Óri. And farther to the east flows the Pétres Kamára, which is fed by a southern branch originating with its tributaries on the west-east spine, and also by an eastern branch, the Potamídha, which begins by the Vrýssinas. The west-east spine which borders the region on the south has never been an insurmountable obstacle. Argyroúpoli, at the middle reaches of the Moussélas, is connected by footpaths with the southern coast around Frangokástello. And from Roústika, in the basin of the Pétres Kamára, paths lead to Plakiá and Ayía Galíni in the south.

It is a beautiful area. Apart from the inviting beaches to the east of Yeor-yioúpoli, the most important attractions are the lake of Kourná (the only natural fresh water lake in Crete; a walk around the lake is possible, and there is a lovely walk from Yeoryioúpoli via Alíkambos to the lake), picturesque Argyroúpoli with the ruins of ancient Láppa, the monastery

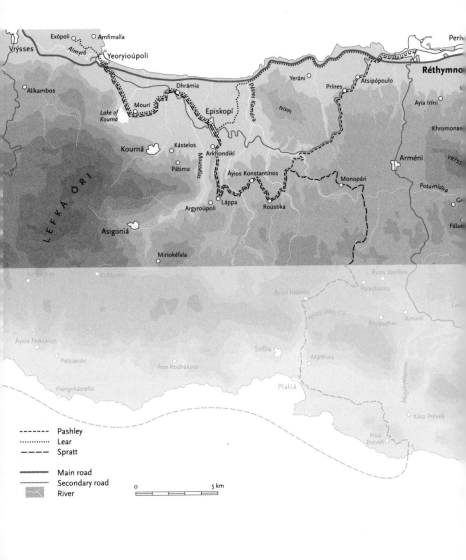

Vrýsses
Exópoli
Amfimalla
Almyró
Yeoryioúpoli
Alíkambos
Dhrámia
Mourí
Lake of Kourná
Episkopí
Kourná
Kástelos
Arkhondikí
Pátima
Áyios Konstantínos
Láppa
Argyroúpoli
Roústika
Asigoniá
Miriokéfala

Yeráni
Prínes
Atsipópoulo
Réthymno
Periv
Ayía Iríni
Khromonas
Arméni
Monopári
Potamídha
Fálar
G

LEFKÁ ÓRI
petres Kamaró
Níppi
Mouséllas
VRÝSS

Áyios Vasílios
Paleolóutra
Áyios Ioánnis
Koxaré
La
ÁYIOS VASÍLIOS
Afsipadhes
Áyios Néktarios
Patsianós
Sellía
Mýthios
Áno Rodhákino
Frangokástello
Plakiá
Megalopótamos
Káto Préveli
Píso Préveli

- - - - - - Pashley
· · · · · · · · · · Lear
- - - - Spratt

━━━━━ Main road
───── Secondary road
River

0   5 km

of Profítis Ilías at Roústika, the church of the Panayía located a bit farther away in Miriokéfala, and the Mycenaean cemetery of Arméni in the
east.

Although the region was undoubtedly inhabited in Minoan times, there
are hardly any traces remaining. An important Minoan peak sanctuary is
found at the top of the Vrýssinas. The cemetery at Arméni, on the western side of the Vrýssinas, dates from the Mycenaean period.

During the Dark Ages the city of Fálanna (by Gouledhianá) flourished, directly south of the Vrýssinas at the headwaters of the Potamídha. There is not much known about the history of the city, but evidently it was important enough to have a basilica during the First Byzantine
Period.

Better known is Láppa, at the site where Argyroúpoli now lies. Láppa
flourished at the end of the Dark Ages, in the 8th century B.C. It was one
of the most powerful cities in western Crete, and for centuries it con-
trolled the entire area between the Lefká Óri and the Kédhros/Vrýssinas
range, from the northern coast to the southern. Láppa was also the city
which in the third century B.C. received the retreating army of Lýttos (or
Lýctos, by the present Kastélli Pedhiádhas), after that city was occupied
by her rivals Knossós and Górtyn (see Part 2 of this series). In 67 B.C., after
violent resistance against the Roman invaders, Láppa was captured and
destroyed. But under orders from Augustus it was restored to prosperity.
This is why there are now traces of the Roman past to be found everywhere in Argyroúpoli. Examples of this are the remnants of an aqueduct
and a 3rd century floor mosaic. To the north of the city was a Roman
cemetery with rock graves, next to the church of the Pénte Párthenes
(the Five Virgins). Close by stands a gigantic, ancient plane tree near a
spring where according to tradition holy water emerges.

To the north of Láppa, at the mouth of the Moussélas, lay Hydramia
(now called Dhrámia), supposed to be the harbour of Láppa.

After the arrival of Christianity, Láppa became seat of a bishopric.
According to tradition the Muslim conquerers of Crete destroyed the
city in the 9th century. After the Byzantines recaptured Crete in 961 the
seat of the bishopric was moved to Episkopí, on the lower reaches of the
Moussélas. During this same period, at Miriokéfala on the upper reaches
of the Moussélas, there was a center established for the spread of the
Orthodox faith. Around the year 1000 the great Ioánnis Xénos lived here,

who spread the Orthodox faith around Crete from this place. He established an important monastery here and its church, the Panayía Antifonítria, can still be admired with its magnificent frescos from around 1000 to 1200. The monastery itself lost its influence in Ottoman times, to the benefit of Profítis Ilías at Roústika, and since the end of the 19th century it has not functioned as a practicing monastery.

On the site of Láppa another regional center grew during the Venetian Period. At the time it was called Pólis. Its Venetian past is still obvious. Among other things there are the remains of villas and workshops, and the Áyios Nikólaos (dating from the 11th century) has beautiful 14th century frescos created by Crete's most famous fresco painter, Ioánnis Pagoménos. More to the east, in Roústika, the church of Panayía and Sótiros Khristós also has exceptional frescos dating from the 14th century. The beautifully situated Profítis Ilías monastery, close to Roústika, was established at the end of the Venetian Period. It flourished during Ottoman times. It is still a functioning monastery, and is well worth a visit.

The military presence of the Venetians in this area is recalled in the castle of Monopári (Bonripari, established by the Genoans when they attempted to occupy the island).

After the capture of Réthymnon by the Ottomans in 1646 the history of the region was closely connected with that of Réthymnon, as it belonged to this province. The region suffered greatly during the uprising of 1821-1830, as did the rest of the island. In the aftermath of this, inhabitants of Sfakiá settled in the empty villages.

In the text, referring to the Sfakian Maniás, the conquering in 1825 of Gramvoússa by the revolutionaries is mentioned. Indeed the rebellion had been rekindled in that year. As explained in the previous chapter, the uprising had been suppressed by Albanian troops from Egypt in 1824. But in August of 1825 Cretans who had fled to the mainland managed to capture the fortified island of Gramvoússa in northwest Crete. In the years to come, this served as a bridgehead to Crete for the rebels.

There are also references in the text to the battle of Navarino. During this naval battle in October 1827 the European powers defeated an Ottoman-Egyptian fleet in the Bay of Navarino (by Náfpaktos). This defeat led to a renewed insurrection and ultimately to the independence of mainland Greece in 1832.

We join Pashley's exploration again at Yeoryioúpoli (Almyró). He arrived there on February 18th, 1834 and in his book he identified the place as either the city of Amfimalla or Amfimatrion. After this he continued to the east.

Pashley, I, p. 71 – 73

I had scarcely passed this supposed site of Amphimatrion, and neighbourhood of Amphimalla, before my guide again lost the road. Ere long we were rambling at the foot of the hills on the south edge of the narrow plain which runs along the shore from Armyró eastward. In somewhat less than three quarters of an hour we arrived at Murní [Mourí], a small hamlet, where we had great difficulty in procuring something to eat, of which we were greatly in want, having most improvidently neglected to take any provisions with us.

There is a small lake near this place, at the foot of the hills: it is called Lake Kurná. The name is derived from a village, consisting of about eighty Christian and five Mohammedan families, situated on the hill above it. The people told me that there are no fish in the lake. Buondelmonti's account, after passing, when at sea, the mouths of the rivers in the plain of Apokórona, is that they saw a rocky coast, and, at no great distance, a river, which his description identifies with this of Armyró. According to his information the little lake Kurná was full of fine eels.

Although I heard of no ancient remains near this lake, it would seem highly probable that the place Corion and a temple of Athene were both in this neighbourhood. This observation has been made by Mr Sieber [a German traveller from the beginning of the 19th century] and also by Professor Hoeck. Stephanus of Byzantium mentions the place, temple, and lake. I can hear of no other lake in the island, and the identity of this permanent physical feature more than makes up for the slight change in the name. Salmasius and Berkelius both wished to read Artemis instead of Athene in the passage of Stephanus, because Callimachus gives to that goddess the epithet of Corian. But, as is observed by Holstenius, both Pausanias and Cicero mention the Corian Athene or Minerva, and therefore no alteration is necessary in the text of Stephanus.

Pashley explains this last passage thoroughly with scholarly footnotes, which we will not cite here (roughly one third of Pashley's book consists of these sorts of footnotes). Twenty years later Spratt also visited the lake.

The only lake in Crete is in this neighbourhood, at two miles south of Almyro. It is deep and nearly a mile in length, situated under the base of the nearest spur of the Askypho Mountains, at the bottom of a crater-like bowl, and surrounded by thickets of brush- and underwood, which hang upon the steep sides of the enclosing hills. The water is as clear as crystal, and fresh; it must therefore have its chief source in the bed of the lake, since no torrent-bed opens into it; and when the rains increase the mountain-springs, this also must increase in its supply, and swell the lake, which, in consequence of its depth and abruptness, has no marshy shore, and, I was told, contains no fish but eels. When an unusual quantity of rain falls, the lake fills and overflows its only low margin on the north side facing the coast, carrying with it numerous large eels, that then become strewed over the plain, thus confirming the statement of Buondelmonte the Florentine traveller, who mentions this fact. Pashley identifies the lake as the ancient Coria, near which was a temple to the Corian Athene or Minerva (vol. i. chap. v. p.73); but I could find no remains or tradition to indicate its true site, although it doubtless stood there.

We return to Pashley, who, as we have seen, arrived at Lake Kourná as a result of his guide being lost.

I ought to have kept close to the shore, towards which I now proceed, and in less than an hour arrive at Dhrámia, a little village entirely occupied by Sfakians, who descend from their homes, on the higher ranges of the mountains, in the month of October or November, and remain here till the following April. If they staid up in Sfakiá, they would be confined to their houses, by the snow, for several weeks in the winter: and those who remain lay in a stock of food and fuel before the heavy falls of snow, just as if they were going to sea for some weeks...

Annoyed as I had so repeatedly been, by the ignorance and stupidity of my Turkish guide, and revolving in my mind plans by which I might hope to succeed in replacing him by a better at Rhíthymnos, I descended the brow of the little hill at the foot of which a river flows [the Mouséllas] between Dhrámia and the village of Episkopé and divides the eparkhías of Rhíthymnos and Apokórona.

I should mention, with respect to this Turk, that he had but recently arrived from Anatolía, and spoke not a single word of Greek; the consequence of which was, that he could not make himself understood by any of the people: and thus in addition to the annoyance caused me by his ignorance of the country, I was not left unmolested by him, even on arriving at our resting place for the evening; but had to act as his interpreter.

As I was passing the village of Dhrámia then, about an hour before sunset, I met a tall and handsome Sfakian, who, after a great deal of Cretan politeness in salutations and compliments, learnt from me, that I was going to travel all over the island, and that I wished to make myself thoroughly acquainted with it. On this he offered to be my guide, assuring me, and he afterwards verified his assertion, that no one could be better acquainted with Crete than himself, and that it would afford him great pleasure to accompany me. Our pecuniary arrangements were easily completed, and he agreed to come on to the village of Episkopé, with mules to replace the horses of my Turk, early in the evening.

Captain Maniás was born at Askýfo, the principal place in the eastern part of Sfakiá, and lost his father when very young. At the outbreaking of the Greek Revolution he was only about sixteen years of age, and, for some time after its commencement, he was always near the person of his uncle Búzo-Márko, who fell in the year 1825, as one of the leaders of the party which attempted to surprise the impregnable rock of Grabúsa, in the night, and to carry it by assault. In constant attendance on his uncle, he soon began himself to take an active part in the affairs of the war, and ere long became a Captain, having a considerable body of men under his standard. In the interval between the submission to Khuseín-bey [in 1824] and the insurrection in 1829 [actually 1828], he armed a kaík, and made descents upon the coast of Crete, chiefly in the province of Sitía, where he made prisoners, in the space of less than two years, sixty-four Mohammedans, if his own story be true, which I believe it to be. The prisoners he sold as slaves, and most of them were soon redeemed. Kasos was the mart where he disposed of them. From 1829 till the period of final submission to the Egyptians, he had his share in the engagements which took place; and, as I have heard from other Greeks, for I must say that he did not sound the trumpet of his own military exploits, he distinguished himself as one of the foremost combatants on several occasions. The life of war, rapine and bloodshed, which he had led, proved of the highest utility to me, for it had made him so well acquainted with every hill and dale, path and river, in the island, that there were few parts of it where he would not have proved an unerring guide even at midnight.

I thought myself fortunate in meeting with such a person, especially since daily intercourse with him would render me better acquainted with that most remarkable part of the population of Crete, the Sfakian mountaineers, than I could possibly have become by a mere ramble of ten days or a fortnight in their mountains.

This Sfakian accompanied me during the greater part of my travels in the island, and proved himself to be a man, who, though entirely destitute of education, was yet possessed of extraordinary abilities, and was certainly, I believe, quite unequalled in most of the important qualities of a guide in such countries.

Maniás would remain Pashley's guide for the rest of his tour. Twenty years later Spratt hired him also, and he also spoke with much feeling about this heir to Achilleus and Herakles. He died from a fever while Spratt was on his way to Ierápetra (see Part 2 of this series). Pashley stayed overnight in Episkopí.

Pashley, I, p. 80

Episkopé now consists of about sixty dwellings: it contained near three hundred at the outbreaking of the revolution, and, as in every other village, the heaps of ruined houses remain as the flames left them, and present a picture of desolation, which, in a country of such fertility and possessing such undeveloped resources, is quite lamentable. On entering the village I was struck with its devastated and lonely aspect; and on my making an observation on the subject to an inhabitant, he replied that 'the Christians had burnt all the houses:' an answer which shewed that he was a Mohammedan, as I learnt that most of his fellow-villagers are. I found half a dozen of them in the coffeehouse of the village, smoking their pipes; the ordinary occupation of followers of the Prophet. I had no little difficulty in obtaining a lodging, although at last I met with very tolerable accommodation in the house of a Christian. Captain Maniás came to me in the evening, and told me that he had found mules, and should be ready, early in the morning, to start for the antiquities, which as I learnt from him, are to be seen at Pólis, a large village on the northern slopes of the Sfakian hills, and a little to the south of our present restingplace.

Lear also went to Episkopí, in 1864. On May 5th he woke up at 4.00 a.m in Exópolis, where we left him complaining.

Rose at four, and at 5.30 (having paid 10 piastres to host) left this piggery, and came out with George to the church above, where I drew till 6.30, a pleasant and fine expanse. During all yesterday, this, and the view from above Karýdhi, are the only two I could have wished to draw, and the latter was not clear as to distance and so useless, as it was mainly a rich olive-covered valley scene. Certainly, Crete has few very picturable scenes hitherto, though it is full of loveliness. I go now to the filthy café of last afternoon, and mean to go and see Kourná. The abundant richness and greenness of the scene before me, and the quiet, are charms not often got nowadays: what fields! what a land of food and riches! O land! O Crete! O morning!

Café, and off at 6.30. Stony descent. Most lovely morning! Fresh green-lanes, as it were. Low olives. And I and George wait to listen to the ἀηδόνια [nightingales] who are wonderful. 7.15 Draw river scene, which at seven I and George forded barefoot – great fun. Freshness and nightingales. 7.30 Ruins of Armyró and fountain with two planes. Great stream. Mills. Plain. 7.45 Leave Rethymnon road and go up hill slightly towards Kourná. Ground very lovely – parky green – large clumps of great oax: δρύϊα [dhrýia] not βελανίδα [velanídha]. Zeriff says there were great numbers of these trees, but they have been cut down; indeed we saw two being burned to make them fall. This spot is quite delightful, cistus and myrtle everywhere.

8.30 We are at the Lake of Kourná – very fine and Cumberlandish – in a nook at the foot of very high hills. Draw, and at nine come to trees not far off, leaving the very beastly-forlorn *metóhi* sort of house close to the lake. 'Ἐκοιμηθήκαμε μαζί μέ τά γουρούνια μιά φορά εἰς τίς εἴκοσι τέσσερις ὧρας καί δέν φθάνει·' ['We've slept with pigs once in twenty-four hours; isn't that enough?'], says George, [who] is gone a-wild grapes getting. (George says, while I was drawing this morning, a man kept taking lice out of his head and killing them with the edge of the coffee pot.) We have sent the chap of the *metóhi*, who has brought us a jug, for a *cuccuma* [coffee pot] – 'ἀλλά δέν εὑρίσκεται' ['but there isn't one to be found'] – also for some glasses, my tin cup being broken. All this morning's walk has been most enjoyable, and the nearer one gets to Ida the more chance there seems of the lines becoming finer, for hitherto they are meagre. At ten we breakfast or lunch: the lamb and *baccalà* are finished, a thousand birds sing, shade of trees delightful; and this pleasure even seems to make amends for past bother and torture. The four sitting

Cretans are wholly tranquil in manner, and discourse a few now and then quietly. I wish I had made a drawing of Ida between the large oaks. 11.15 Lunch is done: the wrens and titmice still sing – still. Zeriff hubblebubbles. The four Cretan creturs sleep, and the sun comes over the oak tree I lie beneath so I must move. Very delightful hours, like those – *somewhat*– of the days that are no more. I hear from George that the real *Hegoúmenos* of the Karýdhi Monastery is in prison, on suspicion of having aided his brother in the death of a man killed in the monastery. I thought something was wrong: but why did Zeriff take us there? The three Cretans opened on this when I praised the monastery wine, and τόσο [much] is offered for the head of the murderer.'

Noon. We prepare to go: lovely air! and most beautiful mountain spot! What blackbirds! 12-12.30 We wind up a myrtle-grown hillside, making towards the sea; this lake evidently lies 'unwholesomely' low, but the mountains about it are fine. Yet, looking back towards Exópolis and Dhrepanon, the scene is very uninteresting and formless. 1 p.m. Always going up a more and more bare hillside: stunty myrtles and cistus – few – and one or two oleander rivulets. At top: nearing Dhramia, which looks a ruin, and behind is the plain I drew this morning from Exópolis; in the middle the long formless promontory of Dhrepanon – right – and the upper part of the Kourná hills – left – with the snow Sphakian range beyond all. At 1.10 pass Dhramia, and see Episkopí beyond. Dhramia is apparently all in ruins, though with signs of former size. 1.30 Ford small river. 2 Ever going uphill, nearing Episkopí, which *looks*, but I dare say is *not*, better than the last hole. A fine open hilly country; olive plantations about, and corn.

Episkopí proved to be, like the last, more than half in ruins, and the streets or lanes more filthy, as being fuller of inhabitants, the place being larger, and Turks many. Along very insupportable places, we reach the Doctor's house, which Zeriff proposes to go to, I having no letter: but he is out. A relation however came, fat and in a swell Levantine dress, and he orders things indoors: a large, decent, stone-paved room; divan at one end, three windows on one side, portraits of King and Queen opposite, books and vials at t'other end. All the women sent off; coffee and water and thenceforth, talk. Doctor, master of the house and brother-in-law of fat man, and very deaf, came in. We all went out to see a view, passing very nasty bazaar and then downhill. After that we came back and sat again, and then I washed in public.

Later, in pure despair, we went to a garden and examined beans and other vegetables, and now – 6.15 – I sit in hopes of change. Supper at 7.15: a rough sort of cove the brother-in-law, but the Doctor, poor fellow, has much of the gentleman in him. Odd mixture of things! He says 'pardon' in French, and talks about Mazzini and Garibaldi. Rice soup, boiled lamb, eggs and stew – roast with capital Kissamos wine and nuts. Fat cove made his little daughter eat extreme before she went to bed, and then talked to me about the Doctor, who supports his mother and grand-mother: "Η γιαγιά του· αὐτή εἶναι ἴσως σχεδόν ἐνενήντα χρονῶν' ['His grandmother; she's perhaps almost ninety years old.'] Fat man wanted George and Zeriff to sit down when we did: 'Εἶναι κι ἄνθρωποι ἐλεύθεροι' ['they are free men too'], but George and Zeriff didn't. Talked as much as I could, and had the bed made in sight of the family, ὥς διδασκαλία [as a lesson]. At nine got the room clear; 9.30, bed.

Back to Pashley, who thirty years before had also stayed overnight in Episkopí. On February 19th he left for Pólis (Argyroúpoli).

Pashley, I, p. 81 – 84

Captain Maniás, who had gone back to Dhrámia for the night, returned to us about half past seven this morning with the mules, and, soon after, we set off for Pólis, which is also called Gaidhurópolis, the City of Asses, and is situated at no great distance from Episkopé. It is within the con-fines of Rhíthymnos, though very near the borders of Sfakiá. My guide, once told that I am anxious to procure all the coins I can meet with, allows no one, man woman or child, to pass us without questioning them whether they have any thing of the sort 'in gold, silver or brass', and thus we advance but slowly...

Before arriving at Pólis we find considerable remains of a massive brick edifice, at one end of which are some buttresses each fifteen feet wide and projecting about nine feet. Close by are remains of an odd cir-cular building, about 60 feet across in its interior... About 300 paces to the south-south-west of Pólis is an ancient cistern 76 feet long and near-ly 20 feet wide. A rapid descent on the western side of the village con-ducts to considerable remains of a Roman brick building, beyond which, in the deep valley between Pólis and the mountain Phterolásko, runs the stream [the Moussélas] which divides the eparkhía of Apokórona from that of Rhíthymnos. Several large caves, containing water both summer and winter, as well as many ancient tombs, excavated out of the solid rock, are said to exist in the neighbourhood of Pólis. Ancient coins are also said to be found in great numbers in the fields about the village, but of those shewn to me the greater part were Venetian. I saw many beautifully shaped ancient earthenware lamps, two of which I purchased. There are remains of some Venetian buildings in the village, one of which was evidently a large palace. Its substructure differs so remarkably from the body of the building, that I cannot but believe it to have belonged to an entirely different age, and to have formed part of a much more ancient edifice...

Pashley devoted several pages of his book to identifying the place with the ancient Láppa. That same day, February 19th, he travelled on.

Pashley, I, p. 88, 96

On leaving Pólis we descend for some time: after seeing several tombs, on our left, we pass the church of Haghíae Parthénoe [the Pénte Párthenes], of which my guide speaks with deep feelings of religious respect; and a hundred paces farther, a most copious fountain, on our right, deriving its name from the same holy and miracle-working virgins to whom the church is dedicated, and who also preside over the waters...

After following, for about two hours, a road unequalled for impracticability by any I have yet seen in the island, we arrived at the village of Hághios Konstantínos, distant about four miles from Pólis, and took up our quarters in the house of a cousin of Captain Maniás. It being Wednesday, the Greeks eat only boiled herbs and bread, to which was added, for us, salt-fish, eggs, and a preparation of camel's flesh, called pástruma, of which I cannot speak very highly. We also obtained plenty of excellent wine; and, during the evening, the two warriors or klefts, by whichever name it is right to call them, amused both themselves and their hearers by recounting several events of the war, especially exploits in which they had themselves a share.

The following day, February 20th, Pashley investigated the region.

Pashley I, p. 96 – 99

Many of the villagers came to my host's house, anxious to conduct me to the Hellenic buildings, which were to be seen, they said, in and about the village; and which proved to be remains of the houses of feudal proprietors, the Venetian Cavalieri of the middle ages. After this, my host, Joseph Russákes, offered to accompany us to a fountain, at which he assured me there were ancient walls and inscriptions. This fountain, a most copious source, is about a mile to the east of the village, and is under two fine plane-trees. It is at the side of a plateau, about a hundred paces long and twenty wide, at the extremity of a little valley, full of cypresses, bay-trees, orange-trees, carobs, platanes, and myrtles. The place is so entirely abandoned that, as Russákes told me, no one comes even to gather the oranges [upon investigation, the fountain turned out to be Venetian].

At the other extremity of this little vale, which is about half a mile long, is another piece of raised ground, with its fountain: the whole was evidently a delightful summer retreat during the time of the Venetians; and, even at the present season of the year, the words of Tasso serve as a faithful description of its beauties.

Se non disdegni il seggio ombroso, e'l monte,
E'l dolce mormorar del chiaro fonte,
Qui siedi, e spazia tra bei fiori e l'erba,
Nella stagione acerba.

About a mile hence is the village of Rústika, and the monastery of Prophét-Elías, which contains thirteen kalógheri and an Hegúmenos, all of whom were absent gathering their olives when we arrived: the news of so unusual an event as a visit from Europeans soon brought the Hegúmenos or Abbot to us...

The Hegúmenos told me, while we partook of wine, fruits, and coffee in his cell, that the monastery was entirely destroyed by the Mohammedans during the war, and that to restore the church, and the few dwellings in which they now live, they had to borrow 15,000 piastres. Their possessions are about 2000 olive-trees and some carobs. In the court-yard of the monastery are suspended three bronze bells of Venetian manufacture, with the maker's name and their dates (1634 and 1636) on them. Little more than a mile from Rústika we crossed a streamlet in a very picturesque valley, where the platane and walnut were the only trees that were not adorned with their green foliage: the former was covered with ivy, and generally had a vine twining round its trunk to a height of thirty to forty feet. We soon traversed a plain near four miles long and about two broad, and from which we had a fine view of the

Sfakian mountains covered with snow, and appearing very beautiful as the Sun shone on their magnificent outline.

From there Pashley travelled on to Réthymnon. In 1853 Spratt, as we have seen, passed this region by ship on his way from Réthymnon to Khaniá. But in 1858 he came back, arriving from the south. In that year he was busy finishing his exploration of Crete. In the summer of 1853, having arrived at Loutró on the southern coast, he had been called away to lend his services in the Crimean War, but in 1858 he had resumed his survey. He used his experiences in 1858 for his description of the route.

Spratt, II, p. 114 – 122

In proceeding to Khania from Retimo the coast-road is both tedious and long, being for a great part upon heavy sand along the strand, or over rugged rocks just above the sea-shore; and if the traveller is not in haste, he may avoid it, and vary the scene by an inland track towards the south and south-west to two ancient sites, the first near Monopari, about two and a half hours from Retimo, and thence to Poli, the site of Lappa, a city that was once one of the most important in Crete, and flourished about the time of the Roman conquest of it: it is noted for having at an earlier period given refuge to the Lyctians, or Lyttians, when their city was surprised and destroyed by the Gnossians during the civil wars which, subsequently to Minos's reign, frequently disturbed the island.

The Monopari kastelli, the first-named of these inland sites, was a small picturesque fortress upon the top of a high triangular-shaped rock, precipitous on all sides but the north, where it is approached by a narrow neck, yet presenting a very bold and steep face on this side also, although not precipitous. There are, however, evidences of a double, if not triple, line of walls to defend its only approach; and these appear to be both of the earliest and the latest style of construction, the more modern parts of the walls having towers and appearing to be of middle-age date…

I visited it [Monopári] in a journey from the southern coast, and not from Retimo. The road to it, however, from the latter is not difficult, although an intervening ridge of mountains above 2000 feet high has to be crossed; and the way will be enlivened by a village or two, and during summer by the incessant song of the nightingale in the groves and valleys near them.

The Monopari kastelli is situated over the eastern branch of the Petro

Kamara, the principal rivulet and valley intersecting the Retimo district; and Poli, the ancient Lappa or Lampa, is on its western branch, which divides the Retimo from the Apokorona district.

The intermediate route is intersected by steep ridges and deep valleys, channelled chiefly in the older yellowish-white tertiary strata, and which lie here in a sort of basin or hollow between the high mountains of grey limestone to the south and those which rise up behind Retimo and partially border the shore to the westward of it, and render the coast-road so tedious and rugged.

There are several villages (that of Rustaki being the principal) through which the traveller has to pass before arriving at the long ridge upon which Poli or Gaiduropoli, is situated, the summit of which is so narrow that the village (which is the most considerable of the district) overlooks both valleys...

The ruins of Lappa or Lampa have been described by Pashley, and appear to be chiefly Roman. One of them, the most perfect that remains, a small circular ivy-covered ruin with recesses, was noticed and a plan of it given by Belli [back from his expedition through and around Crete, Spratt had come into possession of the book 'Museum of Classical Antiquities' by a certain Falkener, wherein excerpts were published, among others a description by the Italian scholar Onorio Belli who had visited Crete in 1583]...

The ancient Lappaeans were evidently characterized by military valour and a generous sympathy for the unfortunate brave, as it is shown, first by their alliance with and hospitality to the Lyttians after the destruction of their city by the Gnossians, and secondly, by the fact that Lappa held out bravely against the Roman conqueror of Crete, after Cydonia, Eleutherna, Gnossus, and Lyttus had submitted, and was then only taken by storm and destroyed by the successful general. It was rebuilt, however, by Augustus for services rendered by the Lappaeans at the battle of Actium. But the modern Lappaeans are said, by their compatriots and neighbours the Sfakians, to be the reverse of their ancestors, having shown a rather pusillanimous disposition during the long revolutionary struggle in Crete, previous to the battle of Navarino; and hence, I was informed, the name of Gaiduropolis, or city of donkeys, is now usually applied to their town, which was previously, and in official records still is, designated Polis – a name significant of its having been at one time the principal city of the district...

When I visited this city in 1858, to obtain some details that were wanting for the completion of the chart of the western division of Crete, I was hospitably received by the family of a resident Sfakiot, but found, nevertheless, that my kindly reception, accidental as I at the time thought it to be, was the result of an intrigue by one of the relatives of that family, who had been deeply implicated as a leader in a revolutionary disturbance of the previous year. As my intended visit was previously known, it was thought a good opportunity to make capital out of the occasion, by impressing the partisans of the Sfakian worthy with the belief that I had come expressly to have a private interview with him, and in support of his cause; for I found afterwards that my muleteer and guide was a relative of this worthy, and that he himself, too, waited in a secluded valley and olive-grove intermediate between Poli and Armyro to meet me on the way, apparently by accident, but in reality in accordance with a well-planned plot that might either have embarrassed me with the local authorities or led the poor duped peasantry into false expectations of a direct sympathy, or more than sympathy, with their cause.

But his appearance and retinue, and other significant indications and expressions which escaped from my guides at the moment he was first seen, put me on my guard before I had quite crossed to the side of the valley where he was waiting for the interview.

I at once questioned my interpreter, on seeing the party, as to the meaning of all this, and then discovered that I had unconsciously been nearly drawn into an interview with a compromised Sfakian chief. Immediately perceiving that all sorts of political surmises might result from the act, and, to suit the views even of parties not connected with his aims, all sorts of constructions might be put upon it, I thwarted the plot by turning suddenly off in another direction, and forbidding the interview, as I would not exchange a word with him or any of his companions, informing the parties near me, at the same time, that my mission was for science and research for their individual information and good, as much as for that of the whole civilized world, and not for local intrigue, and so bade them farewell as I thought. But I was nevertheless conducted to the house of his relative in that village, where I believe he himself slept, unknown to me, as I persisted in my determination not to see him whilst there, little thinking I was then in some degree within the snare he had laid for me to further his objects. The circumstance much annoyed me; and I relate it here as simply one of many I have experienced during the progress of the survey of this island so celebrated for intrigue, both foreign and local, and for internal revolutions. The past education of a Cretan, like that of the oriental and Greek generally, has been so much in this direction, even in the common transactions of business, that it will take generations to direct the mind to more salutary and also ultimately more profitable ways and means of gaining success, since mutual mistrust produces mutual intrigue, and makes progress in prosperity and civilization slow.

The view from Lappa upon the district lying to the westward of it, and upon Armyro Bay, with the headlands of Drepano and Malaxa, is commanding; and the district is in parts very fertile, enclosing several prettily situated villages, as Patenia, Kastellos, and Kurna.

It belongs to the Apokorona eparkhia, although separated from it by a difficult mountain-pass through the range of hills lying over Armyro. It may now, however, be called the lowland territory of the Sfakians, as they have little by little become possessors of considerable land within it since the Revolution, by obliging many of the Mahommedan population that in part peopled it to retire to the towns and sell their lands for what they could get; for the Sfakians so worried them by stealing their cattle or their produce, and so alarmed them by continual night-descents from their mountain-plains of Askypho and Kalikrati above, and by wanton violence and bloodshed, too, when an opportunity offered of indulging in them without detection, that one by one the Mussulman peasants at length succumbed and retired.

Soon we will return to Pashley and join him on his journey, which will take him via Réthymnon to the valley of the Mylopótamos and to Herákleion. But first we turn our attention to the southern sphere of influence of Láppa: the region to the south of the west-east spine, Áyios Vasílios.

4. Between Frangokástello and Ayía Galíni

To the south of the west-east spine between the Lefká Óri and the Kédhros lies the mountainous region of Áyios Vasílios. On the western side it moves into the region of the Sfakians and in the east it is bordered by the Kédhros. This area, rich in natural beauty but limited in history, consists of a series of mountain plains which are connected with the sea by deep gorges. From west to east these are: the area around Asféndhos, with the Asféndhou gorge to Áyios Nektários (a walk here is recommended, possibly starting on the Askyfoú plateau); the area around Kallikrátis, with the Kallikratianó gorge (also a recommended walk, from Asigoniá) to Patsianós and Frangokástello, both of them still in Sfakiá proper; the region around Áyios Ioánnis, with the Kotsifoú gorge to Sellía, Mýrthios and Plakiá (a beautiful route); the area around Áyios Vasílios, Paleoloútra and Koxaré, with the Kourtaliotikoú gorge along the Megalopótamos to the region around Píso Préveli (recommended walk); the area around Kissós, Spíli and Lambíni, with the Kissanós gorge, likewise to Píso Préveli; and the region around Akoúmia and Krýa Výssi, with the Akoumianós gorge to Áyios Pávlos at the foot of the Kédhros (see also the map on page 108). On the other side of the Kédhros

Exópoli · Amfímalla · Periv... · Rèthymno
Ùysses · Almyró · Yeoryioúpoli · Yeráni · Prines · Atsipópoulo
Alikambos · Dhrámia · Episkopí · Ayía Irini
Mourí · Lake of Kourna · Kourna · Kástelos · Arkhondiki · Khromonas
Pátima · Ayios Konstantínos · Monopári · Arméni
Asigonía · Láppa · Argyroúpoli · Roustika · Potamidha · Fá...
Minokéfalo
Asféndhos · Kallikrátis · Áyios Vasílios · Áyios Vasílios · Paleoloútra
Áyios Ioánnis · ÁYIOS VASÍLIOS · Atsípadhes · Koxaré · Lar
Áyios Nektários · Sellía · Mýrthios
Patsianós · Áno Rodhákino
Frangokástello · Plakiá · Megalopótamos · Káto Préveli
Píso Préveli

----- Pashley
············· Lear
--- Spratt

──── Main road
──── Secondary road
〰〰 River

0   5 km

lies the Amári valley (see Chapter 6), with the beach resort of Ayía Galíni at the mouth of the Plátys.

Tourists are attracted to the series of beaches which stretch between Frangokástello and Ayía Galíni. The beach at Plakiá is the most popular of these. Inland the charming mountain village of Spíli attracts the most visitors, but villages such as Mýrthios and Sellía with their brilliant views of the coast by Plakiá, and Rodhákino, farther to the west, are also very engaging. The monastery at Píso Préveli, still functioning, is an attraction for modern travellers with its beautiful location.

Hikers can enjoy the walks through the north-south gorges mentioned above, but also the walks along the coast of Plakiá to Píso Préveli and from there to Áyios Pávlos.

THE PAST

Little is known about the history of the region before the arrival of the Venetians. The area was part of the sphere of influence of Láppa, more to the north. Láppa's southern harbour, Foinix Lampaion, was presumably at Plakiá. However there are as yet hardly any discoveries from Minoan, Mycenaean, Classical, Hellenistic, or Roman times. From the First Byzantine Period remains are known of two basilica's by Frangokástello: the church of the Kharálambos monastery and the nearby church of Áyios Nikítas were both established on the remains of a basilica. From the Second Byzantine Period there is also nothing remaining. However, it is probable that hermits settled around the present monastery of Píso Préveli at this time.

Only from Venetian times is more known. The region belonged to the Réthymnon province (Frangokástello marked the border with Sfakiá). In Spíli and villages in that area Orthodox churches with lovely frescos were established or restored: the Sótiros Khristós in Spíli, the architecturally exceptional Ayía Panayía in Lambíni, the Áyios Yeóryios in Moúrne and the Ayía Panayía in Akoúmia. Spíli also has an extraordinary 16th century fountain.

In 1371 a powerful fort was established by the Venetians on the coast, close to the mouth of the Asféndhou gorge and the Kallikratianó gorge: Castel Franco, called Frangokástello in Greek, which is still one of the best-preserved examples of Venetian fort construction. The fort was built as protection from overseas enemies. It was during this time that the Ottoman Turks began their expansion from Asia Minor in the direction of Europe, and the Byzantines were their allies in these years. But the fort also served to keep the neighbouring Sfakians under control. Indeed, in the 1360's Cretan rebels supported by the Byzantines had shaken Venetian authority. The Sfakians had played a big role in this, and their most important summer dwellings, in the area around Anópolis, were destroyed in 1367 as punishment. The Castel Franco, on the border with Sfakiá, could play a strategic role in keeping the Sfakians subdued.

After the Ottoman conquest of Crete the region fell under the pasha of Réthymnon and just as the rest of Crete it had to contribute to the fiscal machinery of the Ottoman Empire instead of the Venetians. As elsewhere in Crete, this also meant that some of the population converted to Islam.

But Orthodoxy did not disappear. Near Frangokástello the now deserted Kharálambos monastery flourished. And farther to the east the monastery of Préveli developed into an influential and powerful regional center during the Ottoman Period. It was also an educational center. The monastery actually consisted of two monasteries. One was Káto Préveli in the valley of the Megalopótamos, dedicated to St. John the Baptist, which flourished from the 16th century. It was destroyed by the Ottomans right before the rebellion of 1821, as they had discovered that the monastery's abbot was involved in organizing a rebellion (the ruins of the monastery are well worth a visit). The other monastery was Píso Préveli, on a mountainside at the mouth of the Megalopótamos looking out over the Libyan Sea, dedicated to St. John the Evangelist. It was established at the end of the 17th century by descendants of the Prévelis family (it is still functioning and well worth a visit for its magnificent location with a view of the Libyan Sea; the monastery church dates from 1836). It was this Píso Préveli which Spratt visited.

Áyios Vasílios also suffered during the uprising of 1821-1830. The destruction of the Káto Préveli monastery has been mentioned above. During the first years of the uprising the rest of the region seems to have been left in peace, but in 1828 Frangokástello was witness to one of the most famous, and bloodiest, confrontations between the Ottomans and the rebels. After the Treaty of London (July 6th, 1827) it looked as if an independent Greece could be created, but with borders yet to be negotiated. Because the rebellion in Crete had been put down, Greek leaders on the mainland tried to breathe new life into the Cretan uprising in order to make free Greece as large as possible. It was in that connection that the Epirotic freedom fighter Khátzi Mikhális Daliánis landed in January 1828 on the island of Gramvoússa. He was accompanied by 700 fellow fighters. In March he took possession of Frangokástello, but his attempts to create a general rebellion failed. In May the governor of the island, Mustafa Pasha, gathered an army of 8000 men and advanced on the fort. In spite of advice from experienced Sfakians to retreat to the mountains, Daliánis remained at the fort. On May 17th his troops were completely defeated by the Albanian/Ottoman superior forces. He perished, along with 385 other rebels. He is said to have been buried by a nun at the monastery of Kharálambos. Tradition has it that the spirits of the fallen freedom fighters return each year for the ten days following May 17th, and dance in front of the fort.

Incidentally, on their way back to Khaniá via the Ímbros gorge and the Askyfoú plain, Mustafa Pasha's troops were besieged by the rebels and at the entrance to the Askyfoú plain they were driven away. Mustafa Pasha lost 1000 men.

The rebellion did indeed come back to life that year, and fighting broke out all over the island. The Ottoman reaction was fierce. The *pasha* of Herákleion announced that he would offer a reward for every head or limb of a dead Christian. At the beginning of 1829 in the village of Lambíni this led to the massacre at the Ayía Panayía which Pashley writes about when he stays in the village of Piyí (see Chapter 7).

During all of the 19th century the monastery of Píso Préveli played an important role in the region as an economic, cultural, and revolutionary center. During the 1866-1869 rebellion it was a place where weapons and ammunition could be brought ashore and from where fugitives could embark for the mainland. In the decades before independence the region as a whole shared in the fortunes of the rest of Crete.

Pashley visited this region, as can be seen by the map in his book on which he has plotted his tour. Unfortunately he does not refer to it at all, probably because he encountered no ancient antiquities there. Spratt also visited the region, but does not expand upon Pashley's work as we have come to expect him to do. When he had largely completed his investigation of Crete and had arrived at Loutró, he was called away in connection with the outbreak of the Crimean War. He did return to Crete in 1858, but it seems he had less time then, for his

The fort of Frangokástello

descriptions of the island after his return are less detailed. In this year he sailed from Khóra Sfakíon along the southern coast to the east. As the quotation begins he is still off the coast of Sfakiá.

Spratt, II, p. 257 – 260, 268 – 271

To the eastward of the town of Sfakia [Khóra Sfakíon] the mountains diminish in elevation, although not in boldness or ruggedness of character. They are intersected by several deep gorges and ravines that descend from the the eastern shoulders of the Madara Vouna [the Lefká Óri], and render the only roads leading to this south-western coast town of Crete difficult, and even in some parts dangerous, to an equestrian traveller.

The mountain-steeps of this famed province are in general too rocky and abrupt for cultivation, without great industry and labour. The only cultivated land belonging to the comparatively few scattered inhabitants is confined chiefly to the upland basins and plains of Aradena [in Sfakiá, near Anópolis], Askyfo, Asfendu, and Kalikrati, that lie upon the flanks and shoulders of the eastern branch of the White Mountains, all of which, from their elevation and the steep or narrow approaches leading to them, may be considered as the natural fastnesses of this ancient race, from their easy defense by a few resolute mountaineers skilled in the bow or the rifle. The authority of the government in these localities is but feeble, in consequence of such natural advantages favouring a community of men who have little respect for civil laws or social rights not coinciding with their own traditions and customs, or the interests of their own clan; and the power of the law seldom reaches them, in spite of grave offences and deeds of violence.

In the time of the Venetians there was a small fortress or castle at Sfakia; but it is entirely destroyed now, and the Turks have no stronghold in the whole district, in which to lodge a garrison sufficient to awe the proud spirit of the Sfakians and keep them in subjection to the law.

The Venetians had another castle on this coast, called Franko Kastelli, situated upon a rather low part of it, at about five miles east of the town of Sfakia, and just upon the borders of the provinces of Sphakia and Lampe (or Agios Vasiles [Áyios Vasílios]), where the mountains fall back from the shore for a breadth of from three-quarters to more than a mile, leaving between them and the sea an inclined stony plain which extends along its margin for seven or eight miles. Several villages picturesquely dot the craggy steeps rising from the inland margin of the plain, round each of which is some terraced cultivation and a knot of olive- and fig-trees.

Franko Kastelli stands upon the sea-margin of this narrow coast plain. It is a high quadrangular building, with towers at its four corners, conspicuous from the sea, and presents a picturesque appearance where so few buildings of any kind, modern or ancient, exist. The castle is partially in ruins, however, and consequently remains unoccupied by troops; it is also isolated from any habitation. But it is celebrated in Cretan history and song, in connexion with the revolutionary struggle for independence, as the scene of an encounter between the troops of Mustapha Pacha, the Albanian general of Mehemet Ali, and a band of Cretan and Morean patriot Greeks under a famed chieftain named Hadzi Michali.

Being besieged within the castle by the Mussulman troops, he resolved to head a sortie against them, break through their line, and so gain the mountains with some of his devoted band; but he fell in the attempt, a few hundred yards in front of the castle, with most of those who followed him. Hadzi Michali is in consequence a hero in Cretan song, and the record of his gallantry and devotion warms the heart of every Sfakiot and patriot when sung on days of festivity and commemoration or referred to by the stranger…

I must now close this chapter with a few words upon the most interesting features of the remaining eparkhia of Agios Vasiles, or Lampe, lying eastward of Sfakia, and between it and Mount Ida.

Agios Vasiles comprises the most mountainous portion of the western contraction or isthmus of Crete, and throughout its whole length of about 22 miles is bordered by the shore of the Libyan Sea. Its breadth averages 5 miles.

Enclosed between its mountains are some fertile valleys and plains, which are all at moderate elevations above the sea as compared to the Sphakian plains. They are those of Palaio Lutro, Kissos, and Preveli, besides some of less dimensions near the coast. About three-fourths of its inhabitants are Christians, and one forth Mahomedans. Some of the villages are exclusively Mahomedan, of which Atzipades is the largest, numbering about eighty families; among those having only a portion Turkish are Kissos, Speli, Lambine, and Koxare.

One small bay indents its coast nearly in the centre of its extent, called Plaka. A bold rocky point of lime-stone forms its eastern headland, and affords it shelter from the S.E.; but it lies directly open to the S.W., and therefore is only a summer anchorage. A magnificent gorge opens into the bay, at its head, which derives its name of Myrtos from a village situated about halfway up one of the slopes near its entrance [Mýrthios].

This village is Greek, and therefore Christian, as are all those near the coast, the Mahomedans occupying the better land in the interior.

To the east of Plaka Bay is the narrow enclosed valley of Preveli, with a monastery at its eastern extreme, opposite to which are two pictur-esque ravines that give outlet to the waters from the upland districts of Palaio Lutro and Kissos.

The monastery of Preveli is thus situated in one of the most retired and picturesque vales in Crete; for crags of various forms, venerable and grey, beetle over gentle swelling slopes, olive-groved glades, and open fields and vineyards in such proximity that a stranger's first impression on viewing it is to pronounce it the paradise of Crete, and one of the most happily chosen spots for a retreat from the cares and responsibili-ties of life…

The monastery too is clean and inviting, and the monks hospitable. I have twice visited this valley, and twice gone through the central valleys of Agios Vasiles, but each time made the journey by the bad road through the gorge of Myrto [the Kotsifoú gorge], as there is no good road through the Preveli gorges, but only over the high mountain which intervenes between this coast-valley and monastery and the upland district of Palaio Lutro. The road by the gorge of Myrto is sometimes rendered impassable by rains, being contracted to only a few yards' width at its head, where it then forms the bed of a torrent…

It is a singular fact regarding the eparkhia of Agios Vasiles, that throughout its whole extent not any ancient city has been discovered; and yet there can be no doubt that in one or two of the most populous of these valleys there must have been a town of more or less importance. To all my inquiries, however, in my two journeys through the greater part of the province, I could learn of no ruins or traditional site of any Hellenic city. I am induced to call the attention of any future traveller to this absence of any recognized ancient site in so large a district, whilst so many were found of which the names only were known in Selinon [see Part 3 of this series] and other parts, and several have been noticed that yet want discovery and identification.

In the following chapter we return to Pashley, on his way to Réthym-non.

Réthymnon

Fortetsa

PARALIAKI LEOFOROS

PALEOLOGOU

Venetian
Harbour

MELISINOU

PLATEIA
YEORYIOU

Rimondi
fountain

DIKASTIRION

Nerace
Mosque

Loggia

Municipal beach

PARALIAKI LEOFOROS

ETH. ANTISTASEOS

PETIKHAKI

EL. VENIZELOU

AYIAS VARVARAS

ARKADHIOU

DIMAKOPOULOU

Megali
Porta

KOUNDOURIOTOU

PLATEIA
MARTIRON

YERAKARI

Kara Mustafa
Mosque

IGOUMENOU GAVRIL

City park

DHIMITRAKAKI

KOUNDOURIOTOU

250 m

5. Réthymnon

After our visit to Láppa's former sphere of influence, we move on to Réthymnon. Crete's third city (population 25,000) is a fascinating place. Both the Venetian and Ottoman influences are present in attractive ways, and give the city an Oriental-Mediterranean flavour. One striking detail is the minarets that rise up over the city (these are still standing because the city sustained less damage than Herákleion and Khaniá from the earthquakes of 1856 and 1926 and from attacks during World War II). A wide sandy beach by the city center welcomes visitors. In the northwestern section of the city the Fortétsa rises, with the Sultan Ibrahim Mosque. To the east of this is the small Venetian harbour. And to the south of that stretches a row of attractive Venetian houses. The old high street ran from the square by the Rimondi fountain to the partially preserved city gate, the Megáli Pórta (or Porta Guora).

To the south of Réthymnon rises the Vrýssinas. This mountain shuts off the region around Réthymnon in the south. In the west the hills of Níppi form a watershed with the basin of the Pétres Kamára. In the east the Potamídha, which flows through the rugged Prassinós gorge here forms the border with the fertile areas of Stavroménos and Mylopótamos.

The region was inhabited in the Neolithicum, as can be seen by traces of habitation in a cave in the Níppi hill by Yeráni. The peak sanctuary on the Vrýssinas dates from Minoan times. And in the southwestern suburb of Mastabá a rock grave was discovered from Mycenaean times, which points to habitation during that period. Apart from this not much is known about the ancient history of Réthymnon. On the site of the present city lay a less important harbour, Rhithymna, for which Réthymnon is named. Nothing is known about the city during the First Byzantine Period and the Muslim Period. According to some sources, Nikifóras Fokás, after his capture of Crete from the Muslims in 961, reestablished the city. In any case, around the year 1000 A.D. there were activities being carried out by the great Orthodox missionary Ioánnis Xénos: at Khromonastíri, on the northeast slope of the Vrýssinas, he established the Áyios Eftíkhios church with its extraordinary 11th century frescos. Another church in the neighbourhood of Khromonastíri which has special frescos is the Panayía Kirá, from the same period. Apart from that Khromonastíri is also an exceptional village because of its architecture from the Venetian Period.

Réthymnon really only flourished after the island had been occupied by the Venetians in the 13th century. The city had the best, or rather the least poor, harbour for Venetian shipment to take on export products from the fertile agricultural areas between the Lefká Óri and the Ida. The trading vessels could anchor outside the harbour while the harbour itself was suitable for transport boats to receive and deliver the merchandise to the ships at anchor.

After the fall of Constantinople in 1453, the city received a large number of Byzantine refugees, many of whom were well educated. It appears that the city's fame as the cultural center of Crete dates from this time.

When Herákleion and Khaniá were fortified in answer to the increasing Ottoman threat in the 1530's, Réthymnon also received a fortified wall. The Megáli Pórta is all that remains of it. And after the Ottoman marauding raid of 1571 the Fortétsa was built (1573-1578), although not according to the plans which Michele Sanmicheli had earlier drawn up, but simplified and without a moat.

Just as Herákleion and Khaniá, Réthymnon knew a period of prosperity in the 17th century. The Rimondi fountain and the Loggia are proof of this, as are repairs of two of the major churches, the San Francesco and the Santa Maria.

A number of Orthodox monasteries flourished in the neighbourhood of Réthymnon during Venetian times. The best examples of these are the monastery of Khalévi (the monastery itself is ruins, but the simple Theotokós church still stands) and, farther to the south, the beautifully situated monastery of Ayía Eiríni (also important in Ottoman times, and now a lovely convent).

In 1646 the Ottomans arrived. One year after the capture of Khaniá a force of 40,000 troops landed in the Bay of Soúdha on July 2nd, 1646. The troops moved off immediately in an easterly direction. In September of that year the siege of Réthymnon began. Just as at Khaniá it appears that the Venetian authorities gave the city up in advance. They forced the civilian population to leave the city (the refugees sought refuge in Herákleion, where they were not allowed in, whereupon they submitted themselves to the Ottomans). There was only a small garrison in the Fortétsa for defense. On October 11th the city itself was captured, and on November 13th the Fortétsa surrendered. The garrison survivors and the few remaining inhabitants fled by boat to Herákleion and the Ionian islands.

The Ottomans took over the governing of the city and province. The *pasha* of Réthymnon took up residence in the Fortétsa (he was, just as the *pasha* of Khaniá, subordinate to the pasha of Herákleion). A mosque, the Sultan Ibrahim Mosque, was constructed right after the capture. The Ottomans also transformed the Santa Maria and the San Francesco into mosques (the Nerace Mosque and the Kara Mustafa Pasha). In the cited text the Ottoman cemetery lay where the city park is now located.

During the uprisings of 1821-1830 Réthymnon was one of the bases from where the Ottoman rulers tried to maintain their power. When the rebels defeated the *pasha* of Khaniá on June 15th, 1821, Ottoman troops including an army from Réthymnon tried to help the *pasha*. They were held back by the rebels at Áyios Konstantínos and Roústika. One of the warriors who died on the Ottoman side was Glémedh-Alí, who is mentioned in the text. Affendúles, also mentioned in the text, is Mikhaíl Komnínos Afendoúlis, the commander-in-chief of the Cretan rebels. In July and August an Ottoman force of 8000 men was gathered together by the *pasha* of Réthymnon. This army first marched destructively through the Apokórona and at the end of August finally reached the villages of Sfakiá and destroyed them. In spite of this success the Ottomans were not able to definitely suppress the uprising by the end of 1821. In March of 1822 the rebels besieged Réthymnon, but without success. As mentioned earlier,

The Venetian Harbour of Réthymnon

Albanian troops under the leadership of first Hassan Pasha and then Huseyn Bey were necessary in order to crush the rebellion.

~~⌒

On February 20, 1834 we left Pashley on a plain by Roústika, on his way to Réthymnon.

Pashley, I, p. 99, 100

The first village through which we passed is Priné: it is not above two miles from the northern sea, and contains many indications of the Venetian rule. Above one doorway is a mutilated coat of arms and an inscription:

TRAHIT SVA QVEMQVE VOLVPTAS
ANN. DMN. MDCXLIII. PRID. KAL. IVL.

A good many cypresses are scattered among the olives by which the village is surrounded, and produce a very pleasing and picturesque effect.

Leaving Priné and passing Alitsópulo [Atsipópoulo], we soon descended to a curious bridge [the bridge was built in storeys so that the road would remain horizontal]. The principle of its construction is one of which I do not suppose any instance to exist in England: it costs the builder much less to content himself with a single row of arches, and to make the road descent to them at each end of the bridge. But though this method is unemployed at the present day, the ancient Romans made use of it very frequently, especially in carrying an aqueduct across a valley: and sometimes, as at the Pont du Gard near Nismes, and elsewhere, they built three series of arches one above the other, raising the bridge to the level of the water. Near this bridge are excavations in the rock, one of which is a chapel of Hághios Antónios.

We arrived at the gates of Rhíthymnos a little after sunset, and after making the Arab sentries understand that we wanted admission, a messenger was dispatched to the Governor, who, however, did not think proper to order the gates to be opened, and we were therefore obliged to sleep at a little hamlet about a mile from the city.

On the following day, February 21st, they were allowed in.

Pashley I, p. 103 – 110, 113, 114

Wishing to walk over the citadel, to do which the Bey's permission was requisite, I determined to visit him; although I had hardly forgiven his want of courtesy last night. His seraglio, as it is called, is a large and dilapidated building, near the port. Near its entrance were a number of straggling Arab regular soldiers, and some sentries. I found the Bey walking about the room as I entered it; a sure sign that a Turk belongs to the old school of ignorance and prejudice, and wishes to avoid having to rise from his seat when an European traveller enters his apartment. He was very tall, very fat, and very dull: was greatly surprised at my talking Greek and a little Turkish, and suggested that I had only to perfect myself in Turkish, and to learn Arabic, in order to know all existing languages. He was profuse of apologies for last night's incivilities at the gates, and assured me that had he been aware that it was I, they should have been immediately opened.

It being Friday, the Mohammedan sabbath, and the chief day on which visits of ceremony are paid in every part of Turkey, the principal officers of both the regular Arab troops and the Arnauts, visited the Governor, each of the latter accompanied by a few of his rough followers in their shaggy white capotes. These attendants remained in the room, standing of course, during the whole interview. On leaving the Bey I visited the citadel, the guard at the gate of which was turned out as I entered. I found it just like most other Turkish forts: such guns as are not absolutely dismounted being either broken or unserviceable from rust and neglect. I noticed several large bronze Venetian swivels among them.

The present population of Rhíthymnos is upwards of three thousand souls, of whom only about eighty families are Christians. Here the character of the bazárs, and streets, which are better than those of Khaniá, is entirely Turkish.

I have already spoken [quoted in Chapter 1] of the general apostasy, which began to take place in Crete soon after the Turkish conquest, and in consequence of which about half of the whole population of the island consisted of Mohammedans at the outbreaking of the Greek revolution, thirteen years ago.

It is not only in modern Crete and Albania that a Christian population has shewn this readiness to abandon the religion of their forefathers. The early Saracenic conquerors of Christian principalities and kingdoms seem every where to have brought about the rapid conversion, to their own faith, of those among whom they established themselves...

Thus also the acquisition of Crete by the Saracens of Spain in the ninth century [see the introductory notes in Chapter 8], seems to have led to the rapid conversion of nearly the whole population to the faith of the Crescent: and when, at length, this long lost jewel was restored, by the valour and good fortune of Nicephorus Phocas, to the Imperial Diadem, the canonization of Nicon the Armenian became the hardly earned reward of his zeal and success, 'in extirpating the false doctrines of Mohammedanism' from the soil of the island.

On the second conquest of Crete by Mohammedan invaders, some of the wealthier inhabitants of Megálo-Kástron [Herákleion] and its neighbourhood are said, after openly renouncing Christianity, to have retained, in secret, the faith in which they had been baptized; and to have handed it down, in the same manner, to their descendants. Their exoteric doctrine alone was the faith of Islam, their esoteric was still that of the Cross. Among such families that of the Kurmúlidhes is celebrated, throughout the whole island, both for what was done by them before the Greek revolution, and for what they have suffered since. They were a powerful and wealthy house or clan, established at Khusé, in the fertile plain of Messará. They had conformed to the newly introduced religion, almost immediately after the Turkish conquest; but, unlike the majority of the new converts, had their children secretly baptized, and bestowed on them *Christian* names. On subsequent circumcision, each of them received his Mohammedan appellation of Ibrahím, Khuseín, and so forth: thus every Kurmúlis was nominally a Mohammedan, and in reality a Christian.

According to the general testimony of all the Cretans, this distinguished family used to exert a great influence in the whole plain of Messará, and invariably protected the Christians against all violence and oppression from their Moslem neighbours. Still, now and then, fears would arise in the breast of each Kurmúlis respecting his prospects, with reference to the other world: and, at length, one of them, the uncle of the present head of the family, some years before the outbreaking of the Greek revolution, determined to make a pilgrimage to the Holy Sepulchre, and to ask 'the Bishop' there, whether a sincere Christian, who professed Islamism and was supposed to be a true believer in it, could be saved. The Bishop sternly answered, that any Christian who shunned the open profession of his faith, had no chance of salvation: and, on this, the

old man immediately took a resolution, which was also adopted by nearly half the members of his clan. Thirty Kurmúlidhes determined at once
to go to the Pashá at the Kástron, to confess that they were Christians,
and to endure the ignominious death which would immediately await
them. On their arrival in the city, out of respect for the Archbishop, they
went to his residence, 'the Metropolis,' before presenting themselves at
'the seraglio' of the Pashá. The Metropolitan, on learning their intention,
naturally saw the question in a very different light from the Bishop at
Jerusalem; and remonstrated with them, in strong and energetic terms,
against their design. He easily shewed them, that it was not only their
own martyrdom on which they had determined, but that of many others
whom they would leave behind them. Every priest who had married one
of those, who, while in reality Christian dogs, had still usurped the tur-
ban and enjoyed the rank of true believers, would be compromised; and,
undoubtedly, his life would be required as an atonement for his crime.
Many priests would thus inevitably be put to death: every bishop, too,
who had at any time granted a licence for the celebration of such a marriage, would be involved in the same ruin. Moreover, the suspicion excited would doubtless point, not only to the real accessories, but to many
who knew nothing of their secret faith; so that such a step as they thought
of taking would inevitably cause much innocent Christian blood to flow.
The Archbishop likewise alluded to the use they had ever made of their
power, to protect their Christian brethren; and ended by assuring them
that he differed from the Bishop at Jerusalem, and believed they might go
to heaven, though they lived and died in ostensible communion with the
followers of Mohammed. His arguments and exhortations at length prevailed, and they consented to leave the city without divulging their
secret to the Pashá .

One of the most remarkable members of the family was Khuseín-agá,
whose personal exploits before the outbreaking of the Greek revolution
would fill a volume, and who also distinguished himself as a leader in the
early history of the war with the Turks, under his Christian name of
Captain Mikháli Kurmúlis. He was the Greek Arkhegós of all the Kas-
trina [the region surrounding Herákleion], and died at Hýdhra in 1824.
He was succeeded by his son, Rhiziván-agá, or Captain Dhemétrios, who
was killed at Athens. His brother, Mustafá-agá, or Captain Manóles, subsequently fell at Mokhó in Crete. Of sixty-four men of the family, only
two have survived the murderous war of the revolution.

In the year 1824, three Kurmúlidhes, two brothers, and one of their cousins, were executed, outside the walls of Rhíthymnos, by Mustafá-bey, the Turkish general. They had been made prisoners at Mélabes [Mélambes], along with their wives and children, all of whom experienced the usual lot of the war, and became slaves. The men were brought before the Bey, at his palace within the city: he offered them their lives on condition of their abandoning their religion. The proposal was instantly and indignantly rejected by the eldest of the prisoners. On this they were conducted to the place of execution, near the Turkish cemetery without the walls. When every thing was ready, the Bey again asked the eldest whether he would become a Mohammedan: No! his faith was firm: he replied, 'I was born a Christian, and a Christian I will die;' and, in an instant, his two companions saw his head severed from his body. The second, nothing shaken in his resolution by the sight, when asked to choose between the Crescent and the axe, answered that he would follow his brother: on this he also was beheaded. The cousin of these two sufferers was very young, and, though firm of purpose, was unable to make any answer, when the same proposal was repeated to him. He was seized by the attendants, and, the next moment, his body likewise was a headless bleeding trunk.

The Bishop of Rhíthymnos went near the spot that night, and also the two next evenings. Each time he saw a light descend on the bodies of the two, who, with so holy and fervent a zeal, had earned the crown of martyrdom. The blood-stained clothes of all the three unfortunates were cut off, and distributed: a very small portion of any part of them, if burnt in a sick chamber, used to effect the invalid's immediate restoration to health.

I will now give the story of a Mohammedan chieftain's death, which happened near this city a few years earlier, in an action with the Christians under Captain Rússo and Papá-Anagnóstes. Glemédh-Alí was my hero's name, and he was one of the most celebrated native leaders whom the Cretan Mohammedans ever had in their sanguinary contest with the Christians of the island. The beauty of Glemédhi's person, the tallness of his stature, the splendour of his arms, the loudness of his voice, and the swiftness of his feet, are all themes of praise even to my Sfakian companion [Maniás].

In listening to the recital of this chieftain's exploits, I am constantly reminded of the different characteristics of Homer's heroes. Glemédhi's personal beauty, his swiftness of foot, and his incomparable valour, are all traits found in the well-known picture of Achilles; his loud and sonorous voice is spoken of so as to remind me of several of the Grecian warriors at Ilium, and even of the brazen-voiced and brazen-hearted Stentor himself: the exclamations addressed by the Cretan hero to the enemy, in the contests, which, for sometime before his death, used almost daily to take place between Christian and Mohammedan combatants, resemble, in no less striking and interesting a manner, the speeches exchanged between the contending warriors on the plain of Troy.

Glemédhi had five brothers, one alone of whom died a natural death, the others having all fallen by the sword in the bloody contest with the Christians.

The following are parts of a popular song on the death of this distinguished leader. The Commandante spoken of in its first stanza, is Affendúles, who was then residing at Lutró in Sfakiá.

THE SONG OF GLEMÉDHI

No man has ever yet been found,
 The truth to learn and tell,
Whether the Chieftain at Lutró
 Did justly plan, and well.

'Twas to the province of Rhíthymnos
 A firman that he sent;
To seize upon Glemédh-Alí,
 That warlike man, he meant.

  * * *

Behold him, sword in hand, advance
 In conflict close to fight:
At once they all upon him rush,
 Swift as the swallow's flight.

An instant more, from scarce seen foe
 A fatal blow was sped;
And, lo! a Sfakian's right arm
 Struck off Glemédhi's head.

The Sfakian struck off the head
  Of Glemedháki true,
And, like a standard, in his hand
  He held it up to view.

Thy honour'd head, Glemédh-Alé,
  Exulting next they bore,
To Rússo, their renowned chief,
  All stained as 'twas with gore.

And gold, at once, from his own purse,
  On them the Chief bestowed,
Because by their successful fight
  Glemédhi's blood had flowed.

For many hearts with grief he had racked,
  And would have racked still more:
So may each man his eye-sight lose
  Who shall his fate deplore!

Glemédhi! now thy head, that erst
  Courageously would dare,
At Rhíthymnos and at Khaniá,
  The brunt o' th' fray to bear;

Glemédhi! Now thy head, that erst
  With flowers thou didst deck,
Is by the Sfakians possessed,
  A mark for each tufék!

Ye Turks and Janitsáries all
  To th' mosque why don't ye fly?
To gaze upon Glemédh-Alí,
  The pride of every eye!

On that same day, February 21st, Pashley left Réthymnon and travelled east. Spratt, who visited Réthymnon in 1853, supplemented Pashley's information.

Retimo has a commanding fortress of some strength and size, surmounting a rocky eminence upon its extremity, but which was not built by the Venetians until after the town had been surprised, sacked, and burnt by the arrival and hostile attack of some Turkish vessels in 1597 [Spratt means 1571], the need of such a defence having been thus shown when it was too late.

The promontory is also partially defended by a cliffy and steep shore on the west side of it, and by batteries on the east. There is a small artificial port on that side, but with its entrance so near to the sandy shore and shallow water at the root of the point, that it is difficult to keep it open, and consequently it is only available for vessels of very light draught.

Retimo has a population of about 10,000, and some trade in oil, valonea, and soap. It has barracks for the Turkish troops, the usual bazaar, some few good houses that were built by the Venetians, as well as churches and a handsome tower near the port, that have withstood the inroads of decay and the shocks of many earthquakes, since they quitted it two centuries ago.

Pococke also visited the city, in 1739.

Pococke, p. 260, 261

Retimo is situated on the bay antiently called Amphimale. It is on a peninsula that runs northward into the sea, at the north end of which there is a high rock, strongly fortified. To the south of it there is a level spot of ground, on which the town is built, defended by a wall built across the neck of the peninsula, which on the west side extends to the hill on which the castle is built. Though the city is almost encompassed by the sea, yet they find plenty of good fresh water wherever they dig, and a fine stream is brought to the town from a spring that is near, which runs like a river from a handsome conduit made by the Venetians. And though it is a rocky soil, and there is no morass near it, yet, I know not for what reason, it is accounted an unhealthy air. The situation is delightful, and on the east side, facing the sea, there are some very fine houses of the Venetian architecture, with gardens behind them extending to the sea side. There is a Doric door to one of the houses, which may vye with any piece of modern architecture. There is also a fine tower, where there seemed to have been an entrance to the port, on which there was a clock in the time of the Venetians. The port is a small basin to the east, into which large boats only can enter; but the ships anchor abroad in a good road.

There are here some French factors for the merchants of Canea and Candia, in order to export oil. But there are no priests of the Latin church in the city. They compute that there are about ten thousand souls in the town, three thousand of which are Turks who bear arms. There are about five hundred Greek families, who have a church and a bishop residing here. There are six or seven families of Jews, but they have no public synagogue.

They have an old proverb which mentions the people of Retimo as given to letters, but probably it may have no other foundation than that this town has produced a great number of priest and monks.

The grand vizier Ibrahim Pasha, who enjoyed that office at the beginning of the present grand signor's [grand signor = sultan, it refers to Mahmud I, 1730 – 1754] reign, was in exile in this place. I was told that he was first of all caia, or minister to the black eunuch, who advanced him to this office, and when he was in it, he was so sensible of the exorbitant power of that favourite, that he had laid a scheme to send him off in a galley, which he had prepared for that purpose; but his design being discovered, he was himself sent away in that very galley to be a pasha in Negropont [Euboea]. It seems the vizier had obtained a promise from the grand signor not to touch his title or estate, so he was ordered to the honourable pashalic of Romelia, on purpose to put him to great expences, and about six years ago was sent to this place, where he lives in a very honourable retirement. The pasha sometimes goes to his levy, but the station of the vizier exempts him from returning the compliments even of the governor of the province.

When I was at Retimo I heard of a German slave, a native of Silesia, who was taken in the wars with the emperor, and I agreed for him with the Turk his master for two hundred dollars. Every thing being concluded, the property of him was transferred to me by kissing the feet of his old proprietor, and then of his new master. I proposed to give him his choice either to remain with me as a servant, or to be given up to the priests at Constantinople who redeem captives, on their returning me the money. The love of his native country made him choose the latter, and I delivered him up into their hands about a year afterwards.

Lear also visited the city, complaining as usual, in 1864. He had spent the night in Episkopí and left for Réthymnon on May 6th. The doctor and the fat friend to whom he refers at the beginning also figure in his quotation in Chapter 3. The George Kalokairinós whom he mentions later was British vice-consul in Réthymnon and brother of the famous Mínos Kalokairinós who was the first person to excavate at the site of Knossós.

Lear, p. 58-63

Slept well; few fleas, and the two men were quiet. Rose 4.30. The Doctor is Odhyssévs Stravroianídhis, and the fat friend Vasílios Dhrandhákis. Coffee and leave-taking. Off 5.45. Horrid lanes of stones, impeded by sheep, etc. etc. etc. State of ruined villages. 6.15 Open out on cultivated hills with sea beyond and the two capes. Day cloudy. 6.30 Descend nearer the sea: the view here would be magnificent were not all the mountains quite invisible. 6.45 Seashore. 7 Arrive at the Petrés Kamára river, coming through a grand dark gorge and broken bridge. Cross on ass.

7.45 We have been going up and coming down the Kakó Vounó [Bad Mountain], by most execrable stone staircase roads. The coast east is full of long point-promonteries with a foreground of black and gray any-part-of-English-coast rocks. West, the long strip of Dhrepanon and the Akrotíri hills – hidden. All much trouble and little gain. 8.15 Same bother. A more horrid coast edge of sharp rocks can't be! 8.40 Leave sea, but ever on grim dry rox, over vast undulations. 8.45 Ravine, opening on sea, dreadful hard rocky path: half way.

10 Rethymnon seen afar. 10.15 Ever this horrible Murgie [in Apulia] endless stone path! We have met an Arab girl, then an enquiring black, then anxious elderly female. 10.30 Send on Zeriff to Rethymnon, and stop to suck a lemon and draw. Got down to the sea at 11.10, where there is some water, which aids us to eat some bread and O! cheese! in a shady kiosk, overflowing with goats. We return to rocks above the sea, where I draw till 12.30. Town relieves from sea in dark bits and bright sparkles here and there. At the town, passing by leper village, and at Mr George Kalokairinós's house by 1.30. Complimentary and fussy old cove.

I have come to a (*very*) inner room, to write a bit after a lunch of beef-steaks; olives, eggs and good wine. The long road brought us towards Rethymnon: the fortress is a large but not very picturesque affair, but the wide cemeteries seem to speak of more Mussulman life here than hitherto. At 1.20 Zeriff met us on the walls, with a fat, similarly-habited man, some retainer of the Kalokairinós' and him we followed by diabolical pavements through a dark arch and very bothery empty dirty bazaars to the Vice-Consular house. Immediately Kyrios George Kalokairinós met me, an elderly and rather vinous great Cerigotto [[native of Cerigo, or Kythira]], but far too fussy – removing my hat, sack, etc. – more than was bearable. However; he seemed willing to be good natured, only rather drunky. Small child and fat man (son-in-law) and George and Zeriff sat by. After much fuss, which I ignored in quiet (the room was pleasant and large), I was taken to lunch, and that meal was very satisfactory so far as food went. But the old gent wants me to visit the Governor and the Bey, and I *won't*. There is an elderly wife, small and bird-like, and a rather handsome daughter, wife of the fat man, and many others. Mr Kalokairinós proposes to walk with me this evening, and to go to some villages tomorrow – where, I don't know. In so short a stay of two or three days in such places it is a toss-up if one gains or loses more by not giving in to a cumbrous destiny of this kind, let it be that the civility of such houses demand some self-denial. Meanwhile I am here, but George is gone out with Zeriff and this small room is literally a heap of φορτώματα [baggage]. (None of the people here seem to have the least idea of distances towards Kastro or Gortyn. Foolishness abounds.) When George came back I got a thorough wash and went out to the sitting room, when George did likewise. Came a son of Mr Kalokairinós – Levantine – civil. Coffee, and at five the old gent came with two boys and his son-in-law and we all 'went out for a walk'. Very little sufficed to show me that there is little to do at Rethymnon: but we went up a gully and above to a saint's tomb and old Kalokairinós nearly bored me to death; returning by another gate and street and declining to see the port. At the house, found they had six men putting up a bed! – and all the children and women besides – so the room is useless for the present. Was wroth and irritated, but sat with the old cove who is a *frightful* bore, and talks of the 'Governo' ad *nauseam*. Supper proclaimed. Two Anatolic sea-captains, and a gawky son at school at Syra: two captains seemed to me far better bred than all the rest, who clawed food out of the dishes, etc. etc. It cost me an effort to break up the party at nine, when lo! I found George had made up my own little bed! He says the other 'fell all to pieces'. 9.30 Am in bed, but people rush in and out, and altogether Rethymnon is a bore.

Horrid hot box of a room! Yet I slept tolerably. Bugs alas! Rose at five, dressed, left bed, etc., gave a note to Zeriff, who I regret leaves me here, and paid him for his seven days' horse hire. And at six, came out with George and drew on the east side of the town and in various places till nine. Again, above (and through the village of Perivólia), near Aghios Gheórghios till 10.30. 'What are those birds?' says I to a peasant: 'Εἶναι μελισσοφάγοι' ['They are bee-eaters.'] (Owls also last night.) At 10.30 we suddenly resolved to go to the sands, [it] being as George says, 'Εὐχαρίστησις κοντά στήν θάλασσα' ['a pleasure near the sea'], so down we came; a most clear and lovely sea, with only the long snow-fretted lines of mountains not blue. So we made a lunch of very surprising cold soles and *triglia* [barbels], eggs, bread and cheese and *stupendous* wine, and very pleasant it was till 11.30, when it grew hot and we mizzle at 11.45. We go back to the Perivólia villages where all were occupied *shadoofing* and sit us down below a mulberry tree – a very pleasant hour – to 1 p.m.

2 p.m. Still wandering about the 'gardens' [*perivólia*, literally translated] or sitting in the shade of the mulberry tree. Two wonderful things exist in Crete – facts: 1. no dogs bark or bite, except at other dogs; 2. nobody bothers you. Few or none of these peasants can ever have seen two Europeans so clad and acting, yet they only say, 'Is the shade pleasant?' and then 'καλό' ['good'], walking away with no further sign. How are we to get through tomorrow? and most of Monday? However, nearly half our mournful task is done already. These garden folk seem to live a pleasant life, and sing to their *shadoofs*: vegetable marrows and various vegetables appear to thrive well.

It is now four, and we have come to the end of the walls, and as George is athirst I have sent him in for water. Certainly, a most meagre place is Rethymnon, and what to do tomorrow I know not. Anatolian sheep. Went up the hill partly we ascended last night, and drew till six: and now I have exhausted all the feeble resources of this place, the which is a bore. We returned slowly and by the filthy lanes; got home by 6.30. Wash and dawdle till seven; at 7.30 supper and suffering. Draw a whale over my torchers. The converse was mostly on soap. O dirt! Bed at 9.30.

Rose at five. In council with George it was fixed as 'too brutto' to leave the family all today; so we arrange to come back before noon. Coffee at 6.15, and at 6.30 we wander on the ramparts, the world being clear and blue. Then we come down to the sea, which is perfectly calm and like a large opal mirror, and we sit on the sand and asphodels till 9.30, I writing to Spiro and T. Cooper, and my journal up to April 30; but it grows hot, and we must prepare to face an afternoon at Rethymnon. Meanwhile, as I walk about, little boy brings me large bunch of lettuces (μαρούλια). I thought he was taking them somewhere else, but he came up and said, 'Πάρε τούτα' ['take these'], and when I only said I would take one: 'Πάρε όλα' ['take them all']. So I took them and George has gone to wash them in the sea. (A small sort of aloe with yellow flowers grows here plentifully.) Little boy ran away quickly, and was no more found.

10.30 We dawdled back, heat already beginning to be great. The long lines of Rethymnon are a bore, but the clear sparkle of the city and the broad band of Sphakian snow white separating lilac and blue is fine, in the mountain distance. Back by 11.15 and I retired to arrange paper and wash. At twelve, food – O lord! what a piggy feed! – the matter tolerable, the manner loathsome. At 1.30 we have come out, and I sit writing, or read Pashley till four, or slept. Afterwards, coffee; the children all get to George, who is kind to everybody always. Went with Mr Kalokairinós to see his son: pleasing wife, nice baby, roomy new house. Sit in gallery and sketch Ida, which in colour is lovely. Returned at 6.30, the elder Kalokairinós bemoaning life in Rethymnon as 'barbaro', among 'barbari' – as, poor man, well he may. His smaller son takes a fancy to George and won't leave him. The elder Kalokairinós says he knows many cases of leprosy coming on at 30 or 40 years of age, without parental descent, and believes it to be caused by overmuch oil and salt diet. Ἀλάδανο [Aládhano] or dittany, a perfumed herb, is gathered about Melidhóni and sold; much valued by the Turks.

After half an hour's talk with Mr Kalokairinós and the two Anatolical captains (who are waiting for their ships to have a cargo of oil), also with the handsome and amiable married daughter, whose husband Harálambos is piggy and good-natured, we went to supper. Boiled lamb, some Turkish dish, and a vast heap of μυζηθρόπηττες [cheese pies] (and to see Mr Harálambos eat these – twelve – one at a single mouthful! and last night to see him similarly eat raw beans!), with two sorts of wine, both *good thoroughly*. There came in also a big Sphakiot man, like John Gould and Thackeray piled together; and also another whose face expressed more cunning and silliness than could be portrayed. So we talked and smoked, but very little was drunk, till 9.30 – then bed. George has, as usual, made my bed and bedroom perfectly comfortable, and considering the bore, 'pare un'anno oggi', has been totally patient and good; all the children going to him in swarms by instinct. So much for my fourth week in Crete.

Before we follow Pashley to the east on the continuation of his exploration along the northern side of the island, we turn our attention to the Amári valley.

6. The Amári valley

Our journey through Crete continues with a visit to the Amári valley. This is an exquisite area. Idyllic natural beauty, excavations, and the loveliest churches in Crete compete with each other for the attention of the modern traveller. The fertile valley, the basin of the Plátys, lies from northwest to southeast between the Kédhros in the west and the imposing peaks of the Ida in the east. On the northwestern side the Sóros, the Katsoníssi and the Véni form the steep watershed with the basin of the Potamídha. On the northern side of the valley a low back forms the watershed with the region of Mylopótamos; the monastery of Arkádhi lies on this back. Picturesque villages surround the valley, and Ayía Galíni at the mouth of the Plátys is a favourite beach resort.

The valley suffered greatly during the German occupation in the Second World War. The villages on the western side, against the Kédhros, were largely destroyed by the Germans as retribution for the abduction of General Kreipe in 1944 and were rebuilt after the war. A number of churches, however, survived the destruction.

Hikers can find good starting points for walks to the top of the Ida at Fourfourás and Thrónos. Thrónos is also the starting point for a walk to Arkádhi.

Réthymnon

Pánormos

Stavroménos

Pérama

Perivólia

Plataniás

Piyí

Adhéle

Loutrá

Arméni

Amnátos

Eléftherna

Arkhéa Eléftherna

VRÝSSINAS

Moní Arkádhi

Potamídha

Gouledhianá

Potamídha

VÉNI

Klisídhi

PSILÓ (IDA)

Pantánassa

Sybrita

Thrónos

Kalóyeros

Patsós

Apóstoli

Yénna

Asómatos

KATSONÍSSI

Méronas

Monastiráki

Platánia

Lambíni

SÓROS

Amári

Kíssanos

Spíli

Elénes

Lambiótes

Elliniká

Fourfourás

Vizári

Kardháki

Smíles

Vríses

Kíssos

KÉDHROS

Áno Méros

Kouroútes

AMÁRI VALLEY

Níthavri

Akoumianós

Krýa Vrýssi

Ayía Paraskeví

Apodhoúlou

Akoúmia

Orné

Pláti

Vathiakó

Mélambes

Plakýs

Áyios Pávlos

Ayía Galíni

ME

- - - - - Pashley
.... Lear
— — — Spratt

———— Main road
———— Secondary road
River

0   5 km

In the Protopalatial Minoan Period inhabitants had already settled in the Amári valley. Below Patsós, in the basin of the Potamídha, the cave of Áyios Antónios was a continuous place of cultic worship (and still is today). But it is below Monastiráki, in the Amári valley itself, where an extremely important Minoan archaeological site is located: from 1800 B.C. until the end of the Neopalatial Period there was a city here. There are also excavations from the Mycenaean Period, in a village below Apodhoúlou which has a beehive tomb.

From the 5th century B.C. onwards the beautifully situated Sybrita, close to Thrónos, was the most powerful city in the region. The city dominated the entire valley, as far as the harbour city of Soulia (next to Ayía Galíni), and after the arrival of Christianity it was the seat of a bishopric. In Thrónos the mosaic floor under the Panayía church, from a 5th or 6th century basilica, attests to this. The ruins at Elliniká near Vizári date from Roman times and the First Byzantine Period. Among other finds, the remains of a late-8th century basilica were uncovered here.

During the Muslim occupation in the 9th and 10th centuries Sybrita, Soulia and Elliniká were destroyed and the bishopric of Sybrita was no longer seated in the city. From the Second Byzantine Period Lambíni (in Áyios Vasílios) was the seat of the bishopric.

The valley only became important again during Venetian rule. A large number of villages in the valley have Orthodox churches with extraordinary frescos. The Panayía of Thrónos (with early- and late-14th century frescos) has already been mentioned. Monasteries also flourished at this time. Clockwise from Thrónos, the most important churches and monasteries are as follows: past Kalóyeros the church of Áyios Ioánnis Theológos (with 14th century frescos, near a hermit's cave). Then the Asómatos monastery. This was the most prominent monastery in the valley. It already existed in the Second Byzantine Period, but as so many other monasteries it came to flourish at the end of the Venetian era and remained an important center of learning during the Ottoman occupation (it is no longer a functioning monastery). Monastiráki, with the Arkhistrátigos and the Áyios Yeóryios (both with frescos) is the next one. Then comes Amári with the beautifully situated Ayía Ánna, with frescos from 1225. And then up again to Platánia, which has the Panayía with its 14th /15th century frescos. Then there is Lambiótes with the Panayía and its frescos from the 14th century. Then Apodhoúlou with the Áyios Yeóryios, which has wonderful 14th century frescos. Then Ayía Paraskeví

The Amári valley

109

with the Panayía which has frescos from 1516. Across from the Plátys, in the direction of Krýa Vrýssi is Orné with the Mikhaíl Arkhángelos, and Mélambes with the Ayía Paraskeví. And then along the slope of the Kédhros there is Áno Méros with a beautifully situated monastery (functioning until 1821, it collapsed in 1993). Then there is Smíles with the Panayía and its frescos from the 13th century. Then Kardháki with the monastery church of Áyios Ioánnis Theológos Fotís. This has exceptional architecture and frescos from the late 13th and 14th centuries. Then comes Elénes, with the Áyios Nikólaos and its early-13th century frescos. Méronas, with the deserted Kirá Panayía monastery and its interesting church, and the lovely Panayía (with 14th century frescos and a very old icon; probably the church of a monastery which no longer exists) in the same village. Then there is Yénna, with the Áyios Onoúfrios and its 14th century frescos.

Farther to the north, outside the valley proper, there were two important monasteries: that of Véni (now deserted) with its cave church of Áyios Antónios, close to Pantánassa; and on the ridge between the Amári valley and the region of Mylopótamos was the strategically located monastery of Arkádhi which flourished from the end of the 16th century. Its monastery church with the imposing Renaissance façade in Venetian style was built during this period, and the bell tower dates from 1587. The monastery had a school and was a center for religious art. It remained a prominent monastery during Ottoman times, and had an important regional function. It played a sad role in the rebellion of 1866-1869 (see below). The monastery is open to the public.

After Khaniá and Réthymnon were taken over by the Ottomans in 1645 and 1646, they soon occupied the rest of the island, apart from Herákleion. The Amári valley also came under Ottoman rule. In all likelihood the valley remained an important agricultural area during this time. We only hear from the valley again in 1821, right after the outbreak of the rebellion in June. In that month the Orthodox clergy of the region, including the abbot of the most important monastery, Asómatos, were summoned to Réthymnon where a number of them were put to death. As mentioned elsewhere in this book, similar incidents were happening in other parts of Crete at the time. Shortly after this the peasants of the valley also became the victims of the Ottomans. From the Messará, where the notorious Janissar Agriolídhis exercised power on behalf of the Ottoman authorities, Ottoman troops marched to the north in July in order to support the *pasha's* of Khaniá and Réthymnon in their struggle against the rebels in the Apokórona and Sfakiá. Belligerant and frustrated by their defeat at the hands of the rebels, they came back through the Amári valley, making victims of the peasants as they went.

As mentioned earlier, the Ottomans were not able to crush the rebellion immediately, and at the end of 1821 neither party had the upper hand (that only happened when the Albanian troops of Mehmed Ali arrived in May of 1822). The strategically located monastery of Arkádhi, on the ridge between the Amári valley and the north coast, was the subject of fighting between the Ottomans and the rebels in the winter of 1821-1822. The valley itself remained under Ottoman rule. In early 1824, however, it suffered greatly during the pacification expedition of Huseyn Bey (see also the introductory notes to Chapter 7).

During the later rebellion of 1866-1869 Arkádhi played a renowned and sorrowful role. On November 9th, 1866, the day that Ottoman troops threatened to force their way into the monastery, one of the refugees (300 rebels and 600 women and children had found shelter in the monastery) blew up the powder magazine. The monastery collapsed, and most of those present were killed, including hundreds of Ottoman soldiers. Since then the monastery has been a symbol of the Cretan struggle against oppressors.

THE TRAVEL DESCRIPTIONS

For modern, motorised travellers Réthymnon is a natural starting point for a tour of the Amári valley. That was not true for travellers in the time of the horse and the mule. In fact it was impossible to reach the basin of the Plátys via the basin of the Potamídha. Thus the Amári valley was pointing south and was only connected to the north coast with a pass across the ridge between the valley and the north, via the monastery of Arkádhi. So it comes as no surprise that on his way from Khaniá to Herákleion Pashley left the valley off of his route, as did Lear. They both reached the valley only after rambling through the Cretan regions to the east and south of the Ida (see Part 2 of this series), and passed through it from south to north. Spratt did enter the valley from the north, but after his discovery of Sybrita he did not go any farther into the valley. He continued his tour along the north coast to Réthymnon.

We enter into Pashley's expedition on March 30, 1834 in Timbáki on the Messará plain, where he arrived after having visited Górtyn.

Pashley, I, p. 299 – 308

We arrived at Dibáki [Timbáki] at noon, having started from Haghíus Dhéka [Áyii Dhéka, close to Górtyn] at nine o'clock. On leaving the plain we crossed a river which flows under Klíma. Advancing further along these south-eastern slopes of Mount Ida, we passed the small Mohammedan village of Sáhta, the first of a district called Abadhiá, and containg eight villages, chiefly inhabited by Mohammedans. The places are Haghía Paraské, Plátanos, Apodhúlo, Vathiakó, Árdhakto, Sáhta, Kurútes and Níthavri. They are spread along the southern and south-eastern slopes of Mount Ida, and the chief wealth of their inhabitants consists in the olive-trees which grow in their neighbourhood. There is likewise some arable land up in the valleys hereabouts, and several of the inhabitants of Abadhiá have also land down in the plain of Mesará. The term *Abadhiótes* is confined strictly to the Mohammedan inhabitants of the district...

The first village seen, after leaving Sáhta, is Plátanos, situated about a mile to the right: after passing through Vathiakó, we arrived at Apodhúlo at three o'clock...

At Apodhúlo I went to the house of the Proestós, Captain Aléxandhros, or, as he is more commonly called, Alexandhrákes, by whom I was hospitably received on a subsequent occasion, and the history of whose fortunes, from the beginning of the revolution [1821] to the present time, is not devoid of interest.

When the Sfakians and Rhizítes [the inhabitants of the region around Thérisso and Lákki, to the south of Khaniá] arose in insurrection against their Moslem lords, early in July 1821, the Mohammedans of Khaniá and the neighbouring districts were not long in finding out, that they were unable to put down the revolt. They were soon joined by very numerous succours from the central and eastern parts, where their correligionaries were more numerous than in the west. Christians were taken as servants by many of the Mohammedans who joined this expedition, and who were also accompanied by spare horses and mules, which they meant to load with the spoils of Sfakiá. They remembered the victory obtained over the Sfakians in 1770, and thought their success would be equally certain now. As these numerous forces passed through the district of Amári, on their way to Khaniá, they did not either murder or even plunder the quiet and peaceful Christian inhabitants. But, on their return, they wreaked vengeance on the defenceless and submissive rayas of Amári, Hághios Vasílios, and the other districts through which they passed, for the sufferings and losses they had endured in the Sfakian mountains. Every Greek whom they fell in with they massacred: the women and children they made prisoners and slaves. No orders to commit such enormities were issued by Sheríf-pashá, the Governor-general of the island and Commander-in-chief of the expedition; but straggling parties of his returning troops spread themselves over the country, and, with the ordinary license of Janissaries and irregular forces, acted in this lawless way, although assurances had been given, both by the Pashá and by Agri-olídhes, that the Amariótes, who were still peaceable subjects, should remain uninjured.

The news of this conduct of the Mohammedans spread rapidly throughout the district, and before they arrived at Apodhúlo, my host and all the male Christian inhabitants of the village had already sought security on the lofty summits of Mount Ida. Two old men, each upwards of a hundred years of age, supposed that their years would protect them, and remained at home, but were both massacred.

My host's family had been suffering severely from that common scourge of every part of the Turkish empire, the plague: no less than four of his children had been its victims. He had placed his daughter Kalítza and his son Ioánnes in a hut, a little to the east of the village, with a woman, who had also with her three of her own children, to be out of the way of contagion, until the plague should have left the village. Aléxandhros went, on the morning in question, to tell his children, and the woman in the hut, of the expected passage of the Mohammedans, and to bid them not to be alarmed. The troops at length passed along in great numbers, and the hut was not examined by any of them. At last, however, a single straggler stopped, and turned aside from the road, to gather herbs in a field close by the place of refuge of the woman and children. The cottage attracted his attention: he cautiously approached it; and, at length, demanded whether there were any men within it. He was of course told that there were none. He then ordered the woman to open the door that he might see within the house; and, on satisfying himself of the defenceless condition of its occupants, he entered. The result was that he carried off with him to Dibáki, as captives, this helpless woman and the five children. Soon afterwards the two children of Aléxandhros were separated from their companions in the hut, and at last from each other. Kalítza, while at Dibáki, saw her mother, and her infant brother Constantine, who had both suffered the same misfortune, and where then, like herself and her other brother, captives and slaves.

For a long time Aléxandhros and his wife could learn nothing of the fate of their children, except that their daughter had been sent to Egypt, and that their son had been disposed of to a Mohammedan within the walls of Megálo-Kástron. At length, however, tidings respecting their daughter, as definite as they were cheering and unlooked for, reached them.

Years rolled on, and, in the month of September 1829, an Englishman, accompanied by his wife and several domestics, arrived at Khaniá: in a few days a meeting took place between the strangers and Captain Aléxandhros's family. It would be as difficult to describe as it is easy to conceive the joy experienced by the parents on receiving this full proof, by the evidence of their senses, of the happy fortune which had attended their child. She who had been for years deplored by them as dwelling in Egyptian bondage, was the wife of an English gentleman. [Pashley is referring to Robert Hay, archeologist and traveller, who in 1828 had bought Kalítza as a slave girl in Egypt and had returned with her to Crete. As for Kalítza's brother, he later managed to buy his freedom from slavery.]

Before I left Crete, I had the pleasure of becoming acquainted with this long-lost daughter and her husband; of spending some time with them in Megálo-Kástron; of visiting them under the roof of Captain Aléxandhros at Apodhúlo, and rambling with them on the slopes of Mount Ida. They were then on their return from Egypt, where they had long resided, to England.

When at Apodhúlo, I was told that at Kastrí, between two and three miles off towards the sea, considerable Hellenic remains are found. The chief port of Amári is Hághio Galéne, which is somewhat to the eastward of Apodhúlo, and is probably the site of the ancient Sulia or Sulena, recorded by the author of the Stadiasmus, as a promontary where there was a harbour and good water...

In half an hour after leaving Apodhúlo, Níthavri is on our right, on the side of Pselorítes, and about half a mile off. We now descend for about twenty minutes, and then cross a torrent which flows from Pselorítes to the south coast. Before reaching the summit of the ascent on the opposite side I saw to some distance down this valley, and observed that, lower down, the river passes through a perpendicular cleft in the rocks. After an ascent of nearly half an hour, along parts of which, as well as in the previous descent, considerable remains of a Venetian paved road still exist, we see spread out before us the fine valley of Asómatos. On the left side of it are the villages of Anómeros, Vrýsis and Monasteráki: to the right, just before us, is Vasári [Vizári], and, on a hill, Fúrfuras, which is about six hundred paces beyond Visári. These villages are surrounded with olive-trees, as at lower elevations. Fúrfuras was the scene of a considerable engagement between the Greeks and Turks, during the first year of the war. We reached the summit at ten minutes past six; and, after traversing the valley till a little before seven, we discerned to our left some cypress-trees and parts of a white building, which proved to be the monastery of Asómatos. In a few minutes we were standing by a blazing fire, lighted up in the chamber reserved for visitors: we soon obtained some refreshments, and excellent wine, which, after a ride of nearly ten hours from Haghíus Dhéka, was most acceptable.

The venerable Hegúmenos tells me that the monastery possessed annals of its history, which were burnt during the revolution. At present its members are only the Hegúmenos, three Patéres and three servants. In former times it had an Hegúmenos, six Patéres and ten servants. Soon after the commencement of the Greek revolution, the Pashá of Rhíthymnos invited the Abbots of several monasteries, as well as many Patéres and Papádhes, (monks and parish priests,) from Mylopótamos, Amári, and the Rhithymnian district, to go into the city that they might each of them receive a written document (bujurdí) of amnesty and pardon to their correligionaries for what had happened. These documents were to be promulgated by the priests in their respective districts, and to be enforced by their own authority and influence, in order to induce the christian peasantry to remain quiet. It was pretended that the tranquility of this part of the island would probably be then ensured. Many of the poor priests trusted the Turks; for, knowing well that the proposed means were likely to produce their object, the tranquility of the island, they thought it natural that they should be adopted. One of those who thus went to Rhíthymnos, to receive instructions from the Turkish authorities, was the Hegúmenos of this monastery. Those who arrived first were detained within the city, and when their number, within its walls, was judged to be sufficiently great, they were all put to death. They thus learnt, when too late, how fatal a mistake they had committed in having supposed the Turks capable of using any menas, but those of force and terror, to appease the revolt.

This account of the Hegúmenos is confirmed by the words of a letter, written on the 15th of August 1821, by Monsieur D'Herculez, the Austrian Vice-Consul at Khaniá, to the Imperial Internuncio at Constantinople.

From that time the monastery remained without either Hegúmenos or Patéres till about three years ago, when, on the restoration of tranquillity by the Egyptians, the present Hegúmenos returned. He had spent five years of the revolution in Síphnos, and the rest in other islands, occasionally visiting Crete. He embraced the first opportunity of returning to establish himself in the country of his birth, although it is still under Turkish sway, 'for,' as he says, 'one's native land is always sweet.'

Thirty years later Lear also visited the Amári valley, accompanied by his attendant George and his mule driver, a certain Konstandís Manosákis (Zeriff had left his service in Réthymnon). He had been to the Messará plain and, depressed as he was, he wanted to return to Khaniá as quickly as possible, where he lodged in a comfortable house with fellow countrymen. Very early on May 18th, 1864 he left Pómbia, where he had spent the night. At 11.00 in the morning he passed through Timbáki and at 1.00 in the afternoon he began the upward climb.

Lear, p. 86 – 89

2.30 Always such a going up. Stop till 2.40 and draw Paximádhi: a very uninteresting view. At three we are over the southward-looking hill, and see a vast valley, Sata village only therein, and olives. Snow Ida-line above. Kedros left. Down hill.

Wide, fine, but gloomy and *piuttosto* commonplace mountain scenery. But Sata – 3.35 – is in a grand quiet verdant mountain valley.

4 Alas! Alas! Green as is the scene and fresh the air, I am sad and cross, having been angry for half an hour (along of Konstandís stealing artichokes, which I seized and threw away), and of being wholly and totally disgusted. We dip into vast deep valleys, and are to ascend great hills, but I brood over leaving Crete the very soonest possible. At 5.15 after tremendous pulls, passing another ruinous village (Vathiakó), we got to Apodhoúlou, which doubtless contains more or less picturesque, but somehow it was impossible to draw it. In the village, at a wineshop where several Mussulmen were quarrelling, a man in Levantine garments, a hat, etc., was pointed out to me as the son of Aléxandros, and so it turned out: Mrs Hay's nephew [Lear was acquainted with Kalítza's purchaser Robert

Hay; Hay had left with his Cretan wife for Scotland when Lear visited Apodhoúlou]. He seemed to make me very welcome, but one of the *Mussulmen* would make him and me drink, and the scene was not pretty. We were taken to the *konak*, a stout well-built house, but uncared for, and we sat in an open gallery, into which shortly came two quite drunken Moslim, one with four glasses, two of which he let fall and, they broken, he returned with shame whence he came. The host talked a good deal of his uncle and aunt Hay, who are sixty – he – and she fifty years old: showed me a seal, crest goat, and a watch, all broken more or less. This young man is an intelligent fellow, though utterly dirty and neglected. He has a school of 40 children from the village and other villages who sit, some of them shirtless and most shoeless, in what was I suppose the drawing room. Another brother is here, and their father, whom I took for a Moslim – Mrs Hay's brother (not John, who is in Egypt, nor Konstantin, who is dead). We sat in the gallery, and the two drunken Turks made themselves asses. Later we were put into what was once the bedroom, where some good articles of furniture still spoke of other days of wealth and comfort. Then came 'supper': eggs and a rice pilaf, which George had made; George is never out of humour, though tonight sorely tried by the dirt and *scomodi modi* [inconvenient ways] of our dwelling. Artichokes also were there, but the extreme filth of the whole was hideous; so, George having made my bed, we shut up for the night – the muleteer being already asleep – if only to avoid the whole village which had come into the gallery to stare at me, and began to crowd the room. The house is an example of misplaced expense – a ruin. Chairs, a bed and good English bolts, locks, etc. etc. etc., but every part decayed and in the hands of savages. Rabbits, a goat, swallows, etc., rush and flit about the rooms. Part of this is written on the morning of the 19th, which is clear and lovely, and we are up by four.

Amisfield [in East Lothian] is the only address of Mr Hay I can get, but it is known to George Kalokairinós. Off at six, having made a drawing of the house from above, accompanied by Phanoúrios. Very lovely morning. Poor good people! they are half savage. Ida is seen, but by no means pleases me: dome-like, and too near. Very probably from the road to Preveli, it would be finer, but then hardly ever clear. As things are, Haniá is my aim.

7.15 We are stopping, along of the luggage falling. Konstandís having whacked the mule, which jumped and shook off articles. The route has been between Ida – an ugly dome – and immense green valleys, olive dotted: not a scrap to draw; great ascent and descent to Amári Kastélli – fine valley – Ida more drawable now, but of course has become clouded, 8.45.

'Gheórghios Saounátis – Manouél Saounátis of Rethymnon': name of man at a roadside *khan* where we stop and have some good wine at 9-9.15. (A sort of general shop, and I buy a bridle.) Good Aghios Myron wine costs 200 to 250 piastres – the barrel, which is 100 or 150 *okádhes*.

Pleasant walk, Ἀηδόνια [nightingales]. Myrtles, great size; always a very rich yellow green. Clouds increasing. Meronas and other villages, all of which Konstandís knows the names of. They make much silk. Ida always covered, the truth being that she is unwilling to have comparisons made by a distinguished landscape-painter.

10 Going through great olive groves, all property of the Monastery of Asómatos, at which George says he is sure they will say they are poor and have only two eggs, George also bursts out resolving to buy a fish at Haniá, and to roast it himself without oil. 10.30.

10.45 We arrive at the Monastery of Asómatos, but are sorrily received in a dirty bare room and by very dirty lay *kalógheri*. As nobody came, and as they said the *Hegoúmenos* was just going off to Preveli, I thought it fit after 20 or 25 minutes to send the Pasha's letter, which speedily brought the *Hegoúmenos*, but he was a man of no appearance of manner or friendliness, while the other clown *kalógheros* sat staring and yawning. Nothing being said, except a suggestion that Arkádhi was near, I asked for something to eat, when the *Hegoúmenos* said, 'Have you not eaten today?' and shortly after he went away. Presently they brought us a small plate of stewed pigeon, one of eggs, and one of nasty παστάχι [pastáhi] with a sweet wine – not very good – and we three sat down to make the best of it. At the present moment, noon, we have made our lunch, and the *Hegoú-menos* has made his adieux, and the clown giant lay monx have tumbled down the ladder: a rather scurvy lot. I have decided to go to Arkádhi, for the head man going away, and faring as we do so ill while he is here, what should we do when he is gone? So, we are to repoge till 1 p.m. It must be said, George's attention and activity are the greatest comforts. Coffee has since been brought, but so bad as to be undrinkable. And the worst of all is, the mountain is always wholly covered, so that here, where naturally the views of Ida would be the finest, not a line can I draw. O churly monx! At one, I wake George and Konstandís and lo! whereas they were both of accord before, i.e., that it is better to go than to stay, now they hesitate.

Konstandís says it is very far, and will rain: George says the mule will suffer. George says pay nothing: I think it better to pay something.

Before we follow Lear on his way to Arkádhi, we go back again to Pashley. We had left him in the Asómatos monastery, where he was enjoying himself more than Lear. After having spent the night there he left for Arkádhi on March 31st.

Pashley, I, p. 308 – 313, 315 – 317, 319

On leaving the monastery of Asómatos we ascended for nearly half an hour, and then a descent of about equal length brought us to the Water of the Stone, a fountain the virtues of which are the same as those assigned to many fountains, by ancient authors, and have probably been the cause of its name. So celebrated is it, that persons sometimes send to the monastery which we have left, even from Constantinople, for a few bottles of it, and it is said to be always highly beneficial to the invalids who take it. The mountain hereabouts is covered with heath and wild strawberry trees.

An ascent of forty minutes brings us in sight of the monastery of Arkádhi, on a little plain and surrounded by many pine-trees. Over the entrance gateway is an inscription, coeval, I suppose, with the erection of the building, in which mention is made of the monk Neóphytos, the Hegúmenos of the monastery.

I ascertained while here, that there are ancient remains near the metókhi Elévtherna, which is less than three miles to the north-east of Arkádhi. Now, supposing the site of Eleutherna to be near this metókhi of the monastery, I was naturally induced to make all possible inquiries to learn the situation of Sybritia. We know from the Peutinger Table that the latter city was eight miles to the south-west of Eleutherna; and its numerous and beautiful silver coins would lead us to suppose it to have been a place of some consideration. Scylax mentions it, along with Eleutherna, saying that Eleutherna is on the north side of the island, and Sybritia on the south; and its name occurs even in Hierocles.

My very diligent inquiries after the city which was situated so near Eleutherna, were at length successful. I discovered that there are vestiges of antiquity on the summit of a lofty hill, about five miles to the southward of Arkádhi. The distance agrees very well with that of the Table, and it is only necessary to examine the sites, in order to be able to decide with confidence on the question. Supposing however as I did, that the

Beacon would reach Khaniá about the first of April, and being anxious to see Captain Copeland [Copeland was travelling on his ship The Beacon, under assignment from the British government to conduct a survey along the coast of Asia Minor, and had orders to assist Pashley in his expedition], I postponed my examination of these sites, for the present.

In the winter after the revolution commenced, the Sfakians began to spread themselves over the district of Amári, and engaged the Rhithymnióte Mohammedans both in Amári and Rhíthymnos. On this Iatimelés, a Mohammedan leader, left Rhíthymnos with eighty picked men, and took possession of the monastery of Arkádhi. He supposed that his presence, with such a party, would tend to keep the neighbouring district tranquil, since the Christians of Amári had not yet revolted, and the Mohammedans were all remaining quiet in their villages. The straggling parties of armed Christians, chiefly natives of Sfakiá, who were dispersed through the neighbourhood, no sooner learnt that Iatimelés had established himself at Arkádhi, than orders to assemble were immediately given by their leaders, and on the evening of the festival of Hághios Antónios, a little while after sunset, the Christians assembled at Thrónos to the number of 400 men. The Mohammedans had then been only a few days in the monastery. Some time before midnight the Christians commenced their march, and in about two hours arrived at Arkádhi. A postern, of the existence of which the Mohammedans in the monastery were ignorant, was opened to them by the Patéres, who were in correspondence with them and expected their arrival. The Mohammedan inmates of the convent knew nothing of the silent entrance of these armed and rebel Christians within its walls. Most of them were lodged in the Hegumenikó, but others were dispersed in different cells around the court-yard of the monastery.

Some time before day-break the Christians made a sudden attack on the unsuspecting Moslems. Those who were sleeping in different cells were most of them dispatched without great difficulty; but a few fought their way to the Hegumenikó, and prepared for a desperate defence. The Christians, however, succeeded in setting fire to the building, and the Mohammedans, who saw that there was no longer a possibility of either resistance or escape, surrendered. In all likelihood the victors promised to spare their lives; 'but when they had come out of the Hegumenikó, the Christians saw that several of themselves had fallen: one of them found his brother slain, and another his cousin, and another his companion; and they therefore put all their prisoners to death.' There were only seven

The Amári valley

Christians slain, while of the Mohammedans no more than eight or ten escaped. The bodies of all these slaughtered Mohammedans were thrown into a well near the monastery. The ordinary rites of Christian burial were performed by the Hegúmenos and Patéres over the remains of the Greeks...

The Mohammedans of Rhíthymnos, on learning the fate of Iatimelés, came here with all their force. The Hegúmenos and his kalógheri felt their character as peaceable rayas so completely compromised, by the events which had happened, that when the armed Greeks left the monastery they too retired to the loftier ranges of mount Ida in the district of Amári. Two very old kalógheri, who were hardly able to walk, thought their age would protect them, and remained behind. When the Mohammedans came to the monastery, they shot them both, and reduced the greater part of the buildings to a heap of ruins.

The Hegúmenos and Patéres remained in the district of Amári till the following Easter. They then returned, and, fitting up a few of the apartments of the burnt monastery, resided here till they heard, the year after, that Khuseín-bey was coming: they then again fled to the lofty mountain summits, and afterwards stationed themselves at their metókhi at Véni, situated near the summit of a lofty hill on which are found the ruins of Sybritia. They dwelt at Véni from October till April. Amári having submitted to Khuseín-bey they returned to the convent, and never fled from it afterwards. They used to have daily visits paid them by Sfakians and other armed Christians, and the Hegúmenos asserts, that they experienced rougher treatment at the hands of the Sfakians, than they had ever met with from the Mohammedans. They were plundered of many sheep and goats, as well as of the plate of the monastery...

We left the monastery of Arkádhi at a quarter before four, and immediately descended into a ravine, which we crossed. Following the path, on its western side, we emerged at its entrance at half-past four, when Amnátos was before us about two miles off. The minaret seen towering above the house of this village, indicated that its inhabitants are chiefly Mohammedans...

For the first half hour of our journey after passing the village of Amnátos, the road lay through groves of olive trees, almost entirely uncultivated. At a quarter before six we crossed a stream, and at six reached the Turkish village of Lutrá; at twenty minutes after six we passed Peghé; and, a little further on, met two Mohammedans who were returning from Rhíthymnos, where they had been spending the day. One of them was in such a state of inebriation, from the quantity of wine he had been drinking in the city, that he could hardly sit on his horse. He professed to wish to communicate something of importance to me; but would not speak while my Christian guide, Captain Maniás, was within hearing. I therefore sent Maniás on, and waited to receive the import communication which he was so very anxious to make to me. His confession was as follows: 'I am a Mohammedan, and yet, while in the city to day, I have drinking the blood of Christ.'

Although the Mohammedans of Crete generally indulge, with the temperance usual among orientals, in the juice of the grape, yet they of course know, that to do so is a peculiar habit of the *Cretan* Musulman, and does not at all improve his character for orthodoxy in the opinion of other true believers. Thus this drunken fellow knew that, by his excess, he had committed an offence against the precepts of his own religion; and the monstrous dogma of transsubstantiation, held by the Greek church as well as by the Roman Catholic, doubtless suggested to him the strange and shocking expression he used...

A little before seven we passed another long tract of uncultivated olives, and, in about half an hour more, arrived at the village of Perivólia, where, since it was then long after sunset, and we should in all probability have found great difficulty in obtaining admission into the city, if we had proceeded to it, we determined to repose for the night.

Maniás conducted us to the house of a relation of his, the greater part of whose family had retired to rest before we arrived. Within the single apartment, on the ground-floor, of which, as is generally the case in all the villages of Crete, the house consists, we find a sort of upper story, or rather a wooden floor, extending along about one-third of the apartment, at a height of nine or ten feet from the ground. This apology for a 'first floor' is reached by a ladder, and is ordinarily used as the sleeping-place of the family. We threw the cottagers into great confusion by arriving after they had retired to rest. They insisted on giving up to us the 'first floor' in question; so we ascended by the ladder, and were fortunate enough to rest extremely well.

Pashley travelled in one day – April 1st - from Perivólia to Khaniá, where he arrived at 7.00 in the evening. Three weeks later he left on his expedition through western Crete, which is described in Part 3 of this series. In this part we direct ourselves again at Lear, who followed Pashley so painstakingly in 1864. We left him annoyed in the monastery of Asómatos. In spite of objections from his travelling companions, they travelled on to the monastery of Arkádhi. The Hegoúmenos Gabriel who received them so hospitably there, was still the abbot at the monastery during the Ottoman siege of 1866. He died struggling against the enemy just before the monastery was blown up. This travel account begins in the Asómatos monastery on May 19th.

Lear, p. 89 – 91

Off at 1.20, cloudy all. Ida hidden. Myrtle thickets. Ἀηδόνια [nightingales]. Richly wooden slopes of Ida – headless Ida. 2.20 Terminate ascent, and begin descent. Always huge rich valleys. No, ascent *not* finished: begins again, and goes on to 2.45. Descent sharp till three. Fountain of the 'Stone' very cold. Konstandís says no one drinks of it. Ascend again, 3.5 – 3.45: long pull. Leave track to Rethymnon and turn to the right. All gray fogg and mist.

3.55 at top – all mist – Arkádhi just visible. We sit and smoke till four. Plain. Pines. Arkádhi at 4.50: fog, almost a small mizzly rain. It is now six, and I am glad to have come here for the *Hegoúmenos* is a very jolly man and hearty, and gave us all sweets, water, coffee and *rakí* in no time. Also I am well washed, and comparatively comfortable. The place seems picturesque but the dark mizzling fog prevents one seeing much. Fleas commence. How to get back to Halépa by Sunday or Monday? George's good humour is always a blessing, and when they brought coffee for me and for him only, he instantly gave half to the muleteer, of his, tired as he was. (This morning, returning to the house at Apodhoúlou for my small box of flea powder, I found Aléxandros and others taking snuff out of it, as they thought!) The name of the *Hegoúmenos* here is Gabriel. There was a long waiting and semi-sleep before supper, which happened at 7.30 in a very remote room. The Gabriel, who is a man of the world, was very jolly and pleasant and apologized, unnecessarily, for the supper, owing to its late coming: stewed pigeons, three sorts of salad, a dish of honey, cherries, beans, cheese, etc. etc. and with very good wine, though a little too sweet. Everything was orderly and hearty. Healths, Cretan fashion, abundant. Afterwards, coffee and smoking. It seems that the walls of the church and monastery are thick as ever; only the inside was burned in 1823. Gabriel has been at Jerusalem, and that fact was a great gain for George and me, *qua* conversation. At nine we retired; I, I am sorry to say, to a square room with no outlet whatever, and though George showed me a *luogo* (*cari luoghi*) I could not afterwards find it when I wanted it. One of the most worrying parts of these Cretan Travels is the impossibility of chamber pots, and lo! when I went out the door shut to, and I had to roam about to get a priest to open it. It is nearly ten; late hours.

Rose before four [on May 20th], having slept very tolerably, thanks to lots of flea powder. Up and dressed 4.50. Coffee: see church – oldish (leave 24 piastres) – then draw on the outside. Ida *would* be lovely, and the whole scene delightful, but clouds stopped all. Then I went up a hill, Gabriel and all the monx too, and drew again, on bits of paper, having put up my large book. Then, at 6.10, we were off. I like Gabriel.

6.30 We have come across, and out of, a very grand ravine, splendidly berocked, beshrubbed and bebirded. The plain is below, and the sea, but foggy and unclear.

7.15 We get to Amnátos: the morning is very hot, close, damp, and the gardens and close olives keep out air. Moslem burying-ground, but no minarets as in Pashley's days.

7.45 Rethymnon is seen afar, and the friendly-ugly Akrotíri once more. All we pass is like a great continual garden: corn, caraba [carob], olives and fruit trees of many sorts, immensely cultivated and rich.

9 We have just passed Pighí, a very large village utterly hidden in olives. All this territory is amazing for richness.

9.10 We pass through Adhele, another large but concealed village: one is quite surprised by the streets and houses, which are invisible till you are close by them. At a wineshop outside we get some wine. There are the noisiest hens here I ever heard. It seems we are trying to lunch at Perivólia.

10.45 We are actually at Perivólia.

From Perivólia Lear went back to his guest lodgings in Khalépa, near Khaniá. The rest of this chapter concerns the discovery of Sybrita by Spratt. As Pashley mentioned, he did not have time to go investigate this important city in the Amári valley. Therefore it is not surprising that Spratt, who was filling in the gaps in Pashley's description, did go searching for Sybrita. As we will see in Chapter 7, on his journey from Herákleion through the Mylopótamos basin, thus to the north of the Amári valley, Spratt had discovered the remains of the powerful ancient city of Eleutherna, which is also mentioned by Pashley. Spratt had then learned from a priest that there were other ruins not far from Eleutherna, to the southwest, in the neighbourhood of the Véni monastery. So he went there to investigate. We join him now at Eleutherna. He had, by the way, the habit of not spending the night at monasteries or in people's homes, but in his own tent brought along for this purpose. His reasoning for this, as he mentions elsewhere in his book, is that because of this he had no trouble with lice or fleas.

Spratt, II, p. 99 – 110

Taking a guide from Prene [now Arkhéa Eléftherna], I started soon after noon for Veni, judging it to be probably the site of Sybrita, from the information I received from the priest, and from the reported distance to it (about eight miles to the south-west) from Eleutherna corresponding with that given in the Itinery table as the distance between those two cities; and as one of them had been already clearly identified, it seemed that the other must be at the next known Hellenic site. We consequently proceeded towards the south, ascending from Prene up the western root of Ida, and crossing it an elevation of more than 3000 feet above the sea. We found here a sprinkling of oaks with small, pointed leaves, but trunks of large girth, showing that at this elevation they found their proper climate. From this ridge, which divides the Mylopotamo from the Amari district and valley to the south, we were about to descend into a rocky ravine, or rather gorge, which cleaves deeply into this face of Ida, and forms the head of a river or mountain-torrent that, after a westward course, turns sharply to the north and finds its exit to the sea near Retimo; but on the top of the ridge we meet a little shepherd-boy, who, in reply to my inquiry, says he knows the place, and points out to us the site of Veni now nearly due west of us, and appearing as a remarkable table-topped hill standing conspicuously in the centre of a wide valley. It certainly looked an inviting site for a city of the old times, from its form and strength, and therefore my expectations were raised regarding it, especially when the little fellow assured us that there were abundance of ruins there. 'It was an Hellenica polis,' he said; 'and my father lives in a metoki on the top.' I therefore halted a few minutes to sketch the glimpse we got of it through the opening of the gorge, imagining that it must be the site of Sybrita. It was apparently a position well fortified by nature; and its exploration promised to be extremely interesting; for the known silver coins of Sybrita, although rare, are of extremely fine art and very beautiful.

After making a considerable descent to a spring by the roadside,

named Nero Petra [Pashley's and Lear's Water of the Stone], from having the reputation of being good for the stone (a malady very frequent in
Crete, among infants as well as adults), we then approach a swelling spur
(extending from the roots of Ida towards Veni), from which rise two small
rocky eminences above some cultivated terraces, and upon which the
two villages of Klisidi and Thronos (the former Greek, the latter Turk)
are situated. Upon the rocky eminence rising immediately above the latter we see some slight indications of a wall, but are assured by our guide
that it is only of a Franko kastelli, and not Hellenic; and as my muleteers
pressed me to go on to Apostolo, because it was nearly an hour nearer to
Veni, and to pitch my tent there for the night, so as to be able to reach
Veni at an early hour the next morning, I consented, and to got my tent
in order, just at dusk, on the west side of the narrowest part of the gap that
separates the two valleys, running north and south, to the Aegean shore
at Retimo, and the Libyan Sea at Messara Bay.

Apostolo is inhabited by Greeks; and as my guides were Greeks, their
pressing me to pass hastily by the Turkish village of Thronos was natural, and the motive plain.

The tent-fire attracted the villagers after their day's work and their
supper, particularly as my interpreter was loquacious; and whilst talking
with them upon the nature of the remains at Veni, and how much of it
was of the old Hellenic time (for they sometimes retain some slight veneration for such, if aware of their being so), one of the most intelligent
replied, to my great surprise, that Veni was only a Genoese castle, and
not an Hellenic site, but that Thronos was the kephala or chief city in the
old time, 'for there are remains of the city all down the hill under it on
every side.' That Thronos, then, and not Veni must be the true site of
Sybrita, was evident if this information were true. But I was disappointed by the statement, as I had seen so little to indicate it in passing, and the
hill of Veni seemed so purely Hellenic and so promising. The priest and
the old men of the village were then referred to by me, and they all confirmed it, but replied that, as Thronos was a Turkish and not a Christian
village, they did not often go into it or upon the fields its inhabitants cultivated. Yet they knew that Thronos was the kephala or head town of the
district in old times, but they did not know it by any other name than
Thronos.

On my then saying that I was looking for an old Hellenic city called
Sybrita, they unanimously told me that the name did not exist locally
amongst themselves; nevertheless I learnt this curious information of its

being the site of Sybrita, through the preservation of the name amongst another community, in the Messara: – 'Oh!' said one of the oldest, 'that is the reason why the people about Metropoli (Gortyna), in the Messara, always call us, as well as the people of four or five other villages near us, the Tzivrites' when speaking of the head of the Amari valley, – a name which the reader will immediately recognize to be Sybrita itself, only modified, as usual, by the vulgar prefix of Tz. The identity of Sybrita was thus apparent, and it only wanted the site to be properly explored to confirm it. I therefore returned to Thronos the following morning, instead of proceeding to Veni, and found the remains indisputably those of an early Cretan city which had at one time been of considerable size, and, from its situation commanding the two fertile valleys lying below it, of considerable importance also.

Sybrita may be said to be now represented by the five villages of Thronos, Klisida, Kaloyero, Genna, and Apostolos, which are situated either upon or within half a mile of some parts of its ancients limits. The beautiful coins known of this city, as I have before remarked, indicate its early importance as an independent republic of Crete. It was also the see of a bishop in the earlier Christian period; and one of its bishops, named Cyrilles, was mentioned at the Council of Chalcedon, and another, Theodorus, at the second Council of Nice.

This ancient city occupied the sides of a steep eminence that stands over the low neck or col which connects the base of Mount Ida with the base of Kedros, the ancient Cedrius, and the rugged chain of mountains extending from it through the western part of Crete, this col being also, next to that over the isthmus of Ierapetra, the lowest in the island.

The hill of Thronos is surmounted by two rocks, one nearly a hundred yards across, the other, three or four hundred yards to the east of it, being smaller; and the village of Thronos stands upon a small terrace or spur in front of the gap between the two rocks, where, amongst the habitations, I saw some remains of an Hellenic ruin (three or four courses of the stones being visible), also several fragments of columns, and a mutilated statue. In the gap between the two rocks there are some Cyclopean remains; and the larger rock had its summit enclosed by walls, part of which appear, however, to be of middle-age date. I saw also, about halfway down the south face of the site, a rock tomb near some remains of massive Cyclopean walls that both supported terraces and apparently formed part of the walls of an acropolis or upper city, independently of the stronghold upon or enclosing the two crags surmounting the city. There are also vestiges of the ancient city around the north and west face of the hill, down the coll or neck which leads to Apostolo, consisting of Cyclopean walls, terraces, marble fragments, and much pottery in the surface-soil.

A finer site for a city I have not as yet seen in Crete, unless it be that of Arcadia [Spratt thought he had found the ruins of the ancient city of Arkadia during his travels through eastern Crete, see Part 2 of this series], which by its two crags it somewhat resembles in its general aspect, as it looks down at once upon the whole of the Amari valley and the valley of Veni, and holds the key of the most practicable communication between the north and south coasts in the whole of the part of the island westward of Ida, the route being by the Nero Petra spring and over the upland plain near to the monastery of Arkadia [Arkádhi]; for the valley which runs to the north of Sybrita and Veni is shut up to the northwest of the latter hill by a precipitous gorge, through which only is there room for the exit of its waters into the bay of Retimo.

After these evidences of the former existence of a large Cretan city at Thronos, I could not expect to find Veni so important as it had been previously represented; but as, from its peculiar appearance, it looked inviting, I proceeded thither the following day, guided by an intelligent native of Apostolo. And it proved, as he had stated, to have few remains of any kind upon it, although I found traces of Hellenic or early Cyclopean walls at its north extreme, where it is easiest of approach, with remains of middle-age masonry built upon them and also on the margin of the plateau in two or three other places, but especially at its south-west extreme, where there are high walls, built of small stones and mortar, to defend a weak part of the approach, and where there was a later entrance to this hill-city or fortress. The whole area of the flat summit of Veni, which is nearly a mile long, is cultivated, and the only vestiges shown me there were those of cisterns. It belongs to the monastery of Arkadia, the monks of which have a metoki or farm upon the east face of the hill, about 100 feet below its summit. The middle-age remains upon the hill-margin may consequently be only those of an early Christian stronghold and monastery, built after the destruction of the earlier city that stood there, of which there are now only a few vestiges. Although the remains were so insignificant, I nevertheless presume it to be the site of a small town of the same name that it at present bears, viz. Bene, which is only casually mentioned by an early author, and quoted by Dr. Cramer as being a small town subject to Gortyna – as Sybrita doubtless was at the same time, which explains how the name of Sybrita, or Tzivrites, is preserved only amongst the traditions of the inhabitants of Gortyna, at the opposite base of Mount Ida, and so distant...

The situation of Sybrita I have before noticed as being one of the most commanding and most suitable of any I have yet seen in the eastern part of Crete; for almost the whole of its cultivable territory is within view, and adjoining. Its modern name of Thronos is suggestive − a throne whence all its possessions could be surveyed. The salubrity of the situation and air of Thronos is such, too, according to the aga of the place (an Albanian, but long a resident there), that 'I have lived here thirteen years, and never had a headache,' was his reply to my questions regarding the healthiness of the spot, which, with the medicinal spring of Nero Petra in its vicinity, before noticed, and the fine scenery around this natural throne imbosomed within the western roots of Ida, was indeed a highly favoured locality in Crete...

Although I journeyed through the Amari valley from the Messara [at some other occasion, probably in 1858], and slept a night in the Asomatos monastery within the valley, as there is nothing of interest to relate of the journey, and Pashley notices the monastery, as well as that of Arkadia, upon the upland plain over Thronos, I shall only briefly describe my return to Retimo from here on this occasion.

It is evident that Pashley missed the discovery of Sybrita by passing through Klisidi instead of Thronos, his Greek guides, no doubt, having led him that way on account of Thronos being possessed by a Mahommedan community.

In crossing the upland basin of Arkadia, I found the superficial deposits to contains fresh- and brackish-water shells. But between it and Retimo, after a little descent, the road crosses over the yellowish-white tertiary ridges of the miocene period, upon which and in the valleys between them was a fine olive-grove, that extended all the way down to the shore, between Retimo and the Mylopotamo district.

Emerging from this grove, after a short ride by the beach near the city-gardens, we enter Retimo.

7. East of Réthymnon

From Réthymnon our journey procedes to the east, to Anóyia and farther. To the east of the Potamídha lies an area which has always been one
of the most important agricultural regions in Crete: the coastal plain
around Stavroménos (formerly known as Agrion), and further on the
valley of the Mylopótamos between the Ida in the south and the
Kouloúkonas ridge in the northeast. The Mylopótamos basin is connected with the area around Herákleion by two passes: the pass from
Dhamásta and Maráthos along the Stroúmbolas to Gázi, and the pass
from Anóyia to Týlissos.

This is an engaging area for modern travellers. Beach resorts such as
the charming Pánormos and picturesque Balí offer hospitable accommodation, and the villages against the north flank of the Ida show Crete
at its best. Here is also one of Crete's most important ancient cities: the
spectacularly situated Eléftherna. The monastery of Arkádhi and the
cave of Melidhóni are historical landmarks, bringing back tragic memories of the struggle for independence against the Ottoman rulers. Not to
mention the cave where Zeus spent his infancy, which from dramatical-
ly situated Anóyia can easily be reached by car. And then there are the

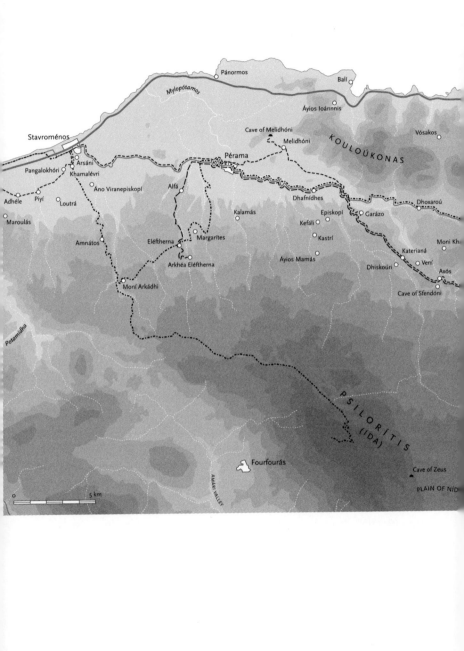

Pánormos

Balí

Mylopótamos

Áyios Ioánnnis

KOULOÚKONAS

Cave of Melidhóni

Vósakos

Stavroménos

Melidhóni

Arsáni

Pérama

Pangalokhóri

Khamalévri

Dhafnídhes

Dhoxaroú

Áno Viranepiskopí

Alfá

Adhéle

Piyí

Loutrá

Kalamás

Episkopí

Garázo

Maroulás

Kefáli

Kastrí

Moní Kha

Amnátos

Eléftherna

Margarítes

Áyios Mamás

Kateriana

Dhiskoúri

Vení

Arkhéa Eléftherna

Axós

Cave of Sfendóni

Moní Arkádhi

Potamidha

P S I L O R Í T I S

(IDA)

Fourfourás

Cave of Zeus

PLAIN OF NÍD

AMARI VALLEY

0   5 km

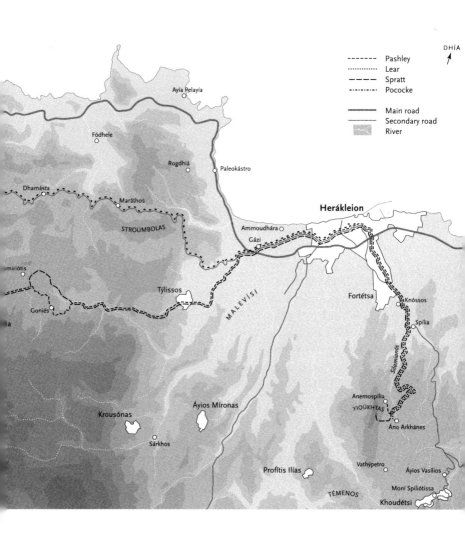

DHÍA

Pashley
Lear
Spratt
Pococke

Main road
Secondary road
River

Ayía Pelayía

Fódhele

Rogdhiá

Paleokástro

Dhamásta

Maráthos

STROÚMBOLAS

Ammoudhára

Gázi

Herákleion

miriótis

Goniés

Týlissos

MALEVÍSI

Fortétsa

Knóssos

Spília

Silamiónds

Anemospília

YIOÚKHTAS

Krousónas

Áyios Míronas

Áno Arkhánes

Sárkhos

Profítis Ilías

Vathýpetro

Áyios Vasílios

Moní Spiliótissa

TÉMENOS

Khoudétsi

ancient Axós and the nearby caves at Sfendóni, and villages such as Maroulás and Episkopí with their memories of the Venetian era. Hikers can enjoy splendid walks, among others through the Kouloúkonas ridge and to the Ida.

THE PAST

The region was already inhabited in the Neolithic Period, as is seen by traces of habitation in the caves of Melidhóni and Sfendóni. And there are also remains to be found from the Minoan Period, among other places in the neighbourhood of Eléftherna and in the Idaean Cave and the cave of Melidhóni. But it is mainly from the Dark Ages and later that important traces can be found. The Idaean Cave by the Nídha plateau, identified by many ancient scholars as the birthplace of Zeus, was a prominent cultic center during this time. In front of the entrance a giant statue of Zeus is said to have stood, and votive offerings have also been discovered. The famous bronze shields that were found there date from the 8th and 7th centuries B.C. The cave continued to be used as a cultic site until Roman times.

On the upper reaches of one of the Mylopótamos' source rivers Axós came to flourish in the Archaic Period (the ruins have hardly been excavated, but the location is impressive). The city remained important until the First Byzantine Period, as can be seen from the remains of the mosaic floor of a 5th-6th century basilica in the church of Áyios Ioánnis. Astále, now the beach resort of Balí, was probably the harbour city of Axós.

Farther to the west was Eléftherna the region's most powerful city for 1600 years, from the 8th century B.C. The centrally located and almost invulnerable city probably dominated the entire region from the Potamídha to the Kouloúkonas. The acropolis, with its exquisite view, is located on a narrow promontory of the Ida, with two gorges on either side. The ruins of the city, including a bridge from the Hellenistic Period, are striking. The 8-meter-high tower at the entrance to the acropolis presumably dates from the late Roman age or from the early Middle Ages. The necropolis in the western gorge below is also interesting, for here the remains of various sorts of burial rituals from the 8th century B.C. have been found, including traces of funeral pyres and of ritual human sacrifice. The city still flourished during the First Byzantine Period and was the seat of a bishopric. The episcopal church presumably lay on the site of the Sótiros Khristós (10th century, with 12th century frescos; a double church together with the 16th century Catholic Áyios Ioánnis).

Pánormos was the nearest harbour city. During the First Byzantine Period Pánormos possessed an important basilica (5th/6th century), the remains of which can still be seen.

Here, as elsewhere in Crete, the time of Muslim rule forms a period of interruption, about which very little is known. During the Second Byzantine Period Eléftherna, Axós, Pánormos and Astále lost their influence. The region has a relatively large number of churches from this period. The bishopric of Eléftherna was now seated in Áno Viran-episkopí, where the Ayía Eiríni church is built on top of the 10th-11th century episcopal church. The nearby ruins of the Áyios Dhimítrios church, from the same period, also deserve a visit. Eléftherna did not lose all its importance, as can be seen by the 10th-century Sótiros Khristós, mentioned earlier. And at the present village of Axós the Stavroménos church was built in this period, partly with ancient building materials. Another Áyios Dhimítrios church, near Piyí, was also built during this period (it has some beautiful 14th century frescos). Kalamás has an 11th century church, the Áyios Yeóryios, also with frescos.

During the time of the Venetians this was an important region. As early as 1212, when the Genoans still possessed large sections of the island, the Venetians placed a Roman Catholic bishop in Episkopí (on the middle reaches of the Mylopótamos). Remains of a 14th century cruciform church can still be seen here. In the neighbourhood of the village the ruins of Venetian country houses still stand, and at Kastrí there are traces of the castle which once stood there. Margarítes, near Eléftherna, was one of the most important villages. Earthenware was made here, as it still is today. The lower basin of the Mylopótamos was ruled from the castle at Pánormos. The picturesque village of Maroulás in the west of the region retains many well-preserved architectural examples of the Venetian era.

And then there are the Orthodox churches and monasteries. At the acropolis of the ancient Axós lies the Áyios Ioánnis church mentioned earlier, with the remains of a 5th-6th century basilica and frescos from the 14th or 15th century. And in the present village lie the Ayía Eiríni from the 14th or 15th century and the ruins of the Áyios Mikhaíl Arkhángelos. Close to Axós are the monasteries of Khalépa and Dhiskoúri, both of which are now deserted. The magnificently situated monastery of Khalépa was a convent until the arrival of the Ottomans; right next to

Cave of Melidhóni

monastery stands the beautifully frescoed church of another convent which is long since gone, the Ayía Marína. On the northern side of the Kouloúkonas ridge lie the deserted monastery of Vósakos (romantically and splendidly located, a recommended walk from Dhoxaroú to Síses passes this monastery) and the beautifully situated monastery of Áyios Ioánnnis above Balí, at the beginning of a picturesque *kaldirimi* to Melidhóni (the monastery, probably dating from the first half of the 17th century, is no longer a functioning one, but restoration has begun). Farther to the west between Stavroménos and Khamalévri is the monastery of Arsáni, which like so many others flourished at the end of the 16th century. It was important because of its school and because of its role as a stopping place between Herákleion and Réthymnon. The monastery is still in use and can be visited. Farther to the south, on the ridge between the Amári valley and the coastal plain, is the monastery of Arkádhi which also had a school and was also a stopping place on an important route (see Chapter 6).

In the 13th and 14th centuries the region was regularly a center of uprisings, led by members of the prominent Kalléryis family. The most dangerous of these took place in the 1360's: part of the Catholic Venetian nobility in Crete declared themselves independent from the home city, and moreover Orthodox Cretan nobility led by the Kalléryis family in Mylopótamos wanted Crete to become part of the Byzantine Empire again. The uprisings were smothered in blood, and the area around Eléftherna was destroyed in retaliation, as was Lassíthi and the area around Anópolis in Sfakiá. After about 1370 there were no more uprisings.

As in the rest of Crete, the region suffered under the increasing Ottoman threat in the 16th century. As mentioned in the introductory notes to Chapter 2, the Ottomans plundered the coast in the summer of 1571, with the goal of capturing prisoners of war to use as galley slaves during the expected confrontation with the Catholic fleet.

Between 1645 and 1647 the Ottomans occupied all of Crete except for Herákleion, which was only taken in 1669. Agrion and Mylopótamos were also occupied, and the Ottomans began the exploitation of the farming population.

It is no surprise that after the revolution of 1821 this fertile and strategically located region was also cause for fighting. As mentioned earlier, in 1822 the Ottoman sultan had called on help from Mehmed Ali, his viceroy in Egypt. In May of 1822 the Egyptian fleet landed in the Bay of Soúdha, with a large military force under the leadership of Mehmed

Ali's brother-in-law Hassan Pasha. In the summer of that same year the *pasha* of Herákleion, Sherif Pasha, tried to defeat the rebels in Mylopótamos. He was not successful; instead, the rebel leaders (among them the Theódhoros mentioned in the text) organized a counterattack in Malevísi, the region east of the Ida.

In August 1822 Hassan Pasha began a long, bloody 'pacification tour' across the island, beginning along the north coast to Mylopótamos. At the end of August he arrived at the monastery of Khalépa near Axós, from where he gained control of the pass at Goniés to Malevísi. The monks in the monastery were slaughtered. From Malevísi he continued his 'pacification' during the following months (see also Part 2 of this series) until he took a fatal fall from his rearing horse in February of 1823. He was succeeded by Huseyn Bey, another brother-in-law of Mehmed Ali.

On his way to Khalépa Hassan Pasha had passed through the village of Melidhóni, where the villagers had sought refuge in the extensive cave above the village. Hassan Pasha left them undisturbed. His successor, however, did not leave the villagers in peace. During the course of 1823 he continued the bloody 'pacification' of the east and middle of the island, until the rebellion in eastern Crete was finally crushed in October of that year. Then, in November, he passed through Melidhóni on his way back. He was, by the way, accompanied by Mustafa Pasha, who would later be his successor as supreme commander and governor of the island. The 370 villagers, mostly women, children, and old people, took refuge in the cave again. But this time to no avail. Huseyn Bey's troops began a siege of the cave that ended in a horrible climax in January 1824: masses of combustible materials were brought to the entrance of the cave, thrown inside, and ignited. All the villagers in the cave died by suffocation. Huseyn Bey left for Sfakiá via the Apokórona and Askyfoú. There he continued his campagne of terror. In May Crete had been subdued, and the Albanian troops crossed over to the Peloponnesos to join in the war there.

Pococke visited this region in 1739, coming from Herákleion. His report, including his account of climbing the Ida, sounds remarkably laconic to modern travellers.

We set out from Candia on the twenty-fourth [of August], and travelling
to the west, went over the mount Strongyle [Stroúmbolas], and laid in a
kane at a village called Damartal [Dhamáste]. On the twenty-fifth we
came into a pleasant country full of small hills covered with oak, olives,
and the plane-tree, having vines twining round them. We travelled
twelve miles to a kane and fountain called Papatebrisy [directly north-
east of Garazo, called Papativrýsi by Pashley farther on], and going two
miles further we saw the high hill of Val Monastere to the right [the
Kouloúkonas], and at the end of six miles came to the village of Perameh,
on a river of the same name. Opposite to this place there is a port called
Astomia [Pánormos], where the Maltese came ashore this year, and carried away above twenty Turks from a village called Delabolou, which is
near a league from the sea. It is said that this descent was occasioned by a
servant of the aga of the village, who having been ill used by his master,
went to the Maltese at Gozo, shewed them the way, and, it is said, had the
revenge to assist in binding his master.

We went three miles out of the high road in a pleasant valley on the
south to a village called Magarites, which was given to the Cuperlis, with
many other villages about Candia, when their ancestor took that city
[that was Köprülüzade Fazil Ahmed Pasha, see Chapter 8]. We were here
directed to an untenanted house where two priests of the convent of
Arcadi came to us, and afterwards the steward of the pasha Cuperli, who
brought me a present of a nosegay and a water melon. And when I went
away he met me at his door, and served us with wine, melon and wallnuts,
and fired a gun at our departure, which were all marks of his civility, for
which I made him a proper acknowledgment. They have here a manufacture of a fine red earthen ware, something like that of the antients.

About a mile further we passed by a church of saint Antonio in a grotto. Travelling still in a pleasant narrow vale, I saw a tower at a distance
called Teleuterna, which I conjectured to be some remains of the old
Eleuterna. Four miles further we passed by the ruined convent of saint
Antony, belonging to the monastery of Arcadi. Soon after we came to a
small plain between the hills about four miles in circumference, in the
middle of which is the large convent of Arcadi, which was erected in the
time of the Venetian government. It is a handsome building, round a
large court; they have a good refectory, and a very fine church in the
middle of the court, with a beautiful front of Venetian architecture. The
convent has a large income, above a hundred caloyers [kalóyeros], and

about twenty priests. I was received here very civilly by the abbot, and conducted to the apartments allotted for strangers; and the abbot always came and took his repasts with me.

On the twenty-sixth I set out in the afternoon with three caloyers to go to mount Ida, which is about six miles to the east of the convent. The road is very bad between the hills, which are covered with ever-green oak. We came to a farm house belonging to the convent, where they killed a sheep for us; we went on further to a grotto, where we made a great fire and lay all night. On the twenty-seventh we went near three hours to the foot of the high mountain.

Mount Ida is now called by the natives Upsilorites [Psilorítis]; it is probable that Jupiter [Zeus] passed great part of his youth amongst these mountains in the manly exercises of hunting and drawing the bow, as he is said to have been educated here. This mountain extends to the north west almost to Retimo, being bounded to the south west by that valley which is to the north east of mount Kedrosè, on the side of which I saw at a distance the convent of Asomatos, and to the north east by those narrow valleys which divide it from mount Strongyle, and so extended to the south east, to the plain in which Gortynia stood. But what is properly mount Ida, is one very high mountain in the middle, or rather towards the south side of them. It is of a grey marble, and the surface being of loose stones, makes it very difficult to ascend. There is no verdure on it, except a few small shrubs or herbs. I was two hours and three quarters ascending to the highest summit, for it has another to the west somewhat lower. I conjectured that this mountain is not so high as mount Libanon, or the Alps. In some hollows, especially in two which I saw, there is snow all the year round, which is carried in summer to Retimo for the use of the pasha.

On the top of the mountain there is a low church built only of loose stones, dedicated to the Holy cross. It commands a glorious view of almost the whole island. And in a clear day, it is said they can see many of the isles of the Archipelago. I saw from it the small islands that are north of Settia [the Dionisádhes, to the north of Siteía]. A little way up the north side of the hill I went into a small rough grotto, which is the only one that I could hear of about this place. As barren a spot at this mountain is, I saw a flock of sheep on the highest summit of it, and I took particular notice of the shepherds laying the snow on stones exposed to the sun, and receiving the water in their bottles as it melted, and they drink it without finding any ill effects from it.

I returned to the convent; and on the twenty-eighth travelling northward, passed through the villages of Amnato, and went to the mouth of
the river Stavromene, on both sides of which there are ruins, and the
place is called Airio [Agrion, now Stavroménos]. We went a mile south-
wards to the rich convent of Arsani, which is subject only to the patriarch
of Constantinople. It is pleasantly situated, and the estate that belongs to
it produces some of the best wines and oil in all Candia. The abbot
pressed me to dine with them, and made a very grand entertainment.
And on drinking certain healths, they chanted some Greek verses. This
convent lying in the road is at a great expence in entertaining strangers.
And the Turks are not content with that, but take away with them whatever they want on the road.

We went eight miles to Retimo, passing over the river Platania [the
Potamídha], and through a beautiful village called Chamaleore [proba-
bly Perivólia]. At Retimo I was received in the house of the English vice
consul.

We return to Pashley, on February 21st, 1834. After visiting Réthymnon he left for Piyí.

Pashley, I, p. 115, 118 – 121

In the evening I rode to Peghé, a village where about 160 Greeks paid the
poll-tax before the revolution: the present number of inhabited houses
does not exceed forty. The Proestós, Spyrídhon Papadhákes, a very hospitable and even intelligent old man, received us most kindly: in a short
time his wife and servant produced an excellent supper, and his wine was
the best I had tasted in the island. On my praising it, and enquiring if it
was abundant, he replied, that he had not much of it, and therefore never
drank it except when a stranger came to see him. In what country of
Europe should we find either a peasant or a gentleman keeping his
choicest wine untouched that he might share it with the wandering
stranger?..

It being Friday none of the Greeks tasted the cheese, eggs or milk,
which, with some excellent caviáre and olives, formed our evening's
meal.

Spyrídhon recounts, to the great annoyance of Captain Maniás, tales of
some of the robberies and excesses committed by the Sfakians during the
revolution. When the arms of Khuseín-bey were so successful, in 1824,
that he was on the point of effecting the general pacification of the island,

Spyrídhon retired, as did many other Christians, to the inaccessible fast-nesses of Haghía Ruméli and Samaría [inaccessible gorge in Sfakiá, at the southern slope of the Lefká Óri] for safety. While he was there, the submission of every district took place, and on this he determined, like every body else, to return to his home. Being unwell, and having his wife with him, he thought it worth while to purchase a mule for the journey. Thus the Sfakians saw that he had money. On his arrival at Lutró [one of the harbours of the Sfakians, on the southern slope of the Lefká Óri] they seized him, and, after tying his hands behind him, held a pistol at each temple, and five or six at his breast. They thus forced him to disclose where his money was, and obtained from him about 1200 piastres, taking also his mule and some of his clothes. Maniás in vain attempted to edge in a word in favour of his fellow Sfakians. All that can be said in their defence is, that they spent their plunder in the struggle, and, like the Hydhraeans, are poorer, to a man, at the present day, than they were at the outbreaking of the revolution. Old Spyrídhon compares the events of the war to a torrent which carries every thing before it; and says that, in consequence of the excesses committed by the Sfakians, he determined, when the last insurrection under Khadjí Mikháli took place [see Chapter 4], to go into the fortified city, and that many other Christians did the same thing, not only in the neighbourhood of Rhíthymnos, but also near Megálo-Kástron and Khaniá.

When Khadjí-Mikháli was at Fránko-Kástello, my host went to see him on the Monday. The Khadjí fell on the Wednesday of the same week [May 17th, 1828]. Spyrídhon attempted to undeceive him with respect to the amount of the Mohammedan force from the Kástron, (already with the Pashá,) which the Rumeliot Chieftain believed to be a body of only a few hundred men: the endeavour to convince him of their real amount was vain: he was bent on fighting, and seemed even to anticipate victory.

After the death of Khadjí-Mikháli the Turks of Rhíthymnos used to make frequent nocturnal expeditions into villages, sometimes at a considerable distance from the city; and, falling on the people by surprise, often succeeded in massacring the men who made any resistance, and in enslaving women and children. Besides a woman-servant, there is in my host's house another female, who seems to be as much his wife's friend as her attendant, and a little child, both of whom were procured by him under the following circumstances.

About twenty days after the Christmas following the death of Khadjí-Mikháli, a numerous party of armed Turks left the town of Rhíthymnos some time before midnight on a Saturday evening. Now at all periods of the war the Greeks were constant in the performance of their religious exercises: they went to church armed; and, if they were to be suddenly attacked, where could they hope better to defend themselves, against the unbaptized Mohammedans, than at God's altar? At the village of Labiní, in the eparkhía of Hághio Vasíli, there was assembled in the church, on the morning after this party left Rhíthymnos, a small congregation of eight Christians, six of whom had also their wives with them. This village is eighteen miles from Rhíthymnos, and the Mohammedans knew well that they should find the Christians assembled at their prayers in its church about day break on the morning of the Lord's day.

Immediately on their arrival they attacked their destined victims, and attempted to force their way into the church: two or three of them paid the price of their temerity, but the others kept up, for about three hours, through the windows and openings of the building, an inefficient fire on the Christians within. At length they adopted a more certain mode of warfare, and heaping up, near the entrance, dry wood and other combustibles, on which oil was poured, they applied a torch to the materials thus collected. The door was soon consumed, and the Christians had no means of escaping from the flames. Resistance and flight being both equally impossible, and their condition in the church becoming insupportable, the men at length surrendered, and were all massacred. One of the women had fainted, half suffocated by the smoke, and doubtless suffering still more from her apprehension of the destiny which awaited both her husband and herself. On recovering from her swoon, she found herself tightly corded on the back of a mule, and already advanced about half way towards Rhíthymnos: her hair, her skull-cap, and her clothes were all stiff with the gore of her murdered husband. The savage who had made her his slave did not succeed in selling her for fifteen days, during all which time she continued to wear the clothes which had been thus soaked and dyed in her husband's blood. She was redeemed by my host, who was then living at Rhíthymnos: and he also purchased the little child from its Turkish owner. The child, if I rightly remember, is the woman's daughter, and the price it cost him was eighty Turkish piastres.

The following day, February 22nd, Pashley travelled on.

Pashley, I, p. 121, 122, 124 – 131, 134 – 137, 140
Our host gives us an excellent breakfast, and, after it, coffee: on my taking

leave of him, he replies to my professions of inability adequately to thank him for his kindness, by saying, 'I will tell you how to thank me: visit my house again when you next come this way.'

An hour after leaving Peghé, we pass through the village of Baga-lokhóri [Pangalokhóri]; and soon after, see on our right the ruins of Khamalévri, another village which, like Bagalokhóri, now contains a population of only ten Christian and five Mohammedan families. A mile farther on is the monastery of Arsáni, which is small and poor. Pococke speaks of this as 'the rich convent of Arsani,' and praises the quality of the wines and oil produced on its estates. It now possesses only about 1800 olive-trees, and owes a debt of 15,000 piastres, for which it pays fifteen per cent. The present coenobites are an Hegúmenos, a patéras, a kalógheros, and a dhiákos. Their possessions were still considerable, a little while before the revolution, but they were obliged to sell the greater part of them to pay off their debts. The church is dedicated to Hághios Gheórghios, and the monastery contains an elementary school, which is conducted on the old system (and not on the plan of mutual instruction,) and is frequented by only a few children...

This morning we see the mouth of a cavern, but the water is too high to allow of entering it. Maniás assures me that a man can walk for *two hours* in it. I should have been glad to see how many hundred feet long it is: the exaggeration of the Greeks on all such topics is very great. About six miles from Arsáni we reach the top of a ridge from which we see spread out before us, to the east, the fertile plain of Mylopótamo. It is almost covered with olive-trees, which half conceal from view the vil-lages scattered over it: five or six however are just visible; and others can be partially discerned peeping from behind the trees. A numerous drove of mules and asses, laden with oil for Rhíthymnos, here passes us. The summit of the conical mountain of Melidhóni, right before us beyond the plain, is covered with snow; a phenomenon which is always regarded by the peasants as an unerring indication that the approaching season will be very productive.

After passing the ruined village of Pérama, we repose for an hour, dur-ing the heat, which is considerable to-day, under the shade of a carob-tree, near a broken bridge, over which people used to cross the river. Per-haps there may be some difficulty in fording this stream immediately after heavy rain, since it flows from the northern ridges of Mount Ida, and must, doubtless, on such an occasion, be greatly swollen. Still the nature of its bed here probably gave the name 'Pérama' or Ford to the spot, long before the wretched modern village was built...

On moving from our resting place, we turned immediately to the left of the regular road between Rhíthymnos and Megálo-Kástron, and, after a short but steep ascent, came on an uncultivated and barren tract, which ends, in about half an hour, in the olive-trees by which the village of Melidhóni is surrounded. I took up my quarters at the house of the Proestós, who was absent, but was immediately sent for and soon arrived. My first enquiry was for the cavern, in the neighbourhood of the village, at the entrance to which an inscription, published by Gruter and Muratori, and in which the Tallaean Hermes is mentioned, ought to be seen. The difficulties encountered by Tournefort, in his endeavour to see the process of collecting *ladanum*, and to visit the inscription in question, of which he heard when at Melidhóni, if compared with the facilities afforded me for every investigation, show how different is the state of the country, under the simple despotism of Mehmét-Alí, from that in which the French naturalist found it.

Half an hour's ascent from the village brought me to the entrance of the cavern; but before I attempt to describe the beautiful stalactites, which make it a worthy rival even of the grotto of Antíparos, I will briefly relate its modern history, as I learnt it during my stay in the village of Melidhóni; and doubt not that it will excite my reader's interest and sympathy.

Near the end of August 1822, Khassán-pashá, the uncle of Mustafá-pashá, the present Seraskier of Crete, passed with his troops through Melidhóni, when on his way from Khaniá to Megálo-Kástron. The unarmed Christians fled before him every where as he approached, and this cavern offered what seemed a secure place of refuge, most of all to such as, from the weakness of age or sex, were unable to retire to the lofty mountains, and there to remain till the storm should have passed over their homes. On this account many of the inhabitants of Melidhóni, especially women and children, as well as people from neighbouring villages, took refuge in the cave, and remained there several days. They found in it plenty of water, and, since a few tuféks sufficed to guard its entrance against any number of troops, they had but little fear of being attacked. The Pashá passed without molesting them, and at length they emerged from their lurking place, and returned in safety to their villages.

Soon after the death of Khassán-pashá, Khuseín-bey, and Mustafá-bey the present Pashá, came to Melidhóni with their troops. The people fled before them, as they had done before Khassán-pashá, on the previous occasion, and now took with them all their cattle, and as much of their transportable property as they could remove, knowing full well that they should inevitably lose all that they might leave behind them. They felt no fear whatever, for they were returning to an impregnable fortress, and had provisions enough to enable them to stand a siege of half a year. The number of those who retired to the grotto on this occasion was upwards of 300 souls.

According to an ancient tradition the caverns of Crete were used in a similar manner in very early times, and Cresphygeton, the Cretan's refuge, became the general name of grottos thus supposed to be places of security from danger.

Khuseín-bey in vain summoned the Christian fugitives to come out of their lurking-place: his messenger was fired on, and fell. He then attempted to force the entrance of the cave: and, in doing so, lost twenty-four of his brave Arnauts, who were killed by shots from the Christians within. On this the Bey sent a Greek woman into the cavern, with a message, that 'if they would all come forth and give up their arms, they should not meet with any ill-treatment.' The woman was shot, and her body cast out from the mouth of the grotto. When the Mohammedan general saw this, he himself took up a stone, and threw it into the cavern's entrance. His troops imitated the example he set them, and thus the only aperture through which light and air could pass to the Christians was entirely filled up. The following morning the Mohammedans saw that a small opening had been produced in their work, during the night. They again filled it up, and their labour was again undone by the Christians the following night. This attempt of the Turks to close the entrance of the cave was repeated twice more. At length they saw that the Christians could still breath and live: they therefore collected wood, oil, chaff, spirit, sulphur, refuse olives, and all other combustibles on which they could lay their hands: they filled up the mouth of the cavern with these materials, instead of the stones and earth which they had before used; and had no sooner completed their work, than they set it on fire. Volumes of smoke immediately rolled along under the spacious vault of the entrance cavern, in which many of the ill-starred Christians were assembled: the dense vapour filled the whole apartment so rapidly that many had no time to escape through devious passages to the inner recesses of the cave. The husband and wife, the parent and child, could only take one last embrace and die. The smoke now forced its way from the entrance apartment into that of which a sketch is given. Here many more fell, but the greater number had still time to escape, through narrow passages, in some of which they must have crept on their hands and knees, into little side chambers, and to the more distant recesses of the cavern. Doubtless, they hoped thus to escape the fate which had overtaken their less active companions. Alas! the passages through which they rushed, suffered the destroying vapour to follow them; and thus, at last, the groups of fugitives who had taken refuge in the inmost depths of the cave, died as their companions had done; and, in a few minutes after their funeral pile was first lighted, all these unhappy Christians had perished. By submission they might, undoubtedly, have avoided this fate, but they were all convinced, that if they once surrendered to their angry and ferocious foes, the men among them would be massacred, and the women and children reduced to slavery; so that one wonders not that they should have refused to listen to the offers which were made them.

The Turks, and the Cretan Mohammedans, distrustful of the effect of their diabolical contrivance, waited patiently outside the cavern for eighteen days. They had with them a Greek prisoner: I might call him a slave, for all those who were made prisoners were considered as such, and used commonly to be sold in the markets of the chief cities. They offered this Christian slave his life, as the reward of his consenting to go down into the cavern to see what his correligionaries were about. He gladly accepted their proposal, and, after venturing, with much fear and anxiety, into the grotto, found in it only the silence of the grave, and soon returned, saying that 'they were all dead'. The Mohammedans, still distrustful of the effect produced by their fire, and fearful of being entrapped if they entered the cavern, sent the man back again, telling him to bring up some arms as a proof of the truth of his account. He did so, and three days afterwards the Mohammedans themselves ventured into the cavern, and stripped the victims of their ferocity of every thing of value which was on their persons, at the same time appropriating to themselves all the stores and other property which they found.

Soon after this, and while the head quarters of the Beys were still at Melidhóni, six Christians, who had all off them both relations and friends within the cavern, impelled by a natural desire to ascertain the truth of the report of their death, went up to see with their own eyes what had happened. Three of them remained outside, to give notice if any Mohammedans should approach, and the other three entered. One of them was called Manúlios Kermezákes: the other two were Melidhónians, whose wives and children had taken refuge in the cavern. Who could describe the anguish of these unhappy men, when they saw lying dead on the ground, and despoiled even of their clothes, those whose safety they had vainly imagined to have been secured when they were once within the grotto? The simple narration of the effect produced on them by this visit, will best declare how heart-rending their grief must have been. One of them never again raised up his head, but pined and wasted, and died only *nine days* after the fatal confirmation, by the evidence of his senses, of his worst fears. The other lived twenty days, and then he too died.

Manúlios, their companion, is still living, and tells me, being at the same time surrounded by a numerous group of his fellow-villagers, of this their visit. Every one confirms his account in all its details, except that one or two of the men maintain that the second death took place eighteen and not twenty days after the visit. I am fully satisfied that I have learnt the simple unadorned truth with respect to all these dreadful events.

When the Greeks were again masters of the village of Melidhóni, and of the district of Mylopótamo, they considered whether they should cause all the dead bodies in the cave to be interred in the usual way; and they thought that no nobler sepulchre could be built for them than that of which they had obtained possession. On this account they only caused the burial service to be read over them where they lay...

From the time when the triple hecatomb of human victims was thus consumed by the flames, in the grotto of Melidhóni, till the hour of my arrival at the village, no one of the people around me has ever ventured to enter the place where their nearest relatives perished. Many of them have wished to do so, but they have been deterred by superstitious fears, which, even without the occurrence of so terrible a calamity, would have been felt to check intrusion, within the sacred cave, by their heathen ancestors...

Twelve or fourteen of the villagers were glad to have an opportunity of gratifying their curiosity, by a view of the cavern, in the safety which they supposed to be guaranteed by my presence. Manúlios was one of them.

The mound of stones and earth heaped up by the Mohammedans at the entrance of the cave, which is near the summit of the mountain, almost entirely conceal from view the ancient inscription, of which I have spoken. The face of the hill is nearly perpendicular, and is not very high above the mouth of the cavern: thus it allowed the Mohammedans to throw down earth and stones from its summit, without being themselves exposed to the shots of the Christians, whose destruction they were endeavouring to accomplish.

On passing the entrance, we find ourselves in a spacious cavern, running east and west and almost as wide as it is long: the ground descends nearly all the way to its eastern end: its vault and sides are so fretted with noble stalactites that they may be said to consist of them; and stalagmites, some of which are of a great size, are seen scattered on different parts of the ground. About the middle of this great entrance chamber, and on its south side, is the mouth of a low and wide passage leading to a room about twenty feet long, twelve feet wide, and from ten to twenty feet high, also full of stalactites. The passage is about thirty feet long, and its stalactites, in some places, come down to the ground: at the entrance is a group of skulls: in the first cavern also are two heaps of skulls and human bones. On the opposite side of this first or entrance cavern is a great passage about twenty feet wide, and, as well as I can judge, somewhat more than sixty feet high. At a little distance from its extremity is a great group of stalactites which so fills it up, as to leave only a pass, six feet in width, unoccupied. Beyond this spot the passage becomes about thirty feet wide and eighty feet high. Among the many beautiful and sometimes fantastic forms, in which the stalactites are seen to hang, I notice here, to the left, what might be almost taken for a gothic church-window, and, a little below it, the entrance of a cavern. Our progress in this passage is suddenly arrested by a perpendicular descent of about eighteen feet: the cave has every appearance of extending to some distance in this direction, but not having a ladder we cannot explore its recesses. The stalactites a little before us in this part, to which we can approach no nearer, hang down in a great cluster as much as thirty feet below the level on which we are standing. Returning hence to the entrance cavern, we turn, at its north or rather north-eastern extremity, along another passage: after continuing for about ten feet, it enlarges into a kind of room twenty-seven feet long, at the further end of which we again enter a narrow pass the length of which is thirteen feet. On emerging from this passage, which we do with considerable difficulty, by clambering round the rock, and letting ourselves down, as well as we can, into another apartment, we find before us a view the grandeur and beauty of which surpasses all that we have heretofore seen. On looking back at the hole in the rock, through which we have just emerged, and where one of my attendants is standing with a lighted taper, the effect is very striking. The apartment in which we have now arrived is about 150 feet long, and varies greatly in width: its height is pretty nearly uniform, and is considerable. Between twenty and thirty feet from the mouth of the pass by which we entered, is a great stalagmite, which rises up and forms a column reaching to the top of the cave, while the stalactites on each side hang in the most beautiful order: near the great central mass the bones and skulls of the poor Christians are so thickly scattered, that it is almost impossible to avoid crushing them as we pick our steps along. On the south-western side of this apartment a complete range of stalactites separates it from a good sized passage; after walking along which we enter a much smaller one, only eight feet long, which leads into a very little room, where we find water and many earthen-ware vessels. They were already firmly and almost inseparably attached to the ground by means of the deposit left by the constant dripping of the water. In the course of a century it would wholly have imbedded them in stalagmites. My Greek companions, with great difficulty, succeeded in rescuing these utensils from the grave which was beginning to swallow them up. Going on from this chamber, we traverse a passage so low and narrow that we are obliged to crawl on our hands and knees, and descend into a small room, the ground in which is literally covered with bones and skulls: in its centre is a columnar stalagmite, which reaches from the ground to the rocks about eighteen feet above our heads. There are also some other considerable stalagmites in the room. A narrow passage leads, by a steep descent, from this chamber to another nearly under it, also small; and on entering which about a dozen skulls, and a proportionate number of bones, are seen spread over the ground. This then was the furthest point to which the unhappy refugees could flee, and here the last of them perished.

The want of a sufficient number of lights, on our first visit, prevented my examining the cavern as I wished: I therefore returned to it on the Sunday morning, having first obtained, from the Papás of Melidhóni, a supply of wax candles, of his own manufacture. The above account is the result of both my visits....

The Proestós of Melidhóni, Konstantínos Konstantidhákes, my host, had two sisters, one sister-in-law, and twelve other relations in the cave: his wife lost a sister with all her children, and two uncles. The other surviving villagers lost their relations in a similar way. Melidhóni, before the Greek revolution, contained 140 Christian and ten Mohammedan families; about four times its present population.

My host had an orphan niece, Iréne, living with him: his daughter, a

lively little girl about three years old, is called Kalliópe. Of these two
female names one is derived from a Christian saint, and the other from a
heathen goddess.

After his visit to Melidhóni Pashley travelled on to the east on February 24th.

Pashley, I, p. 143 – 145

The fine groves of olives, through which I pass for half an hour after leaving Melidhóni, are many of them entirely uncultivated. Soon after
reaching the regular road, which, when on my way to Melidhóni, I left
immediately after crossing the river at Pérama, I pass the village of
Dhafnídhes: it is a quarter of a mile to the right. The valley in which we
now find ourselves is well filled with olive-trees; the river winds through
it, and its scenery is picturesque. Mount Ida is on our right, and the hill
of Melidhóni is still before us. Beyond Dhafnídhes we see the smoke
ascending from the little village of Kefáli, which is entirely concealed
from view by the trees. The road winds along the valley, sometimes on
the banks of the river, sometimes actually in its bed, for near three miles
before we arrive at the Khan Papativrýsi, now a ruin. Rain had begun to
fall in torrents before we reached this place, and, on finding that it afforded no shelter, we ascended on the south side of the valley up to the village of Gharázo. In its neighbourhood there is no such place as 'Lasos,'
which, on looking at Lapie's map, any one would expect to find somewhere near it.

We lodge in the house of a monk who is the resident at this metókhi of
the monastery Vósako, near the village of Sises, at the foot of mount
Kutzutrúli, and where there are fifteen monks. They had twelve pairs of
oxen before the revolution, but now have only four. Before the revolution
the monastery possessed a library, which was destroyed when the church
and other buildings of the society were burnt. This monk, with whom we
lodge, has a female housekeeper whose daughter is ten or twelve years
old: his secular name was Michael, but on becoming anagnóstes, the first
step taken towards the priesthood, he changed it to Melétios. The name
is always thus changed on that occasion.

This village of Gharázo, the metókhis of Omála, Músa and Nesí, being
reckoned with it, is said to have about 12,000 olive-trees, of which
between two and three thousand are uncultivated

One Agá, Khanialúki-Zikní-bey, still receives the seventh of all the produce, as used to be the case [i.e. before Crete was governed by Mehmed Ali], the Pashá only taking the kharátj [the poll tax which Christians and Jews were required to pay] and four parás per oke on the wine [thus excise tax].

Gharázo is celebrated for the beauty of its female inhabitants, and a common proverb asserts, in very plain and unequivocal terms, that

Gharázo's dames are facile as they're fair.

We had rain here, with scarcely any intermission, during the whole day: the old priest produced eggs, fried in oil, olives, cheese, oranges and wine for breakfast: and, a little before sun-set, we were indebted to the zeal of the grammatikós of the village, in my service, for an excellent repast. In consequence of his active exertions, we sat down to a dinner of soup, fowl, stewed mutton, and other dishes, all which was accompanied by most excellent wine, so far superior to that of all parts of the continent of Greece, that we could wish for no better: thus we soon became heedless of the hostile elements, which, on so rainy and windy a day, would otherwise have caused us no slight discomfort in this monk's poor hut, through which the wind whistled and the rain penetrated in half a dozen places. Having listened to some songs of my Sfakian Captain Maniás, we rolled ourselves up in our clokes, and slept through the greater part of the night.

They also stayed the following day, February 25th, in Garázo.

Pashley, I, p. 145, 146

I was again detained in the monk's cottage, throughout the whole of this day, by the incessant rain, which kept dripping heavily through several places in the roof. The discomforts of the lodging continued to be greatly alleviated by the zeal which the priest and the grammatikós of the village manifested to supply our wants; and by the welcome information that there is a village called Áxos, where are many ancient remains, only about four miles off. I learnt, too, that the river which flows near this site, the same that we crossed several times on our way hither, always becomes a torrent, and continues impassable for some time after rain…

Remembering the assertion of Stephanus of Byzantium, that Axos was not far from Eleutherna, I made enquiries after the later city, and learnt, to my great delight, that a village called Elevtherna, is situated somewhat higher up on the ridges of mount Ida, Psylorítes, about twelve miles from áxos, and very near the great convent of Arkádhi, which possesses a metókhi on the site. I was told that Elevtherna will, however, perhaps, be inaccessible, on account of the snow, at this time of the year: at any rate both the sites are clearly determined to be at places which still bear the names of the ancient cities

Among the songs, which my ever-talking and most amusing guide, Captain Maniás, repeated to-day, were one or two which a Boccaccio would have delighted to hear. The immoral consequences of that celibacy, which is enforced on the monks of the Oriental church, have even become the theme of popular songs. Of such effusions of the modern Grecian muse, every Englishman, writing in the nineteenth century, must feel it difficult to publish specimens: and I cannot venture to transcribe those which I heard.

Pashley did not go searching for Eléftherna from Garázo, perhaps because he was frightened off by the description of the snow. On February 26th he finally left for Axós.

Pashley, I, p. 146

At length the weather permitted me to leave Gharázo: the grammatikós of which village accompanied me as a guide. After a gentle ascent of about half an hour, during which I saw, on either side of the road, vineyards belonging to the village which I had just left, the country began to present a more and more barren appearance as we approached áxos. In the rocks, on our right, a few minutes before entering the village, I found five excavations, each of which would seem to have been a tomb. There are some peculiarities about them: they are arched at the top, and are covered over with plaster in the inside. Not one of them is hewn out of the solid rock, as the greater part of tombs, found by modern travellers in countries formerly occupied by the Greeks, usually are. One of them penetrates much further into the side of the hill than the others. The river of áxos flows past the village, through a valley on its north-eastern side, and will be crossed by me when I pursue my journey towards Megálo-Kástron.

After a long, scholarly argument about the identification and name of the city, Pashley describes the ruins.

Soon after my arrival at Áxos, I met with a man who became my guide to the so-called Hellenic walls, situated, as I soon found, about half a mile to the south-east of the present village, and consisting of remains of an aqueduct running across the summit of the little valley, between the hill on the acclivity of which the modern village stands and a loftier hill to the S.S.W. The space between the two hills is about seventy or eighty paces wide. Two pieces of the aqueduct are still standing, one of them about sixteen paces long and thirty feet high, the other a short piece of the same height. The stones of these remains are small, and a great deal of mortar is used: in the smaller fragment is a void, from which my guide assured me that a Frank had removed 'a piece of marble' some years ago. But without placing faith in this account, and inferring that the aqueduct was built after the Venetian conquest, when any monument of ancient art was used, as may be seen in the walls of many fortresses, merely as building materials, it is evident that the work in question was not coeval with the ancient republic of Axos, and cannot be assigned to a more ancient period than the lower Greek empire.

Positive assurances of the existence of an inscription on the loftier hill caused me to mount nearly to its summit, treading on snow during part of the ascent, a fact which gives an idea of our elevation above the level of the sea. The so-called inscription turned out to be a few unmeaning scratches on a stone: a result for which it is necessary always to be prepared, when one's poor guides can scarcely any of them read.

It seemed clear to me that ancient remains were most likely to be found on the hill along the side of which we had wound on leaving Axos, and for the use of the houses on which the ruined aqueduct had plainly been constructed: I therefore ascended its north side, and, in the cultivated fields around it, found the commonest and most certain indication of an ancient site, innumerable fragments of old pottery. The pleasure and hope caused by this discovery were, however, soon damped by my finding remains of the walls of a middle-age fortress running round what undoubtedly was the old acropolis. This was most probably one of the many Genoese forts built early in the thirteenth century. After the establishment of peace in the island, about 140 years later, it fell into neglect, like most of the others, so that in the sixteenth and seventeenth centuries the population of áxos hardly exceeded its present amount. Of course the construction of the fortress must necessarily have destroyed the greater part of the ancient walls of the acropolis, even if they had escaped the ravages of so many previous centuries. I searched, however, diligently throughout their circuit, in the hope of finding something belonging to a better age, and I was successful; for I discovered on the north side of the acropolis, fragments of polygonal masonry, the masses of which are carefully fitted together without cement. They belong to the earliest style of the so-called cyclopean or pelasgic walls. Within these outer walls I also found some remains of what I suppose to have been a fortress within the acropolis.

At some little distance from this ancient acropolis, on the side of the hill, just above the modern village, is the dilapidated church of Hághios Ioánnes: its sides and roof are entirely covered with rude fresco paintings, and a considerable part of its floor consists of remains of mosaic work, of no great excellence, but still of considerable antiquity, and which I should suppose to have belonged originally to the building, the place of which was afterwards occupied by the Christian church. On returning to the village I found in the wall of the church Toú Stavroménou, a beautiful piece of white marble, on which is a sepulchral inscription in the ancient Doric Greek of the island. All its letters are as clear as when they were first cut.

> Insult not this my tomb, O passer by,
>> Lest thou incur Agesilas's wrath,
> And stern Phersephone's: but, passing nigh,
>> Say, to Arate, 'on thee lie light the earth!'

The name Agesilas is here bestowed on Pluto, to whom it is also given by Aeschylus, and other authors…

This virgin daughter of Demeter, Persephone, was usually called Coré: and it is from her name, rather than from that of any other goddess, that one would wish to derive the Cretan Corion, were it not for the former existence of a temple, dedicated to the virgin Goddess Athene, at the place.

In the Orphic poems, and other repertories of those later legends, which delighted in fixing on Crete as the scene of many amours of both gods and goddesses, we find frequent mention of Persephone.

According to the poet Bacchylides, she was carried off by Pluto, not from the shores of Sicily, but from those of Crete. One origin of the name of the Corybantes was derived from the guard which they were said to have kept over Persephone, in order to defend her against the incestuous designs of Zeus. The love which that peculiarly Cretan god had once felt for Demeter, or Rhea, was now transferred to her daughter. The sacred form of serpents was assumed by both the maiden and her suitor, and, in due time, Persephone became the mother of the celebrated Zagreus; who, while yet a child, was placed in the throne of Heaven, and received, with the sceptre and thunderbolts of his father, power over both gods and men. The Curetes were charged to watch over the infant deity, but failed to guard him from the treacherous Titans, by whom he was torn limb from limb.

After his investigation of the ruins Pashley immediately left for Goniés, at the pass to Malevísi.

Pashley, I, p. 157 – 160

On leaving the village we began immediately to descend towards the river, which we crossed to the south-south-east of the acropolis, and soon after commenced our ascent. After passing the river we halted to look back on the district about Axos, which is certainly very barren and rocky. The situation of the city answers well to one of the etymologies of its name given in Stephanus of Byzantium: it was called Axos because the place is precipitous, Axos being used by the Cretans in the same sense as *agmos*, a break, was by the other Greeks.

The vicinity of the village is covered here and there by a few stunted olives, and some patches of tilled land: but the dreary barrenness of its immediate neighbourhood must always have been much the same as it is. I should imagine the district belonging to the ancient city to have extended down past Gharázo, and to have adjoined on the territory of Panormos somewhere in the fertile plain of Mylopótamos. Panormos is a city the remains of which are still seen not far from the shore, on a low hill near the ruins of Castle Mylopótamo, and they still retain their ancient name. The situation of this city might have been supposed to be in this neighbourhood, from the passages of Ptolemy and Pliny in which it is mentioned. The former of those authors places it at some distance to the west of Heracleion, and in the latter's list it is found to the east of Rhithymna...

After halting a little while, to take a distant sketch of áxos and its neighbourhood, we go on ascending, on the north side of a valley bounded by lofty mountains, for nearly two miles, and then turn to our left and cross the ridge. A descent of about twenty minutes brings us to a river: we follow its southern bank nearly a mile, and then cross it and again begin to ascend. As sunset approaches, and we mount higher and higher above the level of the sea, we find the cold become very piercing. We soon see snow scattered in patches over all the mountains about us: at length we reach the lofty level at which the village where we mean to rest for the night is situated. For about a mile our path traverses vine-yards, all of which are partially covered with snow. Just before sunset we arrived, almost frozen, at the village of Goniés, and were soon provided with an extremely wretched lodging in the hut of the Proestós.

Goniés is the first place which I have seen in Crete, that can almost be said to possess no olive-trees: there are only about 150 roots of them in its whole district. As in a village which has no vineyards, we hardly ever obtain wine, so there was actually no oil to be found in this miserable hamlet.

Snow was lying in patches on the ground at Goniés, and some women were greatly surprised at seeing us come 'to the snow', as they called it. Aware that snow is almost unknown near the coasts and in the plains of Crete, the only distant regions with which they have any acquaintance, they were quite astonished to learn that I was familiar with it in my native land, and that I had often seen it there, even without going up 'into the mountains'.

The extreme cold, which penetrated through the hut of the Proestós, could only be kept off by a wood-fire; the smoke of which almost stifled and blinded us, since the cottage was built, in the common fashion, without a chimney. The whole night was spent most uncomfortably, and I was glad to rise, with the very dawn, in order to proceed to Megálo-Kástron.

From Goniés Pashley travelled on to Týlissos and Herákleion on February 27th (the region between these two is described in Part 2 of this series).

Pashley, I, p. 161, 162, 164 – 169

After I left Goniés, the country afforded but few signs of productiveness for miles, except some scattered olive and carob trees in the immediate neighbourhood of the village. After a descent of about half an hour, we began to follow the river, and continued our course, near its bank, for two miles: we then commenced the ascent of a range of rocky mountains, and, from their summit, obtained a view of the plain of Megálo-Kástron, the chief city of the island; the solid walls and lofty minarets of which we at the same time discerned. A somewhat tedious descent brought us to the village of Týlisso, where although I heard of neither coins nor other antiquities, yet I felt little or no doubt that I was standing on the site of the ancient Tylissos.

Unfortunately the passage of Pliny, in which Tylissos is mentioned, proves nothing whatever as to its position; but the supposition that it was here, is confirmed by an examination of its ancient coins. On their reverse is represented a youth holding, in his right hand, the head of an ibex, or wild-goat, as the animal was called by the ancients, and in his left a bow. Now this village is at the foot of a lofty range of mountains, and wild-goats are still found in its neighbourhood...

Týlissos is now reduced to about twenty-five houses, a fourth of its size before the outbreaking of the Greek revolution, and is surrounded by carob-trees and olives, as well as by some vineyards. The rock about it is nearly as full of imbedded shells as that of Malta, or of the south-east of Italy. The day is delightful, and we can hardly believe ourselves within a dozen miles of the cold and snow of yesterday.

After leaving Týlissos we passed a ruined khan, which used formerly to afford good accommodation, and soon arrived at a copious and rather picturesque fountain: here I halted, and listened to a Cretan song, and to some of the innumerable stories, respecting the events of the war, which it seems that Maniás knows for every part of the island. The minuteness of his details, and their invariable agreement with all that I learn from other quarters, prove him to have been an observant actor in the scenes which he describes.

The song which exercised the vocal powers of the Sfakian Captain, while my artist was making a sketch of the fountain of Selvilí, celebrates the heroism and ill-fortunes of the Chieftain Theódhoros, who, during the early part of the Christian revolt in Crete, was arkhegós of the two districts of Mylopótamo and Malevísi. His troops were stationed at Sárko [Sárkhos] and Hághio Mýro: he had with him but few of his fellow Sfakians, having dispatched his brother Russákes, with a detachment, to aid the Greeks of Lassíthi, before he came down towards the plain of Megálo-Kástron. On descending to this mountain of Selvilí, and to the village of Gázi, he fell in with the Mohammedan forces, which were greatly superior in number to his own. The engagement lasted from three hours after sunrise till two hours before sunset. The Christian leader wore a very rich dress, and had most splendid arms: thus he was recognized, and, at length, perished in a furious charge made by the

Arnaut cavalry. The Cretan song, which Maniás sings, commences with
an account of the splendour and value of Theódoros's arms, and of the
beauty of his person, and then proceeds:

To him our Commandante did
   A written order give,
That he permit no Musulman
   In Grecia's world to live:

His mother too had bidden him
   A warrior's part to play,
Nor let a single Arnaut steed
   Escape from out the fray.

   * * *

To Selvilí he did descend
   And there his tents deployed;
And, further onward, Gázi's sports
   His warriors all enjoyed.

   * * *

The warlike Champion of the Cross
   Full many a Moslem slew:
But still the Moslem host was strong,
   While he quite wearied grew.

   * * *

'Our men of Mylopótamo,
   Though dense as groves they be,
When they're resisted all the day
   With evening's sun will flee.

Alas, ill-fated Anoians,
   And ye brave Khrusaniótes,
Who all contend with Moslem foes,
E'en like the Lakiótes!'

'Alas! alas! my brother dear,
  Why sent I thee away?
Thy force, if here, had well secured
  A safe retreat from th'fray.

Alas! alas! my brother dear,
  I would that thou could'st learn
The fatal news of this day's fight,
  My death that thou must mourn!

                    * * *

Salute from me the Sfakians,
  And each brave pallikár,
And tell them how I've vanquish'd been
  In this our Arnaut war.'

As soon as a sketch of the fountain was made, and Maniás' song and stories were ended, we recommenced our journey, and, after finishing what
little there remained of descent, arrived at the bridge of Gázi, the stream
under which is considerable: we passed it, and afterwards, three of four
other bridges, over streams which all discharge themselves into the sea a
little below the places where we crossed them. In rather more than an
hour from the time of our leaving the fountain, we reached the gate of
Megálo-Kástron, and the usual external adjunct of a large Mohammedan town, an extensive burial ground. On entering within the walls of
the city, I saw that I was once more in Turkey: and, the bazárs, though
filled with fewer costly articles of eastern luxury, are still so exclusively
Turkish in their character as to recall to mind those of Smyrna and Constantinople.

Before we continue on with Pashley in Herákleion, we direct our
attention again to Spratt in 1853. We follow him west again, from
Herákleion to Eléftherna.

Spratt, II, p. 64–74

After starting at an early hour from Candia, we proceeded along the
shore of the bay to the foot of the hills near Armyro; an ascent thence of
about a quarter of an hour brought us to the ruined khan and café

[Selvilí] some little way up the mountain, where a spring and some few fig-trees afforded us temporary refreshment and shade from a hot morning sun, and the enjoining café yielded some bad wine and rakee to my thirsty muleteers. Half an hour's ride to the south-west over the shoulder of a ridge which extends from the food of the high peak of Strongilo [Stroúmbolas], rising like a cone immediately over the western coast of Candia Bay, brings us to the modern village of Tylisso, or Dylisso, occupying the upper portion of the site of the old Cretan town of Tylisso, which, from its advantageous situation, must have been once of some size and importance, as it shown by its coins and by the remains of the town itself.

For I was shown where some ancient tombs had recently been opened near the village; and I was told by the inhabitants that foundations of walls, consisting of large blocks, and also ruined arches were often met with there in tilling or excavating. This spot lies a few hundred yards to the north-east of and below the modern village...

Apano Dylisso is two hours and a half from Candia, and is a village of about one hundred and fifty houses; of which thirteen are Turkish. During the time I halted at the village to examine the site and to rest from the heat of the sun, much civility was shown to me by the Greek inhabitants, who pressed me hard to remain with them for the entire day. But, as a long journey over mountains was before me, I determined to push on, as soon as the sun had declined behind Ida, unless prevented by the incapacity of my muleteers, who, I found, had evidently been spending the previous night at some revel, and were not disposed for or equal to a long day in such a hot sun.

The situation of Dylisso is fine – occupying a lower ledge or spur of the eastern roots of Ida, commanding an extensive view over the long and fertile valleys and ridges which formed the western territory of Gnossus, and of the town and fine bay of Candia (now enlivened by a few lateen-sail fishing-boats and a coaster or two); and being situated on the high road between the western division of Crete and its eastern cities, and also with considerable fertile territory in its immediate neighbourhood, it could not fail to become a city of some consequence in the days when Crete was populous. Immediately above it to the west rises a rocky chain of mountains, which, branching from the eastern roots of Ida, extends to the sea at Cape Dia (near which was the ancient Cytaeum), and completes an elevated ridge that forms a natural barrier right across the island. The way over this mountain boundary was thus in the possession of the ancient inhabitants of Tylisso, who possessed also consider-able mountain territory on the route, in the little upland valleys and plains of Gonies and Damasti lying immediatley above it.

It is a ride of nearly an hour and a half to cross this rugged ridge above Dylisso, and then to descend from it into the stony torrent-bed and val-ley of Gonies; and the torrent having only an exit through a very narrow and winding gorge in the mountain some distance to the south of Dylisso, which is impracticable by a road, renders it necessary to cross both the ridge and the valley intervening between Dylisso and the higher ridge of Gonies, in going from the former to the Mylopotamo district...

Gonies contains about thirty houses. Beyond it, at the head of the val-ley to the north-west, we hear of a small hamlet called Kamirotis, and by striking out of the 'vasiliko dromo,' as this mountain-track is called, from being the most frequented road between Candia and Retimo or Rhi-thymna, we reach it in a quarter of an hour. Selecting a level spot in one of the adjacent terraces for the tent, we soon had it erected, and were at leisure to enjoy the scenery surrounding this romantic little spot. We were now above the slaty rocks, and in the midst of the broken up and detached limestone crags that overlie them, with narrow cultivable ledges beneath, descending like a series of steps down their crumbling sides; and upon a few of those in the immediate vicinity of our tent were a variety of fruit-trees flourishing in the irrigation of a copious spring that issued from beneath a neighbouring crag, where we heard again the homely blackbird singing its vespers before retiring to roost.

This was the bright picture of a romantic little mountain location. Now turning to look at the village and its inhabitants, I found a sorry contrast. Four miserable hovels were all that were inhabited out of the twenty-five that belonged to it before the revolution [of 1821]. Of these four, one was occupied by a poor woman widowed since May last, from the inner recess of whose hovel proceeded, as I approached it, the piteous cries of a poor little girl, her only daughter, who, I found on inquiry, was at that moment suffering from a severe paroxysm of fever and ague, recently caught whilst gleaning a few handfuls of corn amongst the fields in the plains of Candia.

Shortly after my arrival, there came also to this hamlet two important-looking travellers in Frank dresses, although one bestrode a jaded mule, and the other a donkey. They, however, proved to be an itinerant Ionian quack doctor and his servant, belonging to Khania, but both natives of Cergo [Kýthira]; and they were now travelling together, dispensing advice and medicine amongst the mountain-villagers, wherever there were unfortunate dupes sufficiently afflicted and able to pay for them.

Their object in coming here, however, was simply to obtain a night's lodging, having arrived too late to proceed to a more populous village. But as the male population of the hamlet were absent, and did not return from their labours till after dark, they were patiently waiting their coming, near the widow's hovel, since none of the wives nor the widow dared to offer them lodgings in the absence of any of the male part of the community.

The poor woman, however, was induced to appeal to me for some medicine for her sick daughter, at the sound of which request the itinerant quack pricked up his ears and approached; but as poverty was so unmistakeably stamped within and without the cottage, he shrugged up his shoulders and walked away, neither revealing his mission to her not uttering a word of sympathy. I had thought of offering him room in my tent, had he failed to obtain a sleeping-place at one or other of the houses of this small hamlet; but this severed our intended friendly acquaintance as fellow travellers, and, taking upon myself to prescribe for the poor girl, I gave a few quinine pills from my own stock, and recommended some absinth tea, as I found that they possessed the herb on the adjacent hills, and knew it, but not its tonic properties.

My mules were ready with their baggage soon after daylight on the following morning, when we proceeded westward, and in a quarter of an hour crossed the pass in the mountain above the hamlet separating the torrents or streams which flow down this root of Ida into the Melavisi on the east and the Mylopotamo on the west side. A sea of ridges stretches before us to the westward for several miles, enclosed between the northern face of Ida and the lofty-pinnacled root of it, which here bends round parallel to the northern shore, and thus, branching round from the eastern base of the celebrated mountain, embraces in its sweep the rich and wooded district of Mylopotamo, formerly called the Avlopotamo.

The height of this pass must be at least 3000 feet above the sea. Descending from it into the head of the Mylopotamo valley immediately after crossing the pass, we asked every passer-by or peasant for information respecting the situation of the villages before us, and of any spot where ancient ruins of any kind existed; for I found that our guides, or rather muleteers, knew only the direct road down the valley to Retimo, and were useless when out of this track.

We at length accost an old woman on a donkey, journeying eastward. Belonging to the village of Anoya, not far distant, she proved of service in directing me to it, as neither of my guides had ever been there; and finding it a large village of 260 houses, I expected that it would prove to be an ancient site also, although the old woman, who said she had been born there, and had also lived there for ten or twelve years since her release from slavery, assured me that she had never heard of such a thing, adding that the only Hellenic places in the neighbourhood were Tylisso and Axo. As she was somewhat more than usually communicative and intelligent, I was led to inquire into the history of her slavery, when she commenced a tale of woe respecting the afflictions she had sustained in the early part of the revolutionary struggle for independence, between 1820 and 1830. Pointing to her wrinkled features, she said, 'These furrows are not the effect of age, but of my griefs. I am not old, although I look it.' She appeared seventy, but was only a little over fifty. 'My husband was killed by the Turks; my four sons were taken from me to Alexandria, whither also I and my only daughter were taken and sold as slaves. My four sons are still in Egypt. I was myself bought from the Turks by the Austrian consul at Megalo Kastron, and lived with him there for seven years afterwards as his servant, as a recompense for the purchase-money. My only daughter also was released, got married, and joined me in my native village; but the husband proved a vagabond, and ran away, leaving her with three children to maintain, and with hardly any means; and I am now going to some acquaintances and friends to beg for them a little bread till the time of the olive-picking.'

The narrative was irresistible; and the manner in which it was related disarmed doubt, especially as I knew that it was a tale not uncommon in Crete of afflictions resulting from the revolution. Thanking the poor dame for her information, and receiving from her the accustomed prayer or benediction and expressions of gratitude and thanks, we parted. Following her directions, we crossed the narrow valley, and fell into a zigzag path leading up the steep side of a ridge of reddish-brown slaty strata; in twenty minutes we reached the village, perched upon the upper edge of the cultivable territory lying on the northern flank of Ida, where the cultivation is chiefly carried on upon narrow terraces along the sides of innumerable narrow ridges, that here, like the fibrous roots of a large tree, shoot out from the base of the mountain.

This, however, is due to the presence of beds of schistose and slaty rocks overlying the grey hippurite limestone, instead of the surface consisting of great masses of the latter, as is the more general character of the slopes of Ida.

Disappointed in not finding any signs of the spot being an ancient site, although so large a village now, I halted in the lower part of it for about twenty minutes, merely whilst asking for information from the few peasants I met with. One at last rose and said he possessed a curious marble, 'covered with inscriptions.' Eager to see it, I followed him to his house-door, preferring to stay at its threshold, however, as it was mean and dirty, to entering within with the surety of returning with a swarm of fleas; for my enthusiasm for a new inscription or an antique did not quite amount to an indifference to such a result.

The mysterious and treasured relic was at last unfolded from the heart of a bundle of rags and presented to me, when it proved to be merely a fragment of a large fossil sea-egg, only somewhat more crystallized than ususal, and with the markings of the ambulacra and spinal pedestals very distinct. These rows of dots upon its surface were the supposed ancient writing alluded to by the possessor, who, when I told him what they were, seemed even more disappointed than I was; for from the geological evidence it afforded me (it being found near the village) that the marine tertiary deposits once overspread these lower hills, as it now does the open districts and valleys below, I found it of more interest than value. Some detached gravelly patches still resting on the summit of a few adjacent ridges had also partially indicated its former existence upon them; had it not been so, these upper shales and schists would doubtless long ago have disappeared, or been much more reduced by denudation and atmospheric degradation.

From Anóyia Spratt travelled on to Axós.

Spratt, II, 75 – 78, 80 – 88

From Anoya I was shown the situation of Axo, distant two or three miles, and immediately proceeded towards it by descending again into one of these narrow valleys; and following it for nearly a mile and a half, I approached a rugged limestone-hill which seems to block up the several ravines leading to it from Anoya and Ida; for seven or eight valleys unite their torrents on the east side of the rock of Axo. But it is seen, on a nearer approach, that the united torrents find their exit through the apparent barrier by a cleft or gorge which divides the rocky hill. The valley near the gorge is lined with some scattered groves of Ilex oaks, which are a small-leaved kind, and only useful for their acorns to feed the village swine. Several of the trees were of large growth, and at the time of our passing they were being thrashed by men, women, and children with long poles and sticks, to gather the ripe acorns from them, the inhabitants being all Christians in this neighbourhood.

On ascending over the limestone-ridge lying to the south of the gorge, we at once perceive evidences of the site of an ancient city, in the heaps of large stones gathered together and cleared on the hill-sides, wherever they were capable of being tilled, and in the abundance of fragments of ruins and ancient pottery in the soil so tilled. An ascent of 200 or 300 feet brings us to the top of the ridge, where, meeting with some Cyclopean walls, I dismount, and, ascending on foot to the top, find myself, on reaching it, close above the houses of the modern village of Axo, and also at the acropolis of the ancient city of Axus.

The hill upon which Axus stood has somewhat the form of a saddle, and vestiges of the Hellenic walls that almost encompassed it may be seen nearly all round it; but as they were not so necessary for defence to the south and north extremes, these being steep, none exist there...

The ancient city thus stood upon and around this saddle-shaped brow, the remains being more particularly abundant on the eastern side of the hill, the way we had ascended. The modern village of Axo, consisting of about forty Greek families, is situated on the west side of the saddle, near a copious spring which, gushing from the mountain into a little marble basin for the use of the damsels of the village, to wash their linen, irrigates some terraced gardens descending to some distance below.

Mr. Pashley not having seen a long inscription which I found upon one of the slabs at this spring, I copied the legible parts of it – which was a task that required some patient labour; for the linen being laid upon this slab (which is of marble) and beat during the process of washing, such ill-usage has greatly worn down its surface, and defaced the inscription. But after trying the patience of a good-natured damsel for more than an hour, whom I had interrupted in this operation, and by keeping the stone constantly wet (for the letters were mostly indistinct from the want of a good light), I at length succeeded in deciphering some parts of this very curious inscription in characters partially reversed and of very early date, whereas, had it been found elsewhere, and no water to aid the copying, not many of the letters would have been made out...

Among the ruins of Axus are six or eight small churches, most of which are left to decay from want of inhabitants to maintain them. They are all several centuries old, and denote times of populousness in the middle ages. The most curious is that of St. Irene, partly excavated into the side of the hill, so that its small cupola of Byzantine architecture is alone seen rising out of the ground. The walls within are painted with rude fresco, but almost defaced by humidity. The church of Joannes, just over it, on the top of the acropolis, is spoken of by Mr. Pashley, it having an ancient tessellated pavement for its present flooring, and it evidently stands upon or within some foundations of an Hellenic building; a broken shaft of a column also is near; so that these combined vestiges seem to point out the site of one of the early temples, which here, as in many other places, have been converted into Christian churches. Walking leisurely in the vicinity of this church, I came suddenly upon the village priest, who was employed in ploughing a small patch of ground adjoining it. Surprised at this sudden appearance of a stranger, and he a Frank, he immediately drove the ploughshare into the soil, to tether his half-frightened cattle, and then poured forth a volume of queries as to where I had dropped from, and what I was in search of; for I was alone. Good-nature, however, was stamped upon his countenance; and a mere hint that I was an 'Inglese' in search of inscriptions, Hellenic remains, &c., at once enlisted him into my service as a willing guide. I was thus indebted to him for enabling me to examine the entire site, and to purchase several of the copper coins of the city, which, as soon as my desire was made known, through him, to the old women of the village, were brought to me by dozens, mixed in general with a greater abundance of Venetian. But in no ancient city in Crete did I ever fall in with a greater quantity of its coins than here. I was indebted also to my friend the priest for a fruitless visit to a cave upon the opposite side of the hill: I was informed by him that I should find an inscription there; and so I did, but I found that it was merely a few rude letters that had been cut or scratched upon one of the fallen fragments. I presume they were the same that had caused Pashley a similar disappointment; but as he does not mention that the 'unmeaning scratches' he was taken to see were in a cave, or that they were in truth Greek characters, I notice it here, in order to prevent some zealous antiquary, who may hereafter visit Axos, from wasting his time and strength in a toil to the 'speli' with 'grammata.' The priest saw my disappointment, and asked me if it did not speak of money (the common belief respecting inscriptions)- showing, by the question, his ignorance of the Greek characters, believing them to be symbols with some mystical meaning known only to the Frank traveller.

I was not surprised at this ignorance, because it is often met with, indeed in half the villages of Crete; but it always awakened astonishment at the preservation of any remnant of Christianity by such benighted ministers in these long-persecuted lands.

On my returning to the village I found our friend the itinerant doctor. As there seemed some hope of doing business here, he had declared his vocation, and opened his baggage to display sundry medicine-bottles, boxes, &c. Desiring now to obtain a good word from me in recommendation of his medical capabilities, he offered gratuitously to give advice and medicine to my interpreter, who was a little indisposed after his revel before starting; but as I rather slighted his attentions, his servant (evidently a co-partner acting in that capacity) began more zealously to extol the skill of the quack, enumerating, in the hearing of all the old women assembled, a long list of cures which, he said, his master had effected during his six months' peregrinations through the Messara and other parts of Crete, finally concluding with the assurance that he was a real medico and had received his diploma at Corfu,– which assertion, of course, confirmed me in the opinion that they were both impostors who, by the possession of a few drugs and some address, had been able, no doubt, to reap a good harvest among the poor credulous peasantry, of whom, unhappily, there are too many whom fever and other diseases through bad living have made easy dupes to such pretenders.

From Axo I descended by a rough, stony road on the south side of the valley which leads to Garisso [Garázo]. On the left we passed the monastery of Lekomi, situated on the ridge, about half an hour from Axo. It affords a convenient position as a halting-place for a traveller who goes unprovided with a tent; but he will find neither accommodation nor food luxurious, the monastery being small, and the monks few and poor.

A steep lane, enclosed by myrtles, leads to the hamlet of Veni, where there is a water-mill. It is prettily situated on a spur of the hill, and surrounded by plane-trees &c. Passing it, we reach the metoki of Kateriana, at a mountain-spring three-quarters of an hour from Axo. Here we pitched our tent in a small garden belonging to a renegade Turk, who occupies a part of the dilapidated but once goodly villa of some Venetian proprietor. The spring irrigates several gardens below, in which thrive oranges and pomegranates.

I descended from here to the Mylopotamo valley, at Daphnes, passing through Garisso, at which place the dark shales and schists of the Axo district end and are entirely replaced by white tertiary strata, which extend along the base of Ida, as far as Retimo, the ancient Rhithymna, and lie nearly horizontal, having a slight dip away from the great central mountain.

We pass between Kastri on our left (hearing that it was only a middle-age or Venetian fortress) and Melidoni within the mountains on the right, where exists the celebrated grotto in which nearly 300 Cretans were suffocated by smoke and fire during the civil struggle for independence between the Turk and Greek. Pashley has fully described this event, and the nature of the cavern; and therefore, although I have been within its deep and dark retreat, and seen the skulls and bones of those that perished there, I shall add nothing to his pages relative to the horrible and barbarous deed. But it is perhaps of some interest to record here, whilst referring to this cavern, that when I visited it, not a quarter of a century after the event, the skulls and bones were in some parts already becoming firmly fixed in the floor by a stalagmitic incrustation resulting from the occasional dripping of water from the calcareous roof; and I thus notice it as a caution to cave-explores upon the fallacy of conclusions as to age deduced from the depth or amount of successive stalagmitic strata in calcareous caverns. I consider, also, that the stalactites of this cavern are far superior to those in the much-extolled grotto at Antiparos...

A priest whom we met in our descent from Axo, well mounted upon a finely caparisoned mule, and whose appearance and manners denoted him to be one of a superior class of local clergy, directed me to Lefterna and Veni as the only places where Hellenic remains existed in the neighbourhood. I immediately determined to proceed thither; and as he belonged to the monastery of Arkadi, situated on a high plateau between them, the information was the more reliable, particularly as both these names were those of ancient cities in the neighbourhood. I was therefore desirous also to learn from him whether Sybrita, a town said to have been only eight miles from Eleutherna, could be discovered and identified by the name being still known at or near its site; but the intelligent pappas had never heard of such a name connected with any place within the whole district, much less at so small a distance as eight miles from Lefterna or Elefterna, which, he stated, was the name of some ruins near a small village called Prene [now Arkhéa Eléftherna].

He also advised me to go first to Alpha, and ascend to Elefterna from there, that I might see the numerous rock tombs on the way. This information made me more desirous to approach it from Alpha, a small village near the mouth of the Elefterna valley; and after we had proceeded southward from it with the tombs referred to, there being a group of nearly a hundred; and at every 200 or 300 yards as we approached Elefterna we found five or six grouped together in the cliff overlooking the valley, and finally, at rather less than two miles from Alpha, others of larger dimensions, intended for families instead of individuals. These were from ten to twelve feet square, and had contained from three to six bodies each. I had time only to visit a few; but as all were excavated in the yellowish-white tertiary sandstone cliffs, were similar in design, and without architectural finish, there was nothing to induce a minute examination.

On reaching the ruins, we hastened through them, as the day was nearly closed; and ascending a narrow but perfectly flat ridge upon which the village of Prene was situated, we pitched our tent for the night in the neighbourhood of the village, near a few scattered well-grown trees of the ilex oak, the presence of which no doubt gave their local name to it.

We were now at the north-western base of Mount Ida, directly in the line of its narrow profile. The venerable and once venerated mountain consequently rose above us as a sharp, bare, whitish cone, majestic and brilliant, as its summit glittered with the last rays of the setting sun above the long, flat, and now shadowless ridges of the foreground, just before the short twilight which in these latitudes intervenes between day and night; and I sketched the view for my portfolio as a memento of the moment.

The village kine and swine were now wending their way home from the wild pasture of the adjoining valleys, without herdsman or call, but instinctively, from habit – and leisurely too, indicating (at this hour of prowling for prey) their conscious freedom from wild animals in this favoured island, in contrast to the neighbouring continents and, indeed, one or two of the Greek islands; for they abound in the former, and occasionally frequent the latter by swimming across some of the intervening channels.

By the return to the village, therefore, of the few milch cows its inhabitants possessed, we were soon regaled with a grateful bowl of new milk for our tea, which we enjoyed the more from being fatigued by the toils of the day.

The following day Spratt visited Eléftherna.

The hills lying around Eleutherna, at the north-west base of Mount Ida, have a remarkable uniform character, consisting of numerous long and narrow flat topped ridges with steep sides, and confined valleys separating them. The whole represents a broad cake of the white tertiary strata, which, having been uniformly elevated around the base of the mountain, with a slight inclination to the north, has become divided into parallel but somewhat irregular strips by the mountain-torrents descending from time to time from the slopes of Ida, channelling and cutting it up into long ribbon-like ridges, with contractions here and there, that vary from a few hundred yards in some parts to a few yards in others.

The termination of one of these so contracted flat ridges was chosen for the site of Eleutherna, on account of the natural strength of the position; for, the upper crust of the ridges being composed of the hardest rock, a fringe of cliffs, varying from twenty to sixty or even eighty feet high, encircles the crests of nearly the whole of them, the softer strata forming gentle slopes beneath, which are terraced and cultivated down to the bed of the valley. There is consequently great fertility over these numerous ridges and valleys; and they are occupied by numerous populous villages, the largest of which is Margarites, about a mile to the east of the old city, but fully an hour's journey across the intervening valleys.

Eleutherna was thus well fortified by nature, although it is by no means a striking or picturesque feature in the landscape. In the form of its groundplan it may be compared to a cricket-bat, or a bottle, the only entrance to it being by a narrow contracted neck of the plateau.

The narrow approach to the terminal plateau of this ridge, on which seems to have stood only the acropolis of the city, is about fifty yards long and from ten to fifteen broad, with the exception of one part, where it is not more than twelve feet across, and at the end of which stand the ruins of a solid tower of mixed masonry, about thirty feet square, thus completely commanding the only apparent and very narrow approach to the acropolis; for the plateau itself was so encircled by cliffs, that it required only a few pieces of wall here and there, where it was scaleable, to prevent access in any other direction than by this narrow neck of land, which a single square tower stopped as completely as a cork would the aperture of a bottle...

The plateau on which stood the acropolis of Eleutherna is cultivated throughout, and has a sprinkling of fine old olives. The remains within, however, are few – mainly the foundations of walls of habitations, and some ruined churches of an early date. On the slope of the hill under the acropolis are remains of numerous terraces, as well as buildings, – the principal buildings of the city having apparently stood there, more especially on the eastern slope...

Upon one of the lower terraces on this side we found a mutilated statue in Parian marble; and near it were the remains of a fine Hellenic platform or terrace that may have originally supported a temple, upon which was a circular altar piece also of white marble, with a carved moulding of eggwork above, and fluted with diagonal and waving grooves down the centre of the altar; it has, however, a circular hollow at the top, like a baptismal font of the present time: but it must be of an earlier time than the Christian, and may be an altar of the Roman period, subsequently converted into a baptismal font. Although it had only recently been discovered in making some excavations there for building-stones, yet it was already in part broken up, for the purpose of being converted into lime, on account of the whiteness and fine quality of the marble; so that I fear none of it now remains.

The most perfect and yet apparently the most ancient ruins at Eleutherna are those of two Hellenic bridges, – one crossing the bed of the stream flowing in the valley just below the above-noticed site of a temple with the statue and altar; the other further down the valley, and below the junction of the streams flowing on either side of the acropolis, immediately under some rock tombs. The arch of each is formed with horizontal layers only, as were all the very early-constructed arches and vaults in Greece. And yet it seems evident that the idea of a circular arch was in the mind of the builder without his knowing how to form it; for there is an excavated arched way over a footpath by the side of the pier of the horizontal one, through the native rock that the bridge abuts against or projects from. This, however, may have been made subsequently; yet the association is curious and interesting. The existence of two such well-built bridges here clearly shows this city to have been both wealthy and populous in early times, although at present the site itself contains so little other evidence of the fact, except its rock tombs.

Each of the cliffs under the acropolis is excavated into sepulchres in several places, some even appearing, from their size and the shape of their interior, to have been intended for the habitations of the living instead of the dead; and one of them is now used as a chapel, dedicated to St. Antonio.

At the turn of the valley close under the little hamlet of Prene, near a copious spring that issues from the hill-side, and picturesquely shaded by a few fine plane-trees, are the remains of a large or double church, dedicated to the Saviour and St. John, with several fragments of ancient columns near. Round the window-sill of the church is a Venetian inscription, showing that the spot was well known to, and inhabited by some Venetian families during their occupation of Crete.

In the vicinity of the spring was found a fragment of an inscription that contained the name of the city, thus aiding in confirming its identity.

It was also in the village of Prene that I found a fragment of an inscription, cut upon a slab of soft calcareous sandstone, making mention of Ptolemy Evergetes, and probably indicating an alliance or connexion between this king of Egypt and Eleutherna...

From Eléftherna Spratt went on to the Amári valley, where he discovered Sybrita (see Chapter 6). In the following chapter we meet our travellers in Herákleion.

Herákleion

Koules

Venetian Harbour

San Pietro

SOFOKLI VENIZELOU

Arsenals

SOFOKLI VENIZELOU

EPIMENIDHOU

St. Andreas bastion

Priuli fountain

KHANDHAKOS

25 AVGOUSTOU

Loggia

Ayios Títos

Sabbionera bastion

Morosini fountain

Armoury

BEAUFORT

Archeological museum

PLATEIA EL. VENIZELOU

San Marco

DHAIDHALOU

PLATEIA ELEFTHERIAS

Pantokrator bastion

KALOKERINOU

KALOKERINOU

Ayía Ekaterini

ODHOS 1821

ODHOS 1866

DHIKEOSINIS

EVANS

Porta Ayios Yeoryios

IKAROU

Porta Khanion

THERISOU

Porta Bethlehem

PLATEIA KORNAROU

Bembo fountain

Vitouri bastion

Bethlehem bastion

Porta Kenouria

DHIMOKRATIAS

Jesus bastion

KONDILAKI

AKADHIMIAS

Martinengo bastion

KNOSSOU

0   250 m

8. Herákleion

THE SETTING

Our tour now brings us to the most important city in Crete, Herákleion. With its 140,000 inhabitants it is a typically Levantine harbour city. Busy, cluttered, with its concrete buildings and hectic traffic it is not a very attractive place at first glance. But a closer look shows that the city is bursting with life and full of tangible memories of a great and centuries-old past.

The city was largely rebuilt after heavy bombing during World War II. It sprawls out on all sides around the original center of the city: the Plateía Eleftheríou Venizélou, with its fountain built by Morosini. Once the palace of the duke, the governor of Venetian Crete, stood here across from the San Marco church. And close by was the Loggia where the Venetian nobility entertained themselves, and the Armoury where the weapons were kept. From this center of government the Odhós 25 Avgoústou goes down to the Venetian harbour with its imposing harbour castle and its Arsenals (shipyards). The Venetian city is circled by a for-midable, still impressive wall which dates from the 15th and 16th cen-turies.

The city's power lay in its location, which, in combination with the

175

island of Dhía off the coast, was the best harbour site of Crete since its establishment by the Muslims in 824. With the prevailing northern winds in the summertime the merchant ships could anchor on the south side of Dhía, under its lee. The merchandise would then be brought to and from the Herákleion harbour by smaller boats. The harbour also suffered less from silting up than either Khaniá or Réthymnon.

THE PAST

It is known that in the Neolithic Period there was a settlement just to the east of the Herákleion harbour, close to the suburb of Póros. There was probably a harbour here in Minoan times also, but nothing is left of it now. There are also no remains of the later harbour of Heraclium, which is mentioned by Roman authors as being on this site. Heraclium is supposed to have been named after the Greek hero Herakles, who according to legend stole one of the bulls of Minos and took it from Crete to the Peloponnesos.

The city's history actually begins when the Muslims capture the island in 824 (or 827, according to some sources) and realize the strategic importance of the location as a harbour. The previous history is as follows. Christian, Visigothic Spain was conquered at the beginning of the 8th century by Arabic and Berber Muslims who fought for the Omayyad caliphs in Damascus. When all but one of the Omayyads had been killed by their successors, the Abbasids, in 750, the only surviving Omayyad was able to escape to Spain. There he established an independent emirate with Cordoba as its capital. As everywhere in Muslim regions, the original inhabitants of Spain gradually converted to the religion of the new rulers. However, these new Muslims considered the third emir of Cordoba, al-Hakam I (796-822), too frivolous and not strict enough (he drank wine, for example). For that reason rebellions broke out against the emir between 805 and 814, especially among the inhabitants of the Rabad district in Cordoba, where many converts lived. The rebellions failed, however, and in 814 the rebels were forced to leave the city. Some of them fled to the recently established city of Fes in Morocco. The rest, some 10,000 people, fled to Alexandria in Egypt. The sources do not explain how such a large group of people was able to make the long voyage across the sea to Egypt, but it is likely that they were helped by experienced sailors from the Spanish coastal cities.

The escapees first settled in Alexandria, but in 824 they were deployed by the Abbasid caliph al-Ma'mun against the Byzantines, probably

because of their skills at sea. Their task was to conquer Crete. They landed at a cape by the name of Kharax, at the Gulf of Messará. From there
they advanced to the north coast under the leadership of the *emir* Abu
Hafs Umar, where they settled on the site of the present Herákleion. Presumably they were attracted by the quality of the harbour and the
favourable location in relation to Byzantine shipping routes and rich
Byzantine cities. In Arabic, the administrative and religious language of
these converts, their settlement was called Rabad al-Khandaq (ususally
translated as 'castle of the ditch' but echoes of their former dwelling
place at Cordoba can also be heard in the name), or al-Khandaq for short.
For one and a half centuries these Muslims (called Agarenes or Saracens
in European sources) had control of Crete, in the name of the Abbasid
caliphs in Baghdad.

There is not much known about the Muslim rule of Crete. Modern
historiography usually attributes the destruction of a large number of
Byzantine cities to these 'Arabic' rulers of Crete, but other causes may
have contributed as well. The cities may have suffered from the series of
catastrophic earthquakes which hit the island between the 4th and 8th
centuries (the last of which occurred in 795), from the widespread plague
epidemic in 642, and from the decrease in trade between Egypt and
Byzantium and the rest of Christian Europe (in 642 Egypt had been conquered by the Muslims). It is not even certain that the Muslims con-
trolled all of Crete. What is certain, though, is that the Muslim fleet
plundered the Byzantine coast and seized Byzantine ships. And it is also
certain that they captured many Christians as slaves.

Al-Khandaq remained the center of Muslim raids until 961. In that
year the Byzantine general, and later emperor, Nikifóros Fokás seized al-
Khandaq and overran the entire island. According to historical chronic-
les he had 200,000 inhabitants executed in the process, which would
amount to nearly the entire population. Traces of the Muslim presence
on the island were destroyed as much as possible. The monastery of
Meyísti Lávra, first of the famous monasteries of Mount Athos, was
established with the yields of the treasures seized from the Muslims.

Not much is known about the history of the city during the Second
Byzantine Period. Under the name of Khándakas the city remained the
governmental and military center of the island and the city was encircled
by a strong wall.

The end of Byzantine rule came in 1204. Alexios Angelos, a pretender
to the Byzantine throne, escaped from Byzantine imprisonment in 1201

and associated himself with a group of Frankish knights in Venice. The knights were readying themselves for a new Crusade – the fourth – against the Muslims, who had reclaimed Jerusalem from the Franks in 1187. With great Venetian endorsement Alexios was able to convince the knights that they should first conquer Constantinople for him. In return he offered them his help and his financial support. The leader of the Crusade, Boniface of Montferrat, would receive northern Greece and Crete as his fee, among other things. Constantinople was indeed conquered by the crusaders in April 1204, and Alexios did sit on the Byzantine throne for a short time. But Boniface had no interest in his new acquisition of Crete. He sold the island to Venice on August 12, 1204 for the sum of 1000 silver marks.

The Venetians did not immediately take possession of the island. The Genoese adventurer Enrico Pescatore, Count of Malta, took advantage of that. In 1204 he was able to occupy large sections of Crete, among others Khándakas. He built forts in a number of strategic locations and by 1205 he appeared to be master of the whole island. The Venetians attempted to recapture the island, but only in 1209 did they gain possession of a bridgehead: the strategic castle of Paleókastro at the foot of the Stroúmbolas, from where they took Khándakas. In 1217 Pescatore's troops were driven out for good.

But the inhabitants did not submit easily to the Venetians. Up until the second half of the 14th century there were large uprisings, and it is estimated that the population of the island dropped to 50,000 during this period. When the rebellions were over, the population rose again, to about 200,000, of whom about 16,000 lived in the city of Candia (Khándakas was corrupted to the name Candia by the Venetians, and the name was thereafter used to refer to the whole island as well).

In 1211 the Venetian administration created the Regno di Candia: Crete was henceforth one administrative unit with the city of Candia as its governing center. The island was divided into six, later four, administrative regions and those into 200 fiefs. Venetians were encouraged to settle on the island, and as many as 10,000 settlers arrived from Venice – about one seventh of the Venetian population. The highest official was the Duca di Candia, the doge or duke, who was chosen by the nobility of Venice. His term of office was two years. In the other major cities authority was wielded by so called *rectors*. In times of crisis the administration in Venice would send a *proveditor general* to Candia with unlimited military authority, but for a term of only two years. After 1569 there was a permanent *proveditor general* in Candia, in connection with the Ottoman threat.

The Venetian aristocracy on the island, descendants of the first Venetians, formed a rich upper class. They were in sharp contrast to the rural population, who as serfs had to work the land, perform various chores, and even serve as oarsmen in the Venetian galleys.

The Venetians brought the Roman Catholic faith to Crete. Henceforth there was a Catholic archbishop (always a Venetian) who, if he left Venice at all, resided in Herákleion. The Catholic cathedral was the church of St. Titus, which stood on the spot where the 19th century Orthodox church of the same name (Áyios Títos) now stands. In the cathedral the head of St. Titus, the patron saint of Crete, was preserved, and this important relic was a center of devotion (when the Venetians left Herákleion in 1669 they took the head with them; in 1966 it was ceremoniously returned and can now be found in the Áyios Títos again). The Dominicans and Franciscans were also present in Herákleion: the 14th century church of San Pietro, close to the Historical Museum, was Dominican, and the Franciscan monastery stood where the Archeological Museum now stands (it was largely destroyed during the Ottoman siege). The San Marco, dating from the 13th century, was the burial church of the dukes.

At first the Catholic Church attempted to make the Orthodox Church subservient. But at the end of the 16th century, because of the Ottoman threat, the attitude towards the Orthodox Church became more tolerant. In this context the flourishing of Orthodox monasteries all around Crete in the 16th and 17th centuries has often been referred to. Something similar occurred in Herákleion. In 1555 the Ayía Ekateríni church was established as a dependency of the Orthodox monastery of St. Catherine in the Sinai. This church, with its monastery school, was the intellectual and artistic center of Orthodox Crete in Venetian as well as Ottoman times. Great artists such as El Greco, the icon painter Mikhaílis Dhamaskinós, and the writer Vitzéntzos Kornáros studied there. Now the Byzantine Museum, with its important icons, is located there.

Herákleion was one of the most important cities of the Venetian seaborne empire. The city lay strategically along the crucial sea route from Venice to Asia Minor and Egypt, and had an outstanding harbour for the Venetian war galleys that had to protect the trade routes from enemies. The Arsenals are reminders of that time. Herákleion's hinterland, moreover, was pre-eminently suited to the cultivation of products for export. These consisted predominently of wine, and to a lesser degree olive oil, timber, cheese, and honey.

The walling-in of Herákleion initially followed the Byzantine wall, from the San Pietro parallel to the Odhós Khándhakos and the Odhós Dhaidhálou to the Plateía Eleftherías. The most prominent gateway lay where the city's most important intersection now lies, at the beginning of the Odhós 1821 and the Odhós 1866. This gateway stood until the 19th century. Initially there was a fortified tower on the site of the present harbour fort.

But stronger fortifications became necessary. This had to do with the Ottoman clash with the Venetian empire after the 15th century. Indeed, the purchase of Crete had been only the beginning of an expansion of Venetian influence in and around the Aegean Sea. On the Peloponnesos, on Náxos, and especially on Euboia (called Negroponte by the Venetians) there are remains of Venetian fortifications which testify to the grandeur of the empire. Khálkis, on Euboia, was the heart of this empire and it was this city which was first hit by the Ottoman expansion after the conquering of Constantinople in 1453. Under the great sultan Mehmed II, the Ottomans used their modern army, armed with firearms, first to overrun the Frankish domains on the Greek mainland. Then, in 1461, they put an end to the last remnants of Byzantine rule in Mistra, on the Peloponnesos. Subsequently it was the Venetian possessions' turn. In 1470 Khálkis fell and during the century which followed, the majority of Venetian strongholds in the Aegean fell into the hands of the Ottomans. But Crete would offer resistance for a long time to come. This was partly due to the modern defences that the Venetians built. As early as 1462 the imposing, five kilometer long wall circling Herákleion was begun, which after the attack of the Ottoman admiral Barbarossa in 1538 (see the introductory notes to Chapter 1) was strengthened with seven bastions, a deep and wide moat, and other defences. The designer of these 16th century defences was the same Michele Sanmicheli who was involved in the fortification of Khaniá and Réthymnon. The wall surrounded the city on all sides, also on the sea side. At the entrance of the harbour the harbour fort was built, currently called Koúles from the Turkish word for fort, and called Rocca al Mare by the Venetians. The construction of the Bembo fountain at the present Plateía Kornárou also dates from this period (1558).

In the first half of the 17th century the island enjoyed a period of calmness, and the Venetian Herákleion which the modern visitor encounters dates mainly from this period. Under the *proveditor* Francesco Morosini the Loggia was built in 1626-1629, as well as the fountain named after him in 1628 on the present Plateía Venizélou. The aqueduct which brings water from Mount Yioúkhtas to the fountain was also constructed on his orders. The primary function of this fountain, just as of the others in the city, was to safeguard the city's water supply.

As mentioned earlier, in 1645 the Ottomans appeared on the island to stay. In that year Khaniá was captured, Réthymnon in 1646, and in May of 1648 Ottoman troops stood at the wall of Candia. But the fortifications did their work. A siege began which would continue more or less intensively for 21 years, and which would cost 30,000 Venetians and 120,000 Ottoman troops their lives. Yusuf Pasha, who had been the first commander, was executed shortly after the invasion. His successor was Deli Huseyn. He commanded the Ottoman troops in their siege of Herákleion until he was called back to Istanbul and eventually executed in 1666. The siege began forcefully, but quickly appeared to be unsuccessful. The Ottoman troops were encamped at what is now Fortétsa and bombarded the city almost daily with their cannons. The city was surrounded on the landward side, but the Venetian fleet was able to keep the sea route to Herákleion free.

In August of 1648, right after the siege began, the Ottoman sultan Ibrahim the Mad was assassinated by his grand vizier. He was succeeded by his 7-year-old son Mehmed IV (deposed in 1687). The first years of Mehmed's reign were chaotic, partly because of the costly siege of Candia, but in 1656 the capable Köprülü Mehmed Pasha became grand vizier. He brought stability to the empire. During his viziership the Ottoman war efforts were directed primarily at the Habsburg empire in the Balkans, and the siege of Herákleion simmered on. That changed in 1661 when he was succeeded as grand vizier by his son, Köprülüzade Fazil Ahmed Pasha. This vizier was able to finish the war with the Habsburgs in 1664, and the Ottoman troops could then be deployed at the siege of Herákleion. In 1666 he personally took leadership of the siege, which was started again in earnest. The Venetians sent the competent Francesco Morosini the Younger (a nephew of the *proveditor* of the early 17th century) to lead the beleaguered city. One of the first measures taken by the grand vizier was the destruction of the aqueduct to the Morosini fountain (the Priuli fountain was then built in the city) and in 1667 40,000 Ottoman troops landed on the island. That was the beginning of the end. The Christian states did send some troops to help (among others a

Morosini Fountain in Herákleion

French contingent under the Duc de Beaufort, mentioned in one of the quotations, who was killed in battle in July 1669), but it was in vain. On September 16th, 1669 the Venetians were forced to give up the city. Morosini, along with all of the city's inhabitants, was allowed to retreat from the city taking archival materials and the head of St. Titus with him, and the Ottomans moved in. Later on Morosini would become Doge of Venice. Köprülüzade remained grand vizier, and a pillar of the Ottoman empire, until his death in 1676 as a result of excessive alcohol use.

From this time on the Ottomans had control of the city and of the island. With the retreat of the Venetians Crete, called Girid in Turkish, became an *eyalet*, an Ottoman province. Kandiya, or Megálo Kástro as the city was called in Greek, was its administrative center (only in 1841 did Khaniá take over that role). The Ottomans took the administrative division of the island over from the Venetians. The island remained divided into four regions, or *sanjaks*. The governor (*pasha*) of the regions of Herákleion and Siteía (thus the centre and the east of the island) resided in Herákleion. He was higher in rank than the *pashas* of the other two regions, Khaniá and Réthymnon, and was *serasker*, commander-in-chief, as well. The *pashas* were assisted in their governing by a council, and for matters concerning the Christian subjects there was a Greek secretary, sometimes called dragoman. The regions were divided into districts where *agas* exerted power. The villages were governed by a *kapetan* or *proestós* on behalf of the Ottoman rulers. All subjects were required to pay taxes; Christians and Jews had an additional tax: the poll tax. In the Ottoman system the tax yields went not only to the central state, but also—as salary—directly to state officials, such as military commanders and functionaries. And parts of the taxes were used for pious purposes such as the maintenance of mosques and public works (an example was the region of Sfakiá: the tax yields there were intended for the holy cities of Mecca and Medina).

The army consisted mainly of Janissaries, who were originally Christian boys from the Balkans who were brought up in Istanbul as Muslims and received a thorough military training. Apart from the Janissaries, there were local troops, recruited from the Muslim population of Crete. In the basically feudal system that existed in Crete, some Janissaries were able to develop their own rural power base. According to a great number of sources, the Janissaries oppressed the Christian population heavily. Opposition to the Ottoman authority came from the so-called *hayyins* who harassed the Ottoman-controlled countryside from their position in the inaccessible mountains. *Hayyins* who were caught by the Ottomans were often executed in a gruesome manner: they were impaled, or thrown onto sharp, crooked hooks.

One of the few good aspects of Ottoman rule was that the Orthodox Church enjoyed much more freedom than under Venetian rule. In the Ottoman system of administration the archbishop of Górtyn, or metropolitan bishop, was regarded as the representative of the Christian subjects in Crete, and had thus a political and influential role. A large part of Crete's population, however, converted to Islam, probably because of the great pressure of taxes imposed on Christians. And a great number of Catholic churches were turned into mosques, by adding a prayer niche and a minaret.

In the first decades following the conquest the economy picked up slowly and the population increased. But in the second half of the 18th century this stopped: the population was terrorized by the Janissaries and the economic situation worsened. In 1770 there was a rebellion. In that year Catherine the Great, tsarina of Russia, tried to provoke an uprising in the Greek regions of the Ottoman Empire. Rebellions did indeed break out, in the Peloponnesos as well as in Sfakiá on Crete, under its legendary leader Ioánnis Dhaskaloyiánnis, but both were mercilessly smothered by Ottoman troops.

That first rebellion did not succeed, but it kept simmering. On June 14th 1821 Crete joined the Greek struggle for independence. The fuse was lit in the region of the Sfakians, but it ignited everywhere, and rebellion broke loose. In response the Ottomans took refuge in the earlier mentioned intimidation of the representatives of the Orthodox Church. However, in 1822 when it became evident that a stalemate had been reached between the rebels and the Ottomans, troops of the viceroy of Egypt, Mehmed Ali, came in to put a bloody end to the uprising. The outcome was that Crete did not become a part of independent Greece. Instead, Crete came under the rule of the *khedive* Mehmed Ali for ten years (between 1830 and 1840), with Mustafa Pasha as *pasha* and *serasker* of Crete, and Osman Bey as *pasha* of Herákleion. They both resided in Herákleion, where Pashley visited them in 1834. Under Mustafa Pasha's rule there was a period of modernization. Herákleion's harbour was dredged, and the city's water supply was secured by a new aqueduct from the Yioúkhtas.

In 1840 the Great Powers (England, France, and Russia) forced

Mehmed Ali to withdraw from Crete because he had become too power-ful in relation to the Ottoman sultan. So the island again came under the authority of Istanbul. In 1841 Khaniá, with its good harbour facilities in the Bay of Soúdha, took over the role of capital of Crete. Mustafa Pasha remained governor of the island, after 1840 on behalf of the Ottoman sul-tan, until he was named grand vizier in 1850. After a short interlude his son Veli Pasha (mentioned by Spratt) succeeded him. He remained governor until 1858.

Between 1841 and the year of independence, 1898, it remained turbulent in Crete. The high point, or perhaps low point, of this turbulence was the previously mentioned uprising from 1866 to 1869 with the martyrs of Arkádhi. The Great Powers demanded from the sultan more and more privileges for the Christians, but Crete remained under Ottoman authority.

Finally in 1898 public opinion in Europe forced the Great Powers (which now included Italy) to grant Crete its independence. It was decided that Crete would not be allowed to join itself to independent Greece, but would become an autonomous protectorate under the pro-tection of England, France, Russia and Italy. On August 25th 1898 an inci-dent occurred, involving the death of British subjects, which helped to speed up the independence process on the island. In Herákleion a Mus-lim crowd, furious about the plans for autonomy and provoked by the arrival of a provisional government, caused a bloodbath among their Christian countrymen, whereby 17 British military men and the British consul, Lysimachos Kalokairinós, were killed. The British reaction was to force the Ottomans, with their troops, to leave the island. On Decem-ber 9th 1898 the High Commissioner, Prince George, landed in the Bay of Soúdha. Crete was no longer an Ottoman province. Kandiya was renamed Herákleion, for the Roman harbour Heracleium. In 1971 Herá-kleion again became the capital of Crete.

THE TRAVEL DESCRIPTIONS

The English traveller Pococke, who visited the island in 1739, gave a description of Herákleion.

Pococke, p. 257, 258

The town of Candia is situated in a plain country on the east side of a large bay, having to the west of it a broad chain of hills, which are called

Strongyle [Stroúmbolas], and make a point out into the sea, which is the Capo Sassoso of Homan, and must be the promontory antiently called Dion. These mountains, together with the eastern parts of mount Ida, and the higher hills towards the plain of Messares, in which Gortynia stands, make a sort of a semicircle, which opens to the north. This country consist mostly of small fruitful hills, which produce great quantities of excellent wines, but it is a level country on the bay [here Pococke describes the area of Malevísi]. Opposite to Candia is the uninhabited isle of Dia, which is said to have its name from Jupiter. It is called Standia by Europeans. There are three good ports to the south of it, where the ships of the Maltese, as well as others, usually anchored during the siege of Candia.

The city of Candia, before it was fortified by the Venetians, was but a small town, encompassing its port, and extended, as it is said, by Tramata gate [the Venetian wall also stretched along the sea, between the St. Andreas bastion and the harbour; the Tramata gate gave entry halfway to the sea] from the north, to Sabionera gate on the east. The present city, which is of a semicircular figure, and very strongly fortified, may be about four miles in circumference, though they affirm that it is twice as much. The city was taken by the Turks in one thousand six hundred sixty-nine, after a siege and blockade of twenty three years, the Venetians having lost thirty thousand men in the siege, and the Turks seventy thousand. In the year one thousand six hundred sixty-seven, twenty thousand Turks and three thousand Venetians were killed. Five hundred mines were blown up; there were eighteen combats in the under ground works. The besieged made seventeen sallies, and the city was assaulted two and thirty times, so that it is deservedly reckoned one of the most famous sieges recorded in history.

There are in Candia six thousand men belonging to the six bodies of the Turkish soldiery, but those include all the Turks who are fit to bear arms, for they all belong to some military body. They have about fourteen mosques, six or seven of which were churches. There are some families of Armenians, who have a church. The Greeks likewise have a church belonging to the convent of mount Sinai, and another at the house of the metropolitan. The capuchins [Franciscans] have a small convent and chapel for the consul and French merchants, and the Jews a synagogue.

The city is well built, though some parts of it near the ramparts lie waste. The streets are broad and handsome, and the shops built after the

Venetian manner. A wall is standing of the antient palace of the governors, and in the piazza there is a fine fountain of the work of Vincenzo. The lower basin is adorned with excellent bass reliefs. The upper basin is supported by four lions, and had in the middle a fine statue by the same hand, which the Turks destroyed. The entrance of the port is narrow and difficult, having only nine feet water, and there is but fifteen within, but there is a good road without the basin. There are several fine arsenals about it which are arched over, in order to build or lay up ships or galeotes, though many of them have been destroyed. The port is made by two points of rocks that run out into the sea on the east, west, and part of the north side, on which walls have been built, and the port is defended by a strong castle.

> Pashley also visited the city. He arrived there from Týlissos, as we have seen, on February 27th, 1834. He stayed for one week, during which time he visited the notables of the city, both Ottoman and Orthodox. We join his story after his description of how 'oriental' the city seemed to him.

Pashley, I, p. 168, 169

I obtained an apartment in the house of Dhemétrio, the Pashá's Greek secretary. My host expressed great delight at receiving in his dwelling an Englishman, who had studied 'the Hellenic language'. The moment he found that I had read Homer, he asked me if I was also acquainted with Synesius [a Greek alchemist from the fourth century A.D.; Pashley explains the connection with Homer in a footnote: 'Before I left Megálo-Kástron I found out the link which united Homer and Synesius in the mind of my host: he possessed a small volume, probably his only Hellenic book, containing extracts from those two authors'].

After establishing myself in these quarters, I proceeded to visit the consular representatives of Great Britain and France. Monsieur Fabreguette [the French consul in Khaniá] had given me a letter of introduction to Monsieur Godebout, the French Consular Agent, who seems to be the person of most consideration among the so-called Frank population of this city. His house is spacious, and is fitted up with some of the ordinary comforts and luxuries of civilized Europe. I declined, however, to accept of his proffered hospitality, since I had obtained a very comfortable apartment with Dhemétrio, and had made arrangements for being duly supplied with dinner, &c. from a kind of locanda in the city.

On a subsequent occasion I became M. Godebout's guest.

I need hardly say that the French agent is a native of the country which he represents here. The English agent, on the contrary, is a Levantine, who was born at Malta, has passed many years of his life as a slave in Barbary [a collective name for Algiers, Tunis and Tripoli, the three Ottoman cities from where large-scale corsairing was practiced, with the corresponding trade in captured Christians]; and, like his principal in Khaniá, is totally unacquainted with English. He is, however, a good-natured old man, and knows enough Italian and Greek to be able to maintain a conversation in either of those languages.

The following morning, February 28th, Pashley visited Mustafa Pasha and Osman Bey.

Pashley, I, p. 172 – 175

On visiting his Excellency Mustafá-pashá, the Seraskier of the island, about nine o'clock this morning, I was accompanied by Monsieur Godebout, and also by the English consular agent. We found the band of one of the Arab regiments, now quartered in the city, playing in the ante-room. The Pashá, who had been forewarned of my visit, rose and descended from his divan, advancing a few steps to meet me, as I entered his apartment. While coffee and pipes were handed round, we conversed on various topics: the Pashá, at first, spoke Turkish, through the medium of a Jewish dragoman; but, after a while, something was said in Greek, from which he found out, equally as it seemed to his surprise and pleasure, that I was acquainted with that language, and immediately began to converse with me in it. Thus all my intercourse with Mustafá-pashá was released from the bonds which usually fetter the conversation of European travellers with men of rank in Turkey. Little can indeed be the communication where every word that is said on either side must pass through the mouth of an illiterate Jew before it can be understood by the other party.

Mustafá-pashá, like his master the Viceroy of Egypt, is a native of Cavallo [Kavala] or its neighbourhood: he is now probably thirty-five years of age, and has become acquainted with Greek since his residence in Crete. Most of the members of his kharém, including the two mothers of his children, are Greek women: and, his daily intercourse with them alone would account for his acquaintance with their language. I was astonished to discover, that, although he reads Turkish and Arabic, he has not thought it worth while to learn the *written* Greek character: and thus, while he speaks the language of the island almost with the fluency of a native, he cannot read even the superscription of a letter...

From the hall of audience of the Pashá I went to see Osmán-bey, a general officer, who is governor of the city and of all the parts of the island which are considered as belonging to it. I found that he speaks French with tolerable fluency: and thus with him, as with the Governor-General, no interpreter was needed. Monsieur Godebout is convinced that Osmán-bey is far the most intelligent person in authority in the whole island. The formation of this opinion has in all probability been aided, if not wholly produced, by the fact that M. Godebout can converse with the General in French. M. Godebout tells me that when his interpreter is the organ of communication between himself and Mustafá-pashá, or the President of the Council, he sometimes looks to the person with whom the Jew enables him to converse, expecting a smile, and sees a grave countenance. I myself discovered that the interpreters here never even try to *translate* the *words* used: they give what they suppose to be the sense of a whole sentence, and since they frequently misunderstand what is said, they equally falsify both the form and substance of what they ought to translate.

After these visits to the Pashá and Osmán-bey, I returned to my apartment in the house of Dhemétrio. My host's late uncle was bishop of Cnossos, and thus the intelligent Greek is naturally full of information on the temporal affairs of the church in Crete. I learn from him the extent of each Episcopal see, and the amount of revenues, both of the bishops and the inferior clergy. On the antiquities of the island, Dhemétrio's knowledge is, as might be expected, much less extensive: he knows only of some ancient remains called Mákro-teíkho, in the immediate neighbourhood of this city, and of 'the sepulchre of Zeus' on Mount Júktas.

Dhemétrio was a widower when he married his present youthful and pretty wife: she is a native of Goniés, the village at which I slept the night before last.

In Chapter 9 we will see how Pashley went to investigate Makritíkhos and the 'sepulchre' of Zeus. First we hear some more about Herákleion.

The most considerable of the Venetian remains, at Megálo-Kástron, next to the massive walls by which the city is surrounded, and the arches seen here, as at Khaniá, near the port, are those of a large building, which I suppose to have been the cathedral church of the Latin Archbishop. It has been totally neglected ever since the Venetians lost the city, and is now in a state of great dilapidation. This cathedral was dedicated to Saint Titus, the peculiar patron of his native island.

The Greeks of Crete, considering St Mark as the protector of their foreign lords, used themselves to raise the standard of St Titus, whenever they rebelled against the Most Serene Republic. This was also done by the Venetian colonists, when they rose against their mother country, and united themselves with the Greeks of the island. According to an old chronicler as soon as Lucchino dal Vermo obtained, at the head of the Venetian forces, a great victory over the rebels, 'he entered into the city of Candia, on the tenth of May 1364, put to death and destroyed many of the traitors, and took away the ensign of St Titus, replacing it by that of the Evangelist St Mark, with great festivity and rejoicing.'

It was in this cathedral that no less valuable a relique than the head of St Titus was preserved during the Venetian rule. According to the Christian legends of the middle ages, the body of the saint, who had been buried in his own cathedral, could never be found after the capture of Gortyna by the Saracens. His head, however, used to be exhibited on certain occasions, and with great solemnity, to the people of Megálo-Kástron. The Latin priests of Candia left not the precious relique within the walls of what, on their departure, became a Mohammedan city; but duly transported the so-called head of Titus to Venice, where it was deposited in the rich *Reliquiario* of St Mark's church…

Among the mosques of Megálo-Kástron is one called after Saint Catherine, its name being Haghía-Katerína-djamé [literally, the mosque of St. Catherine]. I suppose she must have been the saint to whom the building was dedicated before it received the accession of its minaret. The Mohammedans seem never to have had any reluctance to adopt the names of Greek saints, even when given to places of religious worship. Thus the Saint Sophia's church of the Christian has become the Haghía-Sophía-djamé of the Moslem. In Crete many villages continue to be called by the names of well-known Christian saints, even now that all their inhabitants have become Mohammedans: thus St Dionysius, St George, St John, and many other members of the celestial hierarchy, including even the Panaghía, no longer find a single worshipper within the places which were called by their names, and for many centuries were supposed to be under their especial protection.

There is scarcely any perceptible difference, to an eye neither practised nor skilful in observing articles of female apparel, between the dresses of Greek and Turkish ladies in this city. The Christian fair one conceals her charms from every eye, when she once leaves the interior of her husband's house, as completely as any of her Mohammedan neighbours. Before I was aware of this *Greek* concealment of the face, I was not a little surprised to find myself graciously regarded by a pair of eyes belonging, as I supposed, to some unknown Turkish lady, but which, as I afterwards found out, were those of my hostess. Her husband says that he thinks the custom even still more proper for a Greek's wife than for a Turk's; for if she did not observe it, she might attract the gaze of some true believer.

Although the supposition, that the seclusion of Greek women has arisen from an imitation of Turkish manners, is generally received; it may, I think, be shewn to be totally erroneous. The general practice of the ancient Greeks is well known: and, if we find the modern seclusion observed long before the Turkish conquest, we must assign it to its ancient source; and not to the influence of Asiatic manners imported by the Turks. Now there is ample evidence that, while the Venetians were masters of Crete, the Greek women used never to go out of their houses except to perform certain religious ceremonies. The Turks therefore found manners like their own, in this respect at least, on first landing in the island...

Khania possesses a most indifferent khamám or hot-bath. Those of Megálo-Kástron are comparatively excellent. The hot-baths of ancient Greece used to be frequented by both sexes quite as regularly as they are in modern Turkey.

The Turkish ladies seem also to resemble those of ancient Greece in another point: I mean in the extraordinary care which they bestow on their personal cleanliness [the prudish Pashley explains what he means in a learned footnote: 'Tournefort, Voyage, Lettre XIII. Vol. II. p. 94: 'Leur propreté est extraordinaire; elles se baignent deux fois la semaine, et ne souffrent pas le moindre poil, ni la moindre crasse, sur leur corps: tout cela contribue fort à leur santé.' The custom of depilation is also observed by the ladies of Persia: see the Kitabi Kulsum Naneh, or Customs and Manners of the Women of Persia, translated by Mr Atkinson,

Lond. 1832, pp. 17-18']. The peculiar practice to which I more especially allude, was general among the ladies of ancient Greece, at least with the young and beautiful, though not so with older matrons. It has not only been adopted by the female Mohammedans of Greece and Constantinople, but is also preserved, in some few places, among the Christian population.

I went this morning [March 2nd] to visit the Archbishop; whom I found surrounded by several episcopal dignitaries, and a few other persons. The conclave rose as I entered, and I had a seat assigned to me on the divan, to the right of the Metropolitan. The usual cup of coffee, and a modest pipe, unadorned of course by any such precious stones as are usually seen on that of a Turk of consideration, were presented to me: conserves were afterwards handed round.

The Archbishop is a tall and handsome man: his beard is long and his manner dignified. I had the misfortune of finding out, before I left his Holiness, that he is even more ignorant than is usually the case with individuals of his profession in these parts of the world. His Oekonómos however fully made up for the deficiencies of his superior. While I remained at the levee, several Greeks of the city came in to pay their respects to the Archbishop. On approaching the part of the divan, where he was seated, they touched the ground with the right hand: after kissing his Holiness's hand, they again touched the ground as before, while they retreated towards the entrance of the apartment.

The Bishops of the Oriental church are sometimes called Hierarchs, and sometimes High Priests, but more generally Despots. The latter lordly title they have long enjoyed, not, like the Bishops of England, in common with men, most of whom have greater fortunes and higher rank than their spiritual compeers, but as the peculiar address to which the Episcopal Dignitary is alone entitled. These Oriental ecclesiastics have certainly outstepped their western brethren in loud-sounding and pompous appellations, as much as they have fallen short of them in the enjoyment of the more substantial benefits both of a well-paid establishment and of temporal power. Every Greek Bishop, though, in a mere worldly view, sometimes little removed from the condition of Paul and the Apostles, the labour of whose hands ministered to their daily necessities, yet enjoys the title of *His Holiness*, which, at Rome, contents even the successor of St Peter. The Patriarch at Constantinople must, of course, be of superior sanctity to a common Bishop, and is therefore addressed as *His All-Holiness*.

What the peculiar holiness of these mitred dignitaries, under the sun of Greece, really is, may be easily conjectured when it is known that they are *monks*. Although the Greek church not only allows, but, perhaps wisely, *compels* all her working clergy to marry, still her Bishops can be united to the spouse of Christ alone; and are therefore chosen solely from the members of the monastic order.

Thus the Archbishop of Gortyna is, and must ever remain, an unmarried man. His Oekonómos, however, has a wife, who is generally considered, at Megálo-Kástron, as a very beautiful woman. This ecclesiastic, whose house adjoins on 'the Metropolis,' has to spend most of his time in visiting different parts of the Archbishop's extensive diocese; while his wife, of course, remains at home. The scandal of the city assigns a very obvious reason for the episcopal behests, in consequence of which the poor Oekonómos has so frequently to separate himself from the partner of his bed...

In the course of my conversation with the Archbishop, and the other prelates and priests assembled at the palace, I received a confirmation of what I had long supposed to be the case, that *no one* in the island, not even the dignified ecclesiastics with whom I conversed, knew of the existence of any other name than Krété, or Crete, to designate their country. The word Candia has never been pronounced by any Cretan unacquainted with the Italian language...

I learnt, from M. Godebout and other persons, that the Greek Archbishop adopted, on a recent occasion, a practice of the ancient Greeks and Romans, which is seldom observed by Christians, though of common occurrence at the festive entertainments of Mohammedan gentlemen. In order to enliven a party, at which the Pashá and Osmán-bey, as well as the consular agents and the principal Cretans of the city, were present, the Prelate procured the attendance of a number of dancing-girls...

From the levee of the Christian Archbishop I again went to the palace of the Mohammedan Governor-General. His answer to various requests, which I made for permission to excavate on ancient sites, to take sketches, and to draw plans, &c. &c. was uniformly a ready assent: 'Péke!' [Turkish: very well] He had just received information of the loss, by fire, in the port of Alexandria, of a new and beautiful frigate of 62 guns. The general, Osmán-bey, seemed greatly afflicted at the news: he observed to me that he feared they were not yet rightly disciplined, and said that, in the British navy, a lighted candle would not have been left on a wooden table. I mentioned the loss of the Kent East-Indiaman, which proved that, even with English discipline, such an accident might occur, and was therefore a ground of consolation to my Turkish friends.

I found the Pashá engaged this morning in the study of the military art, with a European instructor, a native of Corsica.

Mustafá-pashá has had ample experience in the warfare of *irregular* troops during the long struggle of the Cretans: but till lately was totally ignorant of the regular art of war...

The population of Megálo-Kástron is about 12,000 souls, 11,000 of whom are Mohammedans. Scarcely any change has been produced by the war in the number of its inhabitants. The places of many who perished have been taken by new settlers from the country. The small Mohammedan proprietor used to have his field tilled by his Christian neighbour, and is no longer able, under the rule of Mehmét-Alí, to continue the system of the good old times. Thus, knowing not either how to plough his field, or to dig his vineyard himself, he finds it easier to keep a shop in the city than to dwell on his land in the country. I was assured by many persons that this class of new residents at Megálo-Kástron is numerous.

Now let us hear Spratt's description of Herákleion.

Spratt, I, p. 28, 29, 34 – 42

When Crete came into the hands of the Venetians, the town of Candia was about one-third of its present size, the inner wall of its fortifications of the time of the Genoese being still in parts traceable; and its old land gateway (which led to the south) was, until recently, the town-prison and guardhouse, and stood in the centre of the main street of the present city.

The Venetians not only greatly extended the limits of the town, but embellished it with eight large churches, several fountains, and some fine public buildings, of which latter the Armoury, in the main street, is still a handsome relic, of two stories, combining the Doric and Corinthinian orders. And the large ruined church of St. Titus, over the eastern part of the fortifications, was, for such a town, of cathedral proportions and style of architecture: a handsome entrance and circular window over, and part of an elegant baptistry attached to it, are still standing.

But the wide and noble ditch surrounding the fortifications (and excavated out of the solid rock) which encompass three parts of the city, the fine bastions and high curtains connecting them, as also the several out-works constructed around the extended lines by the Venetians, are still monuments of their wealth, power, and skill.

Candia was consequently the best-fortified and finest city of its time in the Levant. Retiring from the shore upon gently rising land, it has a fine although not an imposing appearance from the sea,– few of its buildings or fortifications, except those near the sea-defences, being very conspicu-ous; for the houses of the upper part of the town, which the Venetians called New Candia, are mostly now, as in their time, of a single story...

The Turks, on gaining possession of the city, took immediate steps to restore its defences and repair its breaches, and also its public buildings and churches, all of which were, excepting the Greek, converted into mosques. But their usual apathy and neglect during recent times, com-bined with occasional earthquakes (more particularly the severe one of 1856, which was felt throughout the East), have greatly damaged both for-tifications and churches, seriously injuring also the public buildings as well as many of the habitations. The principal minarets were at the same time thrown down, and several of the galley-arches within the port fell in, so great were the shocks felt in Candia.

The piers enclosing the old port are for the most part old moles, that formed the later seaport of Gnossus. It was, however, always too limited and too shallow to admit the larger and principal trading-vessels of the Venetians, which in consequence anchored within one of the two eastern bays that indent the southern shore of the Island of Standia [Dhía], lying opposite to it. The bays of Standia were therefore the emporium or prin-cipal trading-port of Crete during its occupation by the Saracens and Venetians, as also during the Turkish occupation; and Candia remained its capital.

The rising of Greece against her oppressors, in 1821, aroused the patri-ots of Crete at the same time, who maintained the struggle, with varied fortune, against the forces of the Sultan and of Mehemet Ali, until the battle of Navarino liberated Greece, in 1828, when Crete was ceded to the powerful Viceroy of Egypt, for the part he had taken against it, and the governorship of the island was given to his able Albanian General Mustapha Pacha, who retained it for twenty years, and who deepened the old port of Candia by dredging, and rendered it available for trade.

But when the island passed back from Mehemet Ali to the Sultan again in 1841, after the fall of Acre, Khania was chosen as the seat of govern-ment, from its proximity to the Bay of Suda, and from possessing also a more capacious and convenient port within it, combined with the other cogent reasons – of policy, and local tranquility.

The town of Candia is now therefore only the second city of Crete, although the largest, the most populous, and the most healthy. It is, however, a separate Sanjak under the Governor-general, who resides at Khania; and the subordinate pashalic of Candia includes the whole of the division of the island lying eastward of the natural limits formed by Mount Ida. It contains about 13,000 inhabitants, Turks and Greeks, the former being the majority...

To the south of the city lies a large Turkish cemetery, which, unlike Turkish graveyards in general, is without a single cypress tree; it is, in consequence, a mere forest of tombstones, of interest only from containing many that fell in the great siege, and for the ancient fragments that may be found in it.

The eastern approach perhaps possesses the greater interest to the stranger, from its being here that the Duc de Beaufort fell. St. George's Gate, which leads to it from near the centre of the lines, was both strongly constructed and well defended; it opens from the parade-ground near the Turkish barracks [now the Plateía Eleftherías]. This gate being much higher than the ditch and valley lying close under it upon this side of the city, the covered way and approach has a considerable descent, and is thus well commanded by the lines above. After passing through this gate, the traveller is sure to encounter a group of miserable-looking objects lying by the wayside and imploring the charity of every passer-by. They are lepers – and in all stages of this terrible disease: on the opposite side of the valley is their village – the location to which all the lepers of the district are driven, and where they pass the rest of their days after the disease has been pronounced to exist upon them.

This day there were eleven lepers waiting at the St. George's Gate for the charity of passengers; and as they were an interesting group, I stopped to make some inquiries of them, which they freely answered. Ten of the group were ranged on the ground, under the angle of the high bastion, just without the gateway; the other, the eleventh, was apart from them, and an object of great commiseration from his disfigured condition and age, being nearly sixty. He had only been twelve years a leper, however; but his disease had been so rapid, that he was perfectly blind, and dreadfully swollen and disfigured in limbs and face, and hid his hands and feet in filthy bags of old rags, to hide their sores and deformities from the public, whose charity he solicited. He was seated in a small shed on the opposite side of the way, apart from his companions, from an apparent consciousness that he was almost too hideous to meet the eye of his fellow-man; and sad and singular it was to learn, that he had only been joined by his daughter about ten days previous. She, at the age of eighteen, and leaving a mother behind, had then, at the age of hope and promise, been driven from her village-home for ever, to be an outcast from friends and relations, in companionship, and with the stigma, of a leper! but yet just in time to become a comfort to her long outcast, and now helpless father, during his fast declining hours of misery. On first seeing her, although seated with the unmistakeable lepers, I could not believe she was one of them, being neatly dressed, of considerable beauty, though pale, and by no means overcast with melancholy, or indicating feelings of mental grief and depression at her new position and miserable prospects. I was induced therefore to ask her if she really was a leper; and she immediately showed me her hands, still delicate and fair, but with two of her fingers slightly bent and stiff. These unmistakeable symptoms, to those who know the early appearance of the disease, had only appeared on her about six months previously, when she was immediately placed under the surveillance of the matrons of the village, who then jealously watch any suspicious spots, from a general belief in its contagious nature. The signs of the foul spot or malady becoming more developed and evident during this time, together with the fact of her father being also a leper, were considered decisive. She was consequently now driven from her home, to become for ever the companion of corruption and misery; and, even on the tenth day of her exile, here she sat, compelled to seek alms on the public approach to a large city, and to meet the cold gaze and indifference of the passers-by. The healthy mind shudders, naturally, at the sight and contemplation of such a condition and future for one so young and attractive.

But perhaps even this change of scene was a relief from the sickening sights of the lepers' village; or perhaps she was buoyed up in spirit by the support and comfort she could now give to her helpless and dying parent. I could account for her apparent apathy from no other cause. 'God tempers the wind to the shorn lamb' – a truth we so often realize; and surely these poor objects need that the sensibilities of the mind should be tempered under the helpless condition of advancing disease and corruption, and, what is worse, the cold neglect of their fellow-creatures. 'To be put under the ground would be better than life,' was, however, the feeling reply of one poor woman, with whom I had exchanged a few words at another gate.

By the side of the girl on the right hand were seated two lepers, man and wife, who had a child, now six or seven months old, and lying in the arms of the latter, and which had been born to them after being married and residents in the leper's village eight years! I learn from them that about seventy families compose this village, of which thirty-two are Turks, numbering in all III persons. What a life and reflections await these poor children on becoming conscious of their condition – burthens to society from their birth! for no employment can be sought for by them, as nothing from their tainted hands would obtain a sale, even if their stiffened fingers could be turned to hard work or handicraft.

It is with satisfaction, then, that I learn that the Turkish Government has recently shown some thought for these afflicted members of the community, by ordering half an oke of bread per diem to be given to every leper. This tardy charity is to them a great boon and relives the local government of this island from a great blot, and was given during the government of Vely Pacha.

Let us now, then, look at their village; for it is close at hand. And what are their habitations there? Why, they are chiefly the walled-up caves and tombs of the ancient Cretans – or the excavations made by the Turks, during the great siege, into the side of a ravine in the low ridge which bounds the valley east of the city, either for their magazines or for winter-quarters.

The lepers' village being only a distance of fifteen or twenty minutes' walk, it is therefore deserving of a visit, if it be only to learn a small lesson of the state of social feeling in this island at the present time, and to feel the sympathy that must be awakened at beholding such a community of outcasts, who are thus living in social degradation, purely because they are the neglected victims of a loathsome and erroneously supposed incurable disease.

Lear also visited the city, on May 9th, 1864. The quotation begins when Lear is still in Réthymnon. Farther along Lear calls Herákleion 'earthquaky.' The reason for this is the great earthquake that hit the city in 1856, traces of which were still visible in 1864.

Lear, p. 63 – 65

Rose at four, and got all things packed. Coffee by five, and off 5.15, sitting on the ramparts drawing till seven. The lepers at both gates are horrible here. We also went on the sands till nearly nine, and then to the port, to

Austrian Lloyd's about the steamer, returning 'home' by 10.15. Pretty hot it is. T'other captain's ship has arrived.

What a pavement is this of Rethymnon! I buy a good blanket of Sphakian make for 300 piastres.

At twelve we dine: George Kalokairinós, Mr Harálambos and the pleasant woman his wife. After dinner talked with Kalokairinós, disturbed by small children's outbreax, about the island, etc. He is after all a kindly cove, but the sneaky Ionian manner is a bore. Abruptiously the steamer is announced. More abruptly a second summons, and we rush out, I beholding three large black men taking all my roba. The children jump and shriek 'all over the place', George endeavours to penetrate the *harem* or γυναικῶν to thank Mrs Harálambos, but only meets the old lady and not the Graziosa. The old lady (who is the most frightful caricature of Lady Farquhar possible) twirls about and says, 'Τί νά κάμουμε;' ['What are we to do?'] Rethymnon life draws to a close. Altogether the proximate advent of the *atmópleon* [steamer] is an interesting circumstance. George, who never forgets those who are kind to him, is bebothered at not being able to thank Mrs H. It is only 1.30 now; steamer not in. Endless fuss. I go to the 'shop' or *empórion*; George looks after the luggage. Fuss at *Dogana* – very ridiculous. At last, off in a boat about 2.30. Found Consul Hay on board (and Henry Moazza), but he is not going ashore, for they say we are to start soon.

And so we did, at 2.45 or 3, to my surprise. Very fine and smooth. Rethymnon soon faded away, and no particular beauty followed.

Dinner. The jokes of the three captains of the *Persia* are not appreciated. After dinner on deck; some views of Ida are fine, but it is soon lost behind the great northern bluff coast cliffs. Near Candia the scene opens out at once, and is at least promising so far as being wide and open, with Mount Juktas very conspicuous. Great delay and immense row in landing, the port being very small. Bore in the boat, and in going ashore: a hustle and savagery not outdone in Jaffa. The landing was a regular misery. We go to the Vice-Consul's house (he having come off for Mr Hay) and preceded by many lanterns thread the dark streets for a short distance and arrive at Mr Kalokairinós' [Lysimachos Kalokairinós], where several courts, etc., lead to a large room: the Consul has a bedroom out of this; I one full of boxes and very nasty, up a narrow stair; a clerk, Moazza and G. Kalokairinós sleeping in closets out of this again. Supper is served. Mrs Kalokairinós speaks a little French and is a nice sort of woman. The Vice-Consul is a pleasant little man, and very rich. Hay not eating, and they pressing him, are mutual bores. Bed at eleven. A most horrible and filthy amount of bugs developed, on my bed and all over the place.

O bugs! I caught 34! Read newspapers. Rose 5.50. Poor George has got no sleep as the hole he is put into is filthier than where I am. Out on the walls at 6.30 with a fat guide. Ruined cathedral, ruined but splendid walls and fortifications. Views of Mount Juktas, and of Ida. Town mealy-ruiny, earthquaky, odious. We return at nine from going round the walls, from which are good views of Juktas and Ida, but the aspect of the distance is rather large than lovely. The Consul has to hear no end of affairs from Kalokairinós, and I found it no easy matter to wedge in questions relating to my own plans. I intend to go round Ida as far as may be coincident with a possible future plan of going into Sphakiá by the south coast...

The walk round the walls this morning: utter ruin and mishmash qua town and forts, but much picturesqueness qua distance; Juktas and Ida, which last however seems only a higher snow range of a long and rather gloomy wall of hills. Below it, looking east, the plains are green; but it is hardly possible to make any drawing of any part of the city, which lies low sloping to the sea, and is of uniformly flat-topped houses, broken mosques and palms here and there. The Venetian cathedral, a ruin-skeleton, speaks of former days. We came back by the bazaars – very ordinary and disagreeable – only the streets are somewhat wider than in other towns. Altogether a nastier and less interesting Turkish town I was never in, and the paved streets are frightful. At ten, having returned, I slept, and Mrs Kalokairinós came and apologized for the B flats.

9. Knossós and Arkhánes

Fifteen kilometers southeast of Herákleion the 800-meter-high Yioúkhtas rises up. From the Yioúkhtas to the north, in the basin of the Kaíratos (also called the Silamianós), lies the heartland of Minoan Crete (see the map on page 132-133). Here lies Knossós, with its gigantic palace complex where the legendary Minos was king and where Theseus once slew the Minotaur. And even now, in spite of the masses of tourists, the palace still inspires feelings of awe and admiration.

In the south rise the two peaks of the Yioúkhtas. According to tradition the tomb of Zeus is here (that the Cretans believed the immortal Zeus could die was reason for the philosopher Epimenides to proclaim that the Cretans were liars; this judgment was repeated by St. Paul in his letter to St. Titus, and it plagued the Cretans for many centuries after that). And the Yioúkhtas did have connections with the gods: on the northern peak is a small Minoan sanctuary (Anemospília) with a view of the faraway palace at Knossós. And on the southern summit was a peak sanctuary, by the present church of Aféndis Khristós. A few remains of the sanctuary are still evident. Both peaks are truly worth a visit, especially for their extraordinary sweeping views. On the southern flank of the Yioúkhtas, by Vathýpetro, there is an ancient Minoan 'villa,' a cultic, administrative, and economic center. Here there is also a wonderful view across the farmlands of Témenos and Malevísi towards the hills of Profítis Ilías and Áyios Thomás.

Above the basin of the Kaíratos, encircled by vineyards against the northern slope of the Yioúkhtas, lies Áno Arkhánes with its fascinating Minoan excavations. It bears sad recollections of World War II when the village's inhabitants were pursued because of the abduction of General Kreipe in 1944, which took place close to the village.

THE PAST

The region was inhabited in the Neolithic Period: on the site of Knossós there was a settlement as far back as about 6000 B.C. And remains of large structures, probably having cultic and administrative functions, have been preserved from the end of the third millennium B.C. In the Proto-palatial Period the so-called First Palace stood here, which was destroyed by an earthquake in around 1700 B.C. At this time, at the sanctuary of Anemospília on the northern peak of the Yioúkhtas, a drama took place which was probably connected with this earthquake. Excavations show that a young man of about eighteen was sacrificed here with a bronze knife. As the priest and priestess who performed the sacrifice soon after became themselves the victims of an earthquake, the sacrifice probably was meant to ward the earthquake off. Against the slope of the Yioúkhtas, by Áno Arkhánes, lay the necropolis of Foúrni where beehive tombs, shaft graves, and tomb buildings from 2500 B.C. until the Mycenaean Period have been found.

In the Neopalatial Period the extensive and complex New Palace of Knossós was built on the site of the First Palace. It is doubtful that this was really a palace with a king and queen, and royal rooms with a bathing room and a throne, as its discoverer Evans thought. More plausible is that the complex had first of all a cultic function, as a temple, with rituals centered around a goddess, religious dancing, and a bull cult. It is plausible that the goddess 'appeared' to the believers, in the form of an image or the guise of a priestess, above the room which Evans christened the 'Throne Room.' The Central Court and the Theatral Area could have been used for the dancing and the bull cult. The lustral basins were perhaps imitations of caves which often had cultic functions in the Minoan religion. Moreover, the 'palace' had administrative and economic functions. Also in Áno Arkhánes remains have been uncovered from a Neopalatial complex which was probably a 'palace.'

Around 1500 B.C. the palace of Knossós was struck by catastrophe. The volcano on the island of Thíra, c. 100 kilometers to the north of Crete, erupted and partly collapsed, sending a dreadful tidal wave to the island and covering the eastern part of the island and the sea between Crete and Rhodes with a thick layer of pumice and ash. The era of the Minoans was over. It appears that the Akhaians [Greek-speaking inhabitants of the mainland who were influenced by Minoan civilization, having Mycene on the Peloponnesos as their center] took advantage of the resulting power vacuum and captured Crete and Knossós, where they rebuilt the palace (the name of the city appears in the Linear B: ko-no-so). The palace of Knossós was, however, once again destroyed around 1350 and then left deserted.

So now the Cretans were allies of, or subservient to, the Greek Akhaians. In all likelihood the Akhaians were identical to the Ahhiyawa from Hittite texts and the Ekwesh from Egyptian sources. So they were part of the so-called Sea Peoples who in the 13th century B.C., as 'vikings,' made the lands around the eastern part of the Mediterranean Sea unsafe with their plundering expeditions. The story of the Trojan War, where Cretans fought on the side of the Akhaians and which has been dated at around 1200 B.C. by both Greek historians and modern archeology, is probably an echo of these marauding expeditions.

But what happened then? Around 1200 B.C. the Mycenaean civilization largely disappeared from Greece, not only on the mainland but also in Crete. Scholars still argue about the reasons for this disappearance. According to some, attacks on the Mycenaean cities by the Sea Peoples were the cause. But there is another possibility, assuming that the Akhaians themselves were part of the Sea Peoples, as mentioned above. In 1176 B.C. the Sea Peoples were crushingly defeated by the Egyptian Pharaoh Ramses III in a sea battle off the coast of Egypt. It is known that their fleet was also destroyed. Apparently without a fleet and far away from home the Akhaian fighters were not in a condition to return to their cities on the Peloponnesos. This may have been the end, thus, to the Mycenaean civilization.

And the Cretans? It is known that in the 12th century B.C. the Philistines settled in Palestine. These Philistines are usually identified with the Peleshet who are named in Egyptian sources as one of the Sea Peoples.

Now, the Peleshet came from Keftiu or Kaftor, one of the names for Crete in that period. So it is possible that after the defeat by Ramses III these Cretans escaped and went to Palestine. In that case it was the descendants of Minoan Cretans who were fought against by the Biblical King David

The temple of Ramses III in Medinet Habu in Egypt, where among other things the victory over the Sea Peoples is noted, probably preserves a remembrance of the tidal wave which had hit Crete earlier, perhaps written down from the mouth of a captive Peleshet:

> The might of the Ocean broke out and fell on our towns and villages in a great wave ... and the head of the cities [of the Sea Peoples] on the sacred island went under the sea; their land is no more.

What happened after the Akhaians disappeared, and with them Mycenaean civilization? Again, there is much uncertainty. Apparently, all around the eastern Mediterranean civilization decreased. This period is therefore usually referred to as the Dark Ages. According to later Greeks there was a huge migration around 1000 B.C.: Greek-speaking Dorians with iron weapons marched into Greece and settled themselves on the Peloponnesos and on Crete, where they put an end to the established civilization. But this migration is often doubted by modern scholarship. Whatever the truth about the migration, what matters here is that at the end of the Dark Ages on the Peloponnesos and Crete mutual comparable city-states flourished, and that those cities were often inhabited by Doric-speaking Greeks. On Crete numerous such city-states came into being, such as Aptéra, Láppa, Eléftherna and Axós. Knossós also flourished again during this time. The center of the city now lay somewhat more to the north than in the Minoan-Mycenaean Period (the remains of it largely disappeared during the building of Candia/Herákleion). From the 8th century B.C. until Roman times and the First Byzantine Period, Knossós was one of the most prominent cities in Crete. It disputed dominion over central Crete with Górtyn and Lýttos. Knossós became the seat of a bishopric after the arrival of Christianity.

In Venetian times the city of Knossós appears to have lost all its prestige, to the benefit of nearby Candia. But the area south of Knossós, around Arkhánes, remained important, in particular because of the wine which was produced there (Arkhánes wine is still famous). Various Orthodox churches date from this time. Among these are the Ayía Triádha,

View from the Yioúkhtas

with 14th century frescos, and the Panayía, with its sculptures on the out-side wall, in Arkhánes; and the Mikhaíl Arkhángelos church (also with extraordinary 14th century frescos) in nearby Asómatos. The cavernous church at the monastery of Panayía Spiliótissa, close to the village of Áyios Vasílios, has frescos which date from before 1500, and in the neigh-bourhood of the monastery the Áyios Ioánnis church has frescos from 1291. Another remembrance from Venetian times is the aqueduct which Morosini the Elder had built in 1628 for the fountain named after him in Herákleion. Remains of this aqueduct can still be seen at Knossós.

The Ottoman besiegers of Herákleion between 1648 and 1669 were, as mentioned earlier, encamped at Fortétsa, close to Knossós, and the remains of Knossós were harmed even more because of this.

After the departure of the Venetians the region kept up its important agricultural function, and wine was still produced. The uprising of 1821-1830 also took its toll here. As elsewhere, the population here was deci-mated.

The still imposing aqueduct over the Kaíratos (called Silamianós here) at Spília, built between 1830 and 1840 for the water supply at Herákleion, is a memory from the rule of the *khedive* of Egypt. As it appears from Spratt's report, the population remained hopeful of liberation from the Ottoman yoke.

THE TRAVEL DESCRIPTIONS

Modern visitors often think that Arthur Evans discovered the ruins of Knossós in 1899/1900. But that was not actually the case. It had long been known that there were ruins at Knossós which had a connection with King Minos. In 1739, for example, Pococke visited the ruins.

Pococke, p. 255, 256

The spot where the small remains of old Cnossus are, is now called Can-dake, doubtless from the trenches which the Turks made there round their camp, that being the meaning of the word in modern Greek. It is a level spot of ground of a small extent, encompassed with low hills. To the south of it there is an eminence, on the top of which is a village called Enadieh [Fortétsa]. The Turks bombarded Candia from this spot, being encamped on the site of the antient Cnossus. It is probable this hill was part of the antient city, and that the fortress was built on it, for the plain is not four miles in circumference.

Strabo [the Greek historian and geographer who wrote an important description of the then known world during the time of the emperor Augustus] describes this place as five stadia distant from the sea, between which and the city there is a rising ground, and two little hills on it, appearing at a distance like barrows. On the east side there is the bed of a winter torrent, which may be the river Ceratus that ran by the city, from which, in very antient times, it had its name.

This city was twenty five miles from Gortynia, and is famous for having been the residence of king Minos, where he had his palace. The labyrinth also was here, concerning which there are so many fables, but even in the time of Pliny there were no remains of it. This city was a Roman colony. Heraclea was its port; but in the time of Minos, Amniso was used as its harbour, where there was a temple to Lucina, which possibly might be at the mouth of the river Cartero near Candia, where Homan has a place called Animos. I take the torrent east of Cnossus to be that which is called Curnos by this geographer.

Cnossus was also famous for its bows and arrows, and for a dextrous use of that sort of arms.

There are some little remains of the walls, especially to the north, which shew its extent that way; and there are four or five heaps of ruins about the little plain, but there is only one which can give an idea of what it was, and it would even be difficult to determine for what use this was intended. It is an oblong square fabric of rough stone, but seems to have been cased either with hewn stone or brick. To the north there are fifteen arches, which are six feet wide. There are the same number of arches on the south side, which are about eighteen feet deep, like the arches on which the seats of theatres are built. The space within the building is about forty five feet wide. About a quarter of a mile to the west of the town there is a building near the road, which is ten feet square within. The walls are six feet thick, and cased with brick inside and out. It seems to have been some antient sepulchre. The people say it is the tomb of Caiaphas, and the most modest account they give of it is, that he landed at this place, where he died and was buried, that his body being found above ground, they buried it again, which happened seven times, and at last they built this strong fabric over it, which, they say, prevented its rising again, to which they add many other circumstances equally ridiculous. I mention this only to shew that the people of Crete have now as great a genius for inventing and spreading fables, as they had in the times of Paganism. It is said that several thousand Venetians sallying out to attack the Turks on the hill of Enadieh, were repulsed with a great slaughter in the valley to the west of it, a pannic having seized them on the accidental blowing up of some gunpowder.

Pashley also visited Knossós, on March 3rd 1834, arriving from Herá-kleion.

Pashley, I, p. 203, 204

I rode, attended only by Captain Maniás, past the village of Fortezza to 'Cave-Bridge,' near which I noticed several caverns, and many ancient sepulchres excavated in the rocky sides of the neighbouring hills.

We are here in the immediate vicinity of the site of Cnossos, and I suppose this stream to be the ancient Tethris, or Theron, in the neighbourhood of which, according to the Cretan tradition, the marriage of Zeus and Heré was celebrated. The event was commemorated by annual sacrifices and ceremonies, performed in a temple erected on the spot, and in which a mimetic representation of the marriage was exhibited to the gaze of the assembled Cretans. Other traditions assigned a different locality to this supposed union of Zeus and Heré, and the words of Theocritus make it obvious that the question was one of recondite mythology in his day.

From Cave-bridge I proceeded to Mákro-teíkho, undoubtedly the site of Cnossos. All the now existing vestiges of the ancient 'metropolis' of Crete, are some rude masses of Roman brick-work, part of the so-called long wall from which the modern name of the site has been derived.

After a long exposé in which Pashley discusses Knossós in the ancient world, but without describing what he saw at Makritíkhos, he ends his visit disappointed.

Pashley, p. 209

The mythological celebrity and historical importance of Cnossos, demand a more careful and minute attention than can be bestowed on them in a mere book of travels. But, since I write as a traveller, and nothing more remains to be examined at Mákro-Teíkho, I shall at once bid farewell to this capital of ancient Crete, which, even after the Roman conquest, remained for some time a considerable city, but, under the Venetian and Turkish rule, has dwindled down into this miserable hamlet, and the few shapeless heaps of masonry, which alone recall to the remembrance of the passing traveller its ancient and bygone splendour.

Spratt also visited Knossós, in 1853.

Spratt, I, p. 58 – 60

It occupied no remarkable site; the spot was not characteristic for its strength nor of striking appearance like the positions of the earliest Greek cities in general: it stood, for the most part, upon a low undulating plain between two parallel ravines, but terminating in two rather abrupt eminences on the south and west, one of which has still vestiges of the walls of a tower upon it, and gives its Italianized name to the small village of Fortezza lying over it, and apparently indicating the position of one of the exterior defences or towers of the city walls, but of a later time. On the north the site of the city was terminated by a lower and smooth-featured eminence,- the city having altogether a circuit of fully six miles in extent. It is bounded on the east by a narrow and rocky ravine, with a rivulet that intersects the white tertiary freestone and marls constituting the chief part of the undulating ridges lying southward of the town of Candia.

The hamlet of Makri Teikos, or Long Wall, is situated within the limits of the ancient city, by the side of the rivulet; and although the identity of the site is not to be disputed, as being that of the capital of Minos, which was also a fine city even in the time of Strabo, who, too, for a time resided in it, yet the only vestiges of Gnossus at the present time are some scattered foundations and a few detached masses of masonry of the Roman time. The entire surface is almost wholly cultivated and unfenced, but throughout indicates the remains of a dense city, from the vast quantity of stones and fragments of pottery that are intermixed with the soil.

This is all that at present remains of Gnossus. But in the time of the Venetians, Belli [also mentioned by Spratt in Chapter 3] shows that there was still existing the remains of a curiously constructed theatre or circus; the plan of it, however, was not sufficiently distinct, to Belli, to be given in the manuscript, the relics of which have been recently published by Mr. Falkener in the 'Museum of Classical Antiquities.' The site of it is now recognizable in the centre of the tract; and the detached masses of masonry before noticed seem to be the very remains of the buttresses of its arches or vaults.

The cause of this great demolition and disappearance of its buildings and fragments is doubtless due to the recent rising up of so large and so well fortified a town as Candia near it; and within its fortifications, therefore, lie the chief relics of Gnossus. The old site is still resorted to, and dug over, for material for the construction or repair of any important building within Candia that may require it, extensive excavations being sometimes made in search of the foundations of its old walls or buildings in consequence.

Knossós may have been a bit disappointing, but that was not true of the visit to the Yioúkhtas. Reading between the lines of the descriptions, it is easy to see how the travellers enjoyed the charms of the scenery, the beautiful panoramic views, and the mystic feeling which the mountain conjured up, even though there were not many antiquities to be seen. We begin with Pashley, who left Herákleion on March 5th, 1834.

Pashley, I, p. 210 – 212

We left Megálo-Kástron early this afternoon, and soon past Fortezza a little on our left. In somewhat less than an hour and a half, we quitted the undulating and cultivated surface of the plain which surrounds the capital of the island, and began to ascend the stony slopes of the eastern side of Mount Júktas. At length we saw before us, on a slightly rising ground, the village of Arkhánes, about which are a few olives and cypresses.

I was of course anxious to hear something of the sepulchre of Zeus; but it was in vain that I enquired of my host, Dhemétrio's brother, for any cave on the mountain. He knew of nothing of the kind; and all that I could learn from him was that, about a mile off, there is a fountain with an inscription on it. When I had thus failed in obtaining any information about the cave, I said, rather meaning to tell him an old story, than supposing that I should learn any thing, that one Zeus, a god of the Hellenes, was said to have been buried there; and that is was his tomb that I wished to see. I had pronounced the very name by which a place on the summit of the mountain is known to all the people in the neighbourhood, although only a few shepherds have ever seen it. My host had never heard it called by any other name than the tomb of Zeus, and therefore had not understood me at first, when I inquired after a cave. It was too late to visit the top of Júktas to-night: so I went to look at the fountain, which is in a stony valley at the foot of the hill, and is distant about a mile to the north of the village. Its waters join those of an aqueduct which passes close by it, conveying a copious stream from Mount Júktas to the city. A Latin inscription tells us that it was the work of Francesco Morosini, the Proveditore of Crete in 1627, when the chief city was in great want of water.

Over the doorway of the church of the Panaghía, at this village of Arkhánes, are bas-reliefs seemingly of the time of the Venetians. Epáno-Arkhánes still contains about 150 houses: at Káto-Arkhánes there are only 30. The government, here as in most other places, now receives the tithe, or rather the seventh, of all the produce. The chief growth of the village is its wine, which is excellent.

What I learn from individuals with whom I become acquainted in my travels, gives me a lively idea of the widely spread misery, and of the destruction of human life, brought about in Crete between 1821 and 1830. My host here lost his father and three brothers: his wife's father and one of her brothers were also put to death by the Mohammedans. The poor woman took these afflictions so heavily, that she died of grief. After losing her my host could not flee to the mountains with two young children, and therefore went and lived for three years in the Kástron.

This village contains no less than nine churches, its population being entirely Christian. In five alone is service ever performed, and of these only regularly at the Panaghías. The people attend at the other churches on the particular festivals of their respective Saints. There is, about two miles off, a monastery of the Panaghía Spelaeótissa which has now only six or eight kalógheri.

The following day, March 6th, Pashley climbed the northern peak of the mountain.

Pashley, I, 212 – 217, 220

I found, as a guide up the mountain, a shepherd who had become acquainted with the tomb of Zeus in tending his flock. A good hour was spent in reaching the summit, towards the northern extremity of which I observed foundations of the massive walls of a building the length of which was about eighty feet. Within this space is an aperture in the ground, which may perhaps once have led into a moderate-sized cave; but, whatever may have been its former size, it is now so filled up, that a man cannot stand in it, and its diameter is not above eight or ten feet.

These then are the only remains of that object of deep religious veneration, the supposed tomb of 'the Father of gods and men' with its celebrated inscription,

All which devouring Time, in his so mighty waste,
Demolishing those walls, hath utterly defac'd:

So that the earth doth feel the ruinous heaps of stones,
That with their burd'nous weight now press his sacred bones.

I now stand on the spot, in which Zeus was supposed to be at rest from all celestial and terrestrial cares, and which was so celebrated during many ages! The testimony of a long series of ancient and ecclesiastical authors, proves fully and distinctly, that the tomb remained an object of curiosity to strangers, and of veneration to the Cretans, from an early period till after the age of Constantine. The legal establishment of Christianity, as the paid religion of the state, by that Emperor, did but little in Greece towards extinguishing the ancient superstitions...

We find that the Cretans continued to worship the old deities of their island, and to venerate the tomb of Zeus, half a century after this legal establishment of Christianity throughout the empire. It was only when the Spaniard Theodosius made himself the blind instrument of orthodox fanatics, and annexed the severest penalties to the celebration of the sacrifices and ceremonies of the old religion, that the corrupted Christianity of the fourth century prevailed...

A well-known couplet of Callimachus accuses the Cretans of being liars, because they asserted that the immortal Zeus had been buried in a tomb, which, as the poet says, was the work of their own hands. I know not why the religious zeal of this learned writer should have taken offence at the Cretan tradition that Zeus was buried in the land of his birth. According to other ancient legends similar fates befell many of the gods. Hermes was interred at Hermopolis, Ares in Thrace, Aphrodite in Cyprus, and the tomb of the Theban Dionysos was long shewn at Delphi. It is evident that, if Zeus was not exempted from the common lot of humanity, he could have no fitter resting-place than in his native island...

Little as I found at this spot to repay me for the trouble of the ascent, I had at all events the pleasure of an extensive view over the whole plain of the Kástron. Dhía lies nearly to the north: and to the north-east is pointed out to me the direction of the village of Khersónesos, and in the mountains to the east of us I learn that there is a place called Lýttos, where, no doubt, I shall find remains of the celebrated Dorian city. Our view is bounded to the west by the mountains, Strómbolo, Khruseanótika-Livádia, and Amurghiéles.

On the eastern side of the mountain, and about a hundred paces from its summit, I found considerable remains of ancient walls. The construction is chiefly of very large stones, among which a good many small ones were intermixed. Some of the latter have fallen out in places. These fragments seem to offer a good specimen of the so-called first cyclopean style. They are four or five in number, and the whole length of the ground, which they partially cover, is between four and five hundred paces, of which not more than fifty paces are occupied by the actually existing remains. It is, however, evident that the old walls extended all round the summit, except where, as on its western side, it is nearly a perpendicular precipice. Above this wall I observed, scattered over the ground, many pieces of ancient pottery, which, as well as the wall, would rather serve to indicate an abode of the living than a restingplace of the dead.

On descending down the side of the mountain, we found in the ground, about half way down, a hole, the diameter of which is twelve feet, and its depth about ninety or a hundred feet. As far as I can judge by visible appearances from the outside, it leads into a cavern; which, since the rock is limestone, is probable full of beautiful stalactites, and is certainly as yet unexplored.

Pashley had no opportunity to examine the cave – undoubtedly to his disappointment, as he was a lover of cave exploration – but had to return to Arkhánes. Spratt also visited the Yioúkhtas, at the beginning of his exploration of Crete.

Spratt, I, p. 78 – 84, 86 – 88

Iuktas is traditionally supposed to have been a mountain that was held in great sanctity by the ancient Cretans, and even long after the Christian era; for it seems to have been regarded as the burial-place of the 'God of men', of Jupiter [Zeus] himself; and the myths and mysteries of that superstition and religion, which Christianity finally swept away, long held this spot in special veneration. And although it is a mere hill, as compared with the lofty Ida that directly overlooks it, its form and isolation amidst lower land give it a striking appearance from all sides, especially in the approach to Candia by sea.

Pashley visited this mountain in 1838 [Spratt is mistaken here]; and as I now tread upon the footsteps of a scholar who has described it and the few remains that he found there, and who regarded it as the site of the sepulchre, or rather states that it was anciently so regarded and venerated, I shall quote his enthusiastic words. 'I now stand,' says Pashley, 'upon

the spot on which Zeus is supposed to be at rest from all celestial and terrestrial cares, and which was so celebrated for so many ages. The testimony of a long series of ancient and ecclesiastical authors proves fully
and distinctly that the tomb remained an object of curiosity and veneration to the Cretans from an early period until after the age of Constantine.'

The spot thus spoken of by the above traveller has some few Cyclopean foundations, at a small cavern situated upon the northern brow of
the mountain, which has two summits, lying nearly north and south of
each other, and nearly of equal elevation. They are distant about a mile
apart; so that from the sea they appear as one sharp peak, but from the
east and west the hill has a saddle-backed form, bare, rugged, and grey
(the characteristic colour of all cliffy and naked rocks of limestone),
especially on its east and west faces. The hill is an insular mass of hippu-
ritic limestone rising out of the surrounding strata of tertiary marls and
whitish-yellow limestone.

As a spot, then, that seems to have been regarded by the Pagan wor-
shippers, of a late as well as an early period, with something of the rev-
erence that Mecca is held in by the Mahomedan, and Jerusalem by the
Christian, I am induced to dwell upon the way to it, recommending a
visit to the mountain by every traveller to this part of Crete, from its easy
accessibility from the town of Candia, and the command of view he will
obtain over the surrounding country, more than from the interest he perhaps will feel in the few old stones to be seen there, either of the supposed tomb of Jupiter or of the habitations for the priests that guarded its
sanctity.

The way to the mountain, after leaving Candia, is through the half
Turkish and half Greek village of Phortetsa, over Gnossus, whence can
again be obtained a glance down upon the undulating ground under it to
the east – the site of this once important and interesting old city. But now
how different the aspect, to what it was then! – either green with the lux-
uriant crops of corn that year by year grow from the fertile soil that has
accumulated upon its remains, or brown from the débris of stones and
rubbish that form its surface when the crop is removed and the summer's
sun has baked it. The remains of an old rough-paved Venetian road are
occasionally met with as we ascend the brow of the ridge from Phortetsa, which our sagacious mules would generally avoid by following a deep,
well-trodden rut they have worn by its sides, to avoid its slipperiness and
shock to their feet; for every stone seems turned the wrong side upwards.

In about an hour and three-quarters ride from the town, we reach the foot of Mount Iuktas; but as it is not accessible from this point, our muleteer tells us we must proceed to the south extreme, and ascend to it from the village of Arkhanes or Arkhanais; to do which we turn towards a narrow valley that runs parallel to the eastern base of the mountain.

But, before reaching this valley, we passed near a somewhat substantial but solitary building upon the ridge-brow leading up to Iuktas from Phortetsa, and which my guides pointed out as being a Turkish monastary for a certain sect of dervishes, accompanying the communication with a muttering of some word of contempt, and with a curse upon the race. In turning off the road into a path that leads to the monastery, which, in spite of my guides' disinclination, I was desirous of approaching, we came suddenly upon three young dervishes, who were seated in a secluded position under a rock, and apparently where they could receive the full force of the sun's rays upon their features during a devotional reverie,- the principal object of which, however, seemed to be to enable them to obtain that tanning of their features and skin for which the mendicant dervish of the East is remarkable. It thus was apparently a part of their training or education for the obtaining a complexion of the skin, as a professional requisite to the exercise of their craft and calling; and I frequently observed afterwards, during my stay in Crete, one of the three so sitting at the hottest time of the day, under the hottest wall, in the hottest part of the town, with breast and face bared to the sun's bronzing influence, and with composed features, indicative of the most perfect absorption, and the most enthusiastic devotion of mind and aim; nothing distracted him. 'Allah is great, and Mahomet is His prophet, and I am his devout disciple,' seemed to be the all-absorbing sentiment on these occasions. And thus as the three young dervishes faced the mountain that had been so venerated in the days of Paganism, as well as the midday sun, the idea could hardly help arising in my mind, that the situation of the monastery might have been chosen from some tradition of its sacredness relative to the tomb of the God of gods...

Quitting then the Turkish monastery, we enter the narrow and stony ravine that leads to the open valley of Apano, or the upper Arkhanais, at the southern base of Mount Iuktas, pitching my tent near a small cottage, amidst the flourishing vineyards for which the Arkhanais district is somewhat noted from the quality of the wine they produce. The vines extend over the upper part of two valleys, called the upper and lower Arkhanais, and contain within them two scattered villages of the same name, their inhabitants being nearly all Christian, and amounting to nearly 300 families. The Venetians conveyed water to Candia from here by an aqueduct; and the fountain whence it came has an inscription to commemorate this public benefit to the town, by Morosini, its last pro-consul, and defender, before its surrender to the Turks [Spratt is mistak-en; it refers to Morosini's uncle, Morosini the Elder].

Mount Iuktas is easiest ascended from the head of the Arkhanais val-ley: for the southern summit of the mount has a Greek chapel upon it; and a mule-track, zigzag and steep, in consequence leads to it from the valley. We ascend the mount therefore by it, and enjoy the fine view its summit commands, more than having our curiosity gratified in seeing the old foundations and stones upon its northern brow which Pashley recognizes as the site of the sacred Tomb of Zeus. But if a contrary opin-ion may be allowed to be entertained by any one, I should be disposed to think that the venerated spot was more probably where the chapel now stands, since it is the most commanding as well as highest point; and the sanctity which is still attached to it being derived from the pre-existence of an older chapel (the present being a recently restored one), seems to favour this view; while local tradition is as much in support of the latter site, instead of the Cyclopean remains on the slope of the northern sum-mit; and some ancient fragments that belong to an early Greek building seem to indicate that it had a temple or tomb upon it...

Arkhanais is one of those upland valleys or basins that nature has scat-tered here and there, as an oasis of fertility and richness, throughout the island. Possessing the charm of seclusion and of luxuriance, an imagined tranquillity and repose to all who live within them is the feeling that first strikes a stranger on beholding these retreats; more especially if he be wearied from his journey and the heat of a southern sun. For, the body wanting repose, as soon as it can obtain it, the mind of man often sympa-thizes in unison, and then lights his fancy with an imagined heaven of peace with all around him – but which, his experience of the world at other moments will teach him, is but vanity, and which, a closer associa-tion with the fifty or sixty families that chance to occupy the place shows him, will be sought in vane. For little minds and large jealousies, little faults as well as large misrepresentations, will be found to have destroyed the existence of that supposed tranquillity where nature seems to have placed so many advantages to promote it.

We pitched our tent near a small Greek cottage upon one of these, at the invitation of the family who inhabited it, who deemed themselves honoured by our doing so, and by our accepting their hospitality in donations of fruit and eggs. A serene summer's evening brought many neighbours around our tent. Some smoked; some played with beads; and all talked – some in reference to the prospective crops, and others of the blight amongst the vineyards; but there was still a strong feeling and thought with all, that occasionally would break forth from the minds of the most earnest or the least discreet: it was that which ever rankles in the heart of a Cretan Greek, viz. the hope that they would be some day freed from the government of their present masters.

But, as I could not tell them a word regarding such a hope, silence was my best policy, although my sympathy in their naturally patriotic wish might have been strongly with them. A fair damsel, too, would some-times lend her voice to the hope – that is, if she were married and her husband present; but even her efforts at feminine eloquence and persua-sion, necessarily, failed to extort any such hope or opinion from me: and thus one by one the party stole away to their own domiciles, and we were at length alone in ours and to the stillness of the night that succeeded. For all nature was soon hushed in slumber and silence, excepting the melancholy and monotonous too, and the occasional coo-coo-vaie of the little Athenian Owl, that was perched upon a neighbouring olive-tree and thus repeating in the latter sounds as the Cuckoo does with us, the very name he is commonly known by amongst the modern Greeks. How quiet is the serenity of a calm Levantine night in such a mountain retreat! and how enjoyable is this serenity! For the air then reigns still as death, and all nature seems hushed into repose and peace – not a breath mov-ing a leaf to produce a rustle, and not a cloud in motion, or even visible, to obscure the tiniest little star to be seen by the naked eye. Such is its usual serenity in such a secluded valley.

We now turn to Lear. He started off on May 13th 1864, in Herákleion, where he stayed at the home of the British vice-consul, Lysimachus Kalokairinós.

Lear, p. 70 – 72

The weather, cloudy yesterday, is again clear and fine. Rose, 4.30, having slept tolerably, spite of bugs, of which I have only caught six. It is now 5.15 and we are utterly packed up and ready, but nobody seems up as yet, no man or mule. We had to wait and wait, in great disgust; sending and jaw-ing and dawdling with George in the lanes by the nasty house. Hay was also up at eight, but groaning from stinx, etc. etc. At 8.45 the original muleteer came, and I can't say I like his face. I sent him with the mule to the Kainoúria Gate while I and George go round by the walls. At the gate, lo! it is not the same man but his 'brother' – one Konstandís Manosákis – whose visage is more promising. Lepers. Smart Cretans on compact trotting horses.

At 9.45 we are at the crevice and tavern of two days back [referring to an outing Lear had made from Her·kleion]. 10.45 Going up stony slope above Fortétsa. Back, the view is all cultivated, and might be Lincoln-shire. 11 Descend to big bridge and Venetian aqueduct; drink good water – it runs over the bridge. Dry white and green hills. Asses and mules laden with great bales of sweet herbs for fuel. 11.15 Winding paths, pale, through herbs and heathy hillsides and a quiet upper valley of corn. 11.30 Silamos – we are near – a village; olives and corn at the foor of the Juktas. Behind is the sea, and Dhia. Konstandís went this road once with a *lordhos.* 'Ἀλλά, μά τόν Θεόν, δέν ἐμποροῦσε νά εἰπῇ μιάν ἑλληνικήν λέξιν· κι' διά τοῦτο νά ἥτανε λόρδος, λοιπόν' ['But, by God, he couldn't speak one word of Greek; and so he must have been a *lordhos.*']

At twelve we get to slopes of detached olives, with a pleasant gardeny village beyond, and here we fix for lunch. We sat below an olive like a Zante olive tree, and were soon well settled. Only Konstandís, a very 'smelly' man is he! – wo is me! – but when he had got some water, I and George had good lunch on bread and meat, English cheese and good wine. The muleteer made great friends, but we thought proper that too great intimacy should not begin the first day, so we gave him three beans and *basta.* Afterwards came two men, supremely picturesque. I went above and drew till two. Some peasants passing stop, and I ask about the ruins on Juktas, which they say they never saw but 'εἶναι πολύ παλαιά' ['they are very old']. There is a church there. I wish I had seen this place by a more favourable light, 2 p.m.

We are off at 2.15 and our new guide takes us to a spring; the loveliest little *buca* [cave] possible, covered with maidenhair fern – a delicious lit-tle grot. Going uphill we come to another *metóhi*, which Konstandís calls 'Ali Bey's Metóhi': great lots of vine and new olives. 2.45 Ever going up: an immense green expanse. 3 p.m. More immediately below Juktas: long dry raviny hill – green – and lines of stone; wild and ugly enough. 3.15 Always up very stony sides of Juktas, but though wild there is little beau-ty in the scene. 3.30 Draw Mount Juktas; very Cumberlandish. (Dead ass – no, mule – by pathway.) 4 After tough ascent, rest; very Noto-ish Sicil-ian hills; no beauty at all.

4.15 Turn a corner and see a wide and separate valley and a really pleasant 'sparkling' neat Greek village: olives everywhere, and even with my glass I detect no ruins in this Epáno Arhánes. 4.30 Descent to valley below Arhánes: ἀηδόνια [nightingales]. Their notes almost our quench our thirst. Bottom of valley: stunty planes – frogs – tadpoles. Fountain, and after, a rise through narrow lanes.

5 p.m. Enquire for Konstandínos Kapládhis, and find his house at top of the village. Dark and dirty entrance; house a single room, with ladder to loft or second floor. Hearty vulgar man, squinty wife. Luggage taken down, we sit in earth-floor room, wooden alcove above. Shown in by one who says, 'Sono Ebraio io, queste son Christiani' ['I'm a Jew myself, these are Christians'], and sits down as if at home. It seems a dismal place but is but for a few hours. George asks for some coffee for me and we wait. The ever-moving Hebrew curiosity bores me. The Hebrew mizzles, which as he speaks Italian, don't displease me. Coffee comes and after, at 5.30, we all go out to look at the town.

This village is very different from those I passed above Rethymnon: the houses and people all in good order, and by comparison comfortable. One narrow alley with an arch and pergola and women sitting might have been in Italy. Mulberry trees abound. We went above the town and I drew the view, very unmolested by several who had joined us (one or two of whom merely asked to look through my glass) till 6.30. A vast yet grand scene, the dark olive groves below, and the villages – very pretty.

Returned at seven, and was the better for a wash and for a lovely nosegay of roses given me by my host who, with the hostess, is most obliging-courteous. Konstandínos Kapládhis. Odd places are these to sleep in, yet somehow I feel relieved to be here after the dreadful place at Kastro. There is no staring nor questions, though my washing must be a novelty. 'It will be found' is the reply to my question about good wine. The supper was spread on a table, brought near, when ready, to the *divan* or wooden long seat I sit on. The supper was *snails*, herbs as salad, and πᾰστάχι [pastáhi], this being flour and milk with oil. Host announces there is but one *trapézi* [table] so we fixed: I, George, the host and the muleteer. Crumbly-bumbly bits of loose brown bread were dealt out all over the table promiscuous by the hostess, who retired into the dark background that effort concluded. The snails, which George as well as I ate for the first time, we found really very decent, boiled in oil. The herbs in oil also were not bad, and the πᾰστάχι [pastáhi] capital. We all set to with small forks and the host and muleteer continually filled glasses, perpetual healths and compliments going on before and after drink; a running fire of ceremony. Wine good. After supper we declined going to 'society' at the 'café' and George began to make my bed, which incited wonder to a horrid amount, and I nearly expected to see my host lie down on it. By degrees they grew quieter, as we arranged ourselves serenely for the night, and by nine I am writing this in bed. George sleeps on a wooden dresser, on his bed; the muleteer and host in a vast square bed at the end of the room; Mrs Kapládhis upstairs with the silkworms, the existence of which has prevented George smoking. As a contrast, the loveliest rosebuds, in a great jug close to me, embellish this queer scene of life.

We leave out travellers in Arkhánes, and find them again in Part 2 of this series, which deals with the eastern and central southern part of Crete.

1. The time of the gods

In a mythical age, before mankind was created, the gods came into being. *Miscellanea* Crete played an major role in this: Zeus, the mightiest of the Greek gods, is said to have been born and raised in Crete. Moreover, according to Cretan tradition he is said to have died in Crete also, however paradoxical that may sound for a god. His tomb is supposed to be located on Mount Yioúkhtas.

The Greek poet Hesiod (8th century B.C.) laid down the canonized version of the birth of the gods in his evocative *Theogony*. We quote here from the first sections. The first part of the quotation is an invocation of the Muses, the poet's sources of inspiration. 'Kronion' refers to Zeus.

Hesiod, *Theogony*, 1 - 35

INVOCATION TO THE MUSES

Begin our singing with the Helikonian Muses,
Who possess Mount Helikon, high and holy,
And near its violet-stained spring on petalsoft feet
Dance circling the altar of almighty Kronion,

And having bathed their silken skin in Permessos
Or in Horse Spring or the sacred creek Olmeios,
They begin their choral dance on Helikon's summit
So lovely it pangs, and with power in their steps
Ascend veiled and misted in palpable air
Treading the night, and in a voice beyond beauty
They chant:

Zeus Aegisholder and his lady Hera
Of Argos, in gold sandals striding,
And the Aegisholder's girl, owl-eyed Athene,
And Phoibos Apollo and arrowy Artemis,

Poseidon earth-holder, earthquaking god,
Modest Themis and Aphrodite, eyelashes curling,
And Hebe goldcrowned and lovely Dione,
Leto and Iapetos and Kronos, his mind bent,
Eos and Helios and glowing Selene,
Gaia, Okeanos, and the black one, Night,

And the whole eerie brood of the eternal Immortals.

And they once taught Hesiod the art of singing verse,
While he pastured his lambs on holy Helikon's slopes.
And this was the very first thing they told me,
The Olympian Muses, daughters of Zeus Aegisholder:

'Hillbillies and bellies, poor excuses for shepherds:
We know how to tell many believable lies,
But also, when we want to, how to speak the plain truth.'

So spoke the daughters of great Zeus, mincing their words.
And they gave me a staff, a branch of good sappy laurel,
Plucking it off, spectacular. And they breathed into me
A voice divine, so I might celebrate past and future.
And they told me to hymn the generation of the eternal gods,
But always to sing of themselves, the Muses, first and last.

The poet continues with a hymn to the Muses, which we do not quote
here. Then he continues:

Hesiod, *Theogony*, 105 - 187
Farewell Zeus's daughters, and bestow song that beguiles.
Make known the eerie brood of the eternal Immortals
Who were born of Earth and starry Sky,
And of dusky Night, and whom the salt Sea bore.
Tell how first the gods and earth came into being
And the rivers and the sea, endless and surging,
And the stars shining and the wide sky above;
How they divided wealth and allotted honors,
And first possessed deep-ridged Olympos.

Tell me these things, Olympian Muses,
From the beginning, and tell which of them came first.

THE FIRST GODS

In the beginning there was only Chaos, the Abyss,
But then Gaia, the Earth, came into being,
Her broad bosom the ever-firm foundation of all,
And Tartaros, dim in the underground depths,
And Eros, loveliest of all the Immortals, who
Makes their bodies (and men's bodies) go limp,
Mastering their minds and subduing their wills.

From the Abyss were born Erebos and dark Night.
And Night, pregnant after sweet intercourse
With Erebos, gave birth to Aether and Day.

Earth's first child was Ouranos, starry Heaven,
Just her size, a perfect fit on all sides.
And a firm foundation for the blessed gods.
And she bore the Mountains in long ranges, haunted
By the Nymphs who live in the deep mountain dells.
Then she gave birth to the barren, raging Sea
Without any sexual love. But later she slept with
Ouranos and bore Ocean with its deep currents,
And also: Koios, Krios, Hyperion, Iapetos,
             Theia, Rheia, Themis, Mnemosyne,
             Gold-crowned Phoibe and lovely Tethys.

THE CASTRATION OF OURANOS

After them she bore a most terrible child,
Kronos, her youngest, an arch-deceiver,
And this boy hated his lecherous father.

She bore the Cyclopes too, with hearts of stone,
Brontes, Steropes and ponderous Arges,
Who gave Zeus thunder and made the thunderbolt.
In every other respect they were just like gods,
But a lone eye lay in their foreheads' middle.
They were nicknamed Cyclopes because they had

A single goggle eye in their foreheads' middle.
Strong as the dickens, and they knew their craft.

And three other sons were born to Gaia and Ouranos,
Strong, hulking creatures that beggar description,
Kottos, Briareos, and Gyges, outrageous children.
A hundred hands stuck out of their shoulders,
Grotesque, and fifty heads grew on each stumpy neck.   *Miscellanea*
These monsters exuded irresistible strength.
They were Gaia's most dreaded offspring,
And from the start their father feared and loathed them.
Ouranos used to stuff all of his children
Back into a hollow of Earth soon as they were born,
Keeping them from the light, an awful thing to do,
But Heaven did it, and was very pleased with himself.

Vast Earth groaned under the pressure inside,
And then she came up with a plan, a really wicked trick.
She created a new mineral, grey flint, and formed
A huge sickle from it and showed it to her dear boys.
And she rallied them with this bitter speech:

'Listen to me, children, and we might yet get even
With your criminal father for what he has done to us.
After all, he started this whole ugly business.'

They were tongue-tied with fear when they heard this.
But Kronos, whose mind worked in strange ways,
Got his pluck up and found the words to answer her:

'I think I might be able to bring it off, Mother.
I can't stand Father; he doesn't even deserve the name.
And after all, he started this whole ugly business.'

This response warmed the heart of vast Earth.
She hid young Kronos in an ambush and placed in his hands
The jagged sickle. Then she went over the whole plan with him.
And now on came great Ouranos, bringing Night with him.
And, longing for love, he settled himself all over Earth.

carries Heaven on his shoulders
onal Museum, Naples, Italy)

From his dark hiding-place, the son reached out
With his left hand, while with his right he swung
The fiendishly long and jagged sickle, pruning the genitals
Of his own father with one swoop and tossing them
Behind him, where they fell to no small effect.
Earth soaked up all the bloody drops that spurted out,
And as the seasons went by she gave birth to the Furies
And to great Giants gleaming in full armor, spears in hand,
And to the Meliai, as ash-tree nymphs are generally called.

The poet continues with a description of the birth of Aphrodite from the genitals of Ouranos, and then a genealogy of dozens of lesser gods and goddesses. The birth of the Olympic gods follows.

Hesiod, *Theogony*, 456 - 508

THE BIRTH OF THE OLYMPIANS
Later, Kronos forced himself upon Rheia,
And she gave birth to a splendid brood:

> Hestia and Demeter and gold-sandalled Hera,
> Strong, pitiless Hades, the underworld lord,
> The booming Earth-shaker, Poseidon, and finally
> Zeus, a wise god, our Father in heaven
> Under whose thunder the wide world trembles.

And Kronos swallowed them all down as soon as each
Issued from Rheia's holy womb onto her knees,
With the intent that only he among the proud Ouranians
Should hold the title of King among the Immortals.
For he had learned from Earth and starry Heaven
That it was fated for him, powerful though he was,
To be overthrown by his child, through the scheming of Zeus.
Well, Kronos wasn't blind. He kept a sharp watch
And swallowed his children.
Rheia's grief was unbearable.
When she was about to give birth to Zeus our Father
She petitioned her parents, Earth and starry Heaven,
To put together some plan so that the birth of her child

Might go unnoticed, and she would make devious Kronos
Pay the Avengers of her father and children.
They listened to their daughter and were moved by her words,
And the two of them told her all that was fated
For Kronos the King and his stout-hearted son.
They sent her to Lyktos, to the rich land of Crete,
When she was ready to bear the youngest of her sons,
Mighty Zeus. Vast Earth received him when he was born
To be nursed and brought up in the wide land of Crete.
She came first to Lyktos, travelling quickly by night,
And took the baby in her hands and hid him in a cave,
An eerie hollow in the woods of dark Mount Aigaion.
Then she wrapped up a great stone in swaddling clothes
And gave it to Kronos, Ouranos' son, the great lord and king
Of the earlier gods. He took it in his hands and rammed it
Down into his belly, the poor fool! He had no idea
That a stone had been substituted for his son, who,
Unscathed and content as a babe, would soon wrest
His honors from him by main force and rule the Immortals.
It wasn't long before the young lord was flexing
His glorious muscles. The seasons followed each other,
And great devious Kronos, gulled by Earth's
Clever suggestions, vomited up his offspring,
Overcome by the wiles and power of his son
The stone first, which he'd swallowed last.
Zeus took the stone and set it in the ground at Pytho
Under Parnassos' hollows, a sign and wonder for men to come.
And he freed his uncles, other sons of Ouranos
Whom their father in a fit of idiocy had bound.
They remembered his charity and in gratitude
Gave him thunder and the flashing thunderbolt
And lightning, which enormous Earth had hidden before.
Trusting in these he rules mortals and Immortals.

The poet continues with a genealogy of the other gods and elaborately
sings about the struggle between Zeus and the Titans. Those passages
are not quoted here.

Callimachus (the 3rd century B.C. Alexandrian poet and librarian) also
describes the birth and rearing of Zeus in his *Hymn to Zeus*. Zeus' death is

also mentioned, although indirectly. The translation tries to catch Callimachus overwrought writing style.

Callimachus, *Hymn to Zeus*, 1 - 53

At libations to Zeus what else should rather be sung than the god himself; mighty for ever, king for evermore, router of the Pelagonians, dealer of justice to the sons of Heaven?

How shall we sing of him – as lord of Dicte or of Lycaeum [a mountain in Arcadia, in the Peloponnesos]? My soul is all in doubt, since debated is his birth. O Zeus, some say that thou wert born on the hills of Ida; others, O Zeus, say in Arcadia; did these or those, O Father, lie? 'Cretans are ever liars.' Yea, a tomb, O Lord, for thee the Cretans builded; but thou didst not die, for thou art for ever.

In Parrhasia [=Arcadia] it was that Rheia bare thee, where was a hill sheltered with thickest brush. Thence is the place holy, and no fourfooted thing that hath need of Eileithyia nor any woman approacheth thereto, but the Apidanians call it the primeval childbed of Rheia. There when thy mother had laid thee down from her mighty lap, straightway she sought a stream of water, wherewith she might purge her of the soilure of birth and wash thy body therein.

But mighty Ladon [a river in Arcadia, like the rivers mentioned later] flowed not yet, nor Erymanthus, clearest of rivers; waterless was all Arcadia; yet was it anon to be called well-watered. For at that time when Rhea loosed her girdle, full many a hollow oak did watery Iaon bear aloft, and many a wain did Melas carry and many a serpent above Carnion, wet though it now be, cast its lair; and a man would fare on foot over Crathis and manypebbled Metope, athirst: while that abundant water lay beneath his feet.

And holden in distress the lady Rheia said, 'Dear Earth, give birth thou also! thy birthpangs are light.' So spake the goddess, and lifting her great arm aloft she smote the mountain with her staff; and it was greatly rent in twain for her and poured forth a mighty flood. Therein, O Lord, she cleansed thy body; and swaddled thee, and gave thee to Neda to carry within the Cretan covert, that thou mightst be reared secretly: Neda, eldest of the nymphs who then were about her bed, earliest birth after Styx and Philyra. And no idle favour did the goddess repay her, but named that stream Neda; which, I ween, in great flood by the very city of the Cauconians, which is called Lepreion, mingles its stream with Nereus, and its primeval water do the son's sons of the Bear [Arkas, the ancestor of the

Arcadians], Lycaon's daughter, drink.

When the nymph, carrying thee, O Father Zeus, toward Cnosus, was leaving Thenae – for Thenae was nigh to Cnosus – even then, O God, thy navel fell away: hence that plain the Cydonians call the Plain of the Navel. But thee, O Zeus, the companions of the Cyrbantes took to their arms, even the Dictaean Meliae, and Adrasteia [sister of the Curetes] laid thee to rest in a cradle of gold, and thou didst suck the rich teat of the she-goat Amaltheia, and thereto eat the sweet honey-comb. For suddenly on the hills of Ida, which men call Panacra, appeared the works of the Panacrian bee. And lustily round thee danced the Curetes a war-dance, beating their armour, that Cronus might hear with his ears the din of the shield, but not thine infant noise…

Another version of the birth of the gods is provided by Diodorus Siculus (a Greek historian from the first century B.C. and an important source of Greek myths and legends) in his *Library of History*.

Diodorus Siculus, *Library of History*, Book V, 64.1 - 66.6, 68, 69.4 - 70

64. The inhabitants of Crete claim that the oldest people of the island were those who are known as Eteocretans ('genuine Cretans'), who were sprung from the soil itself, and that their king, who was called Cres, was responsible for the greatest number of the most important discoveries made in the island which contributed to the improvement of the social life of mankind. Also the greater number of the gods who, because of their benefactions to all men alike, have been accorded immortal honours, had their origin, so their myths relate, in their land; and of the tradition regarding these gods we shall now give a summary account, following the most reputable writers who have recorded the affairs of Crete.

The first of these gods of whom tradition has left a record made their home in Crete about Mt. Idê and were called Idaean Dactyli. These, according to one tradition, were one hundred in number, but others say that there were only ten to receive this name, corresponding in number to the fingers (*dactyli*) of the hands. But some historians, and Ephorus is one of them, record that the Idaean Dactyli were in fact born on the Mt. Idê which is in Phrygia [in Asia Minor] and passed over to Europe together with Mygdon; and since they were wizards, they practised charms and initiatory rites and mysteries, and in the course of a sojourn in Samothrace they amazed the natives of that island not a little by their skill in such matters. And it was at this time, we are further told, that

Orpheus, who was endowed with an exceptional gift of poesy and song, also became a pupil of theirs, and he was subsequently the first to introduce initiatory rites and mysteries to the Greeks.

However this may be, the Idaean Dactyli of Crete, so tradition tells us, discovered both the use of fire and what the metals copper and iron are, as well as the means of working them, this being done in the territory of the city of Aptera at Berecynthus, as it is called; and since they were looked upon as the originators of great blessings for the race of men, they were accorded immortal honours. And writers tell us that one of them was named Heracles, and excelling as he did in fame, he established the Olympic Games, and that the men of a later period thought, because the name was the same, that it was the son of Alcmenê who had founded the institution of the Olympic Games. And evidences of this, they tell us, are found in the fact that many women even to this day take their incantations from this god and make amulets in his name, on the ground that he was a wizard and practised the arts of initiatory rites; but they add that these things were indeed very far removed from the habits of the Heracles who was born of Alcmenê.

65. After the Idaean Dactyli, according to accounts we have, there were nine Curetes. Some writers of myths relate that these gods were born of the earth, but according to others, they were descended from the Idaean Dactyli. Their home they made in mountainous places which were thickly wooded and full of ravines, and which, in a word, provided a natural shelter and coverage, since it had not yet been discovered how to build houses. And since these Curetes excelled in wisdom they discovered many things which are of use to men generally; so, for instance, they were the first to gather sheep into flocks, to domesticate the several other kinds of animals which men fatten, and to discover the making of honey. In the same manner they introduced the art of shooting with the bow and the ways of hunting animals, and they showed mankind how to live and associate together in a common life, and they were the originators of concord and, so to speak, of orderly behaviour. The Curetes also invented swords and helmets and the war-dance, by means of which they raised a great alarum and deceived Cronus. And we are told that, when Rhea, the mother of Zeus, entrusted him to them unbeknown to Cronus his father, they took him under their care and saw to his nurture; but since we purpose to set forth this affair in detail, we must take up the account at a little earlier point.

66. The myth the Cretans relate runs like this: When the Curetes were

young men, the Titans, as they are called, were still living. These Titans had their dwelling in the land about Cnosus, at the place where even to this day men point out foundations of a house of Rhea and a cypress grove which has been consecrated to her from ancient times. The Titans numbered six men and five women, being born, as certain writers of myths relate, of Uranus and Gê, but according to others, of one of the Curetes and Titaea, from whom as their mother they derive the name they have. The males were Cronus, Hyperion, Coeus, Iapetus, Crius, and Oceanus, and their sisters were Rhea, Themis, Mnemosynê, Phoebê, and Tethys. Each one of them was the discoverer of things of benefit to mankind, and because of the benefaction they conferred upon all men they were accorded honours and everlasting fame.

Cronus, since he was the eldest of the Titans, became king and caused all men who were his subjects to change from a rude way of living to civilized life, and for this reason he received great approbation and visited many regions of the inhabited earth. Among all he met he introduced justice and sincerity of soul, and this is why the tradition has come down to later generations that the men of Cronus' time were good-hearted, altogether guileless, and blest with felicity. His kingdom was strongest in the western regions, where indeed he enjoyed his greatest honour; consequently, down even to comparatively recent times, among the Romans and the Carthaginians, while their city still stood, and other neighbouring peoples, notable festivals and sacrifices were celebrated in honour of this god and many places bore his name. And because of the exceptional obedience to laws no injustice was committed by any one at any time and all the subjects of the rule of Cronus lived a life of blessedness, in the unhindered enjoyment of every pleasure...

68. To Cronus and Rhea, we are told, were born Hestia, Demeter, and Hera, and Zeus, Poseidon, and Hades. Of these, they say, Hestia discovered how to build houses, and because of this benefaction of hers practically all men have established her shrine in every home, according her honours and sacrifices. And Demeter, since the corn still grew wild together with the other plants and was still unknown to men, was the first to gather it in, to devise how to prepare and preserve it, and to instruct mankind how to sow it. Now she had discovered the corn before she gave birth to her daughter Persephonê, but after the birth of her daughter and the rape of her by Pluton, she burned all the fruit of the corn, both because of her anger at Zeus and because of her grief over her daughter. After she had found Persephonê, however, she became reconciled with

Zeus and gave Triptolemus the corn to sow, instructing him both to share the gift with men everywhere and to teach them everything concerned with the labour of sowing. And some men say that it was she also who introduced laws, by obedience to which men have become accustomed to deal justly one with another, and that mankind has called this goddess Thesmophoros [law-giver] after the laws which she gave them. And since Demeter has been responsible for the greatest blessings to mankind, she has been accorded the most notable honours and sacrifices, and magnificent feasts and festivals as well, not only by the Greeks, but also by almost all barbarians who have partaken of this kind of food…

69.4 As for the rest of the gods who were born to Cronus and Rhea, the Cretans say that Poseidon was the first to concern himself with sea-faring and to fit out fleets, Cronus having given him the lordship in such matters; and this is why the tradition has been passed along to succeeding generations that he controls whatever is done on the sea, and why mariners honour him by means of sacrifices. Men further bestow upon Poseidon the distinction of having been the first to tame horses and to introduce the knowledge of horsemanship (*hippikê*), because of which he is called 'Hippius.' And of Hades it is said that he laid down the rules which are concerned with burials and funerals and the honours which are paid to the dead, no concern having been given to the dead before this time; and this is why tradition tells us that Hades is lord of the dead, since there were assigned to him in ancient times the first offices in such matters and the concern for them.

70. Regarding the birth of Zeus and the manner in which he came to be king, there is no agreement. Some say that he succeeded to the kingship after Cronus passed from among men into the company of the gods, not by overcoming his father with violence, but in the manner prescribed by custom and justly, having been judged worthy of that honour. But others recount a myth, which runs as follows: There was delivered to Cronus an oracle regarding the birth of Zeus which stated that the son who would be born to him would wrest the kingship from him by force. Consequently Cronus time and again did away with the children whom he begot; but Rhea, grieved as she was, and yet lacking the power to change her husband's purpose, when she had given birth to Zeus, concealed him in Idê, as it is called, and, without the knowledge of Cronus entrusted the rearing of him to the Curetes who dwelt in the neighbourhood of Mount Idê. The Curetes bore him off to a certain cave where they gave him over to the Nymphs, with the command that they should minister to his every

need. And the Nymphs nurtured the child on a mixture of honey and milk and gave him upbringing at the udder of the goat which was named Amaltheia. And many evidences of the birth and upbringing of this god remain to this day on the island. For instance, when he was being carried away, while still an infant, by the Curetes, they say that the umbilical cord (*omphalos*) fell from him near the river known as Triton, and that this spot has been made sacred and has been called Omphalus after that incident, while in like manner the plain about it is known as Omphaleium. And on Mount Idê, where the god was nurtured, both the cave in which he spent his days has been made sacred to him, and the meadows round about it, which lie upon the ridges of the mountain, have in like manner been consecrated to him. But the most astonishing of all that which the myth relates has to do with the bees, and we should not omit to mention it: The god, they say, wishing to preserve an immortal memorial of his close association with the bees, changed the colour of them, making it like copper with the gleam of gold, and since the region lay at a very great altitude, where fierce winds blew about it and heavy snows fell, he made the bees insensible to such things and unaffected by them, since they must range over the most wintry stretches. To the goat [*aeg-*]which suckled him Zeus also accorded certain honours, and in particular took from it a surname, being called Aegiochus. And when he had attained to manhood he founded first a city in Dicta, where indeed the myth states that he was born; in later times this city was abandoned, but some stone blocks of its foundations are still preserved.

Europa and the Bull (Museum, Sparta, Greece).

11. The time of the heroes

After the gods came the heroes. Counting back the generations from the beginning of the Olympic Games in 776 B.C., ancient historians place heroes like Theseus, Herakles, Achilleus and Odysseus in the 14th and 13th centuries B.C. Thus in the time of Akhaian Crete. *Miscellanea*

In legend, the Crete of this time was always connected with Minos, the legendary king who resided in Knossós. Minos was the son of Zeus and Europa, daughter of the king of Tyrus (in Phoenicia, what is now Lebanon). He was married to Pasiphae and was the father of Ariadne. Minos' history is linked to that of the Athenian hero Theseus, who defeated the Minotaur and eloped with Ariadne.

First we give the story of Zeus and Europa as it is told by the first century Roman poet Ovid in his *Metamorphoses*. In Latin Zeus is called Jupiter, and in English also Jove.

Ovid, *Metamorphoses*, Book II, 835 - Book III, 6

JUPITER AND EUROPA

Jove called his son aside and, keeping dark
His secret passion, 'Mercury', he said,
'Trusty executant of my commands,
Make haste, glide swiftly on your usual course
Down to the land that sees your mother's star
High in the southern sky, named by its people
The land of Sidon; in the distance there,
Grazing the mountain pastures, you will find
The royal herd; drive them to the sea-shore.'
And presently (as Jove had bidden) the herd,
Driven from the hillside, headed for the shore,
Where with her girls of Tyre for company
The great king's daughter often used to play.
   Ah, majesty and love go ill together,
Nor long share one abode! Relinquishing

Sceptre and throne, heaven's father, God of gods,
Who wields the three-forked lightning, at whose nod
The world is shaken, now transforms himself
Into a bull and, lowing, joins the herd,
Ambling – so handsome – through the tender grass.
His hide was white, white as untrodden snow
Before the south wind brings the melting rain.
The muscles of his neck swelled proud; below
The dewlap hung; his horns, though small, you'd swear
A master hand had made, so jewel-like
Their pure and pearly sheen; upon his brow
No threat, no menace in his eye; his mien
Peaceful. Europa marvelled at his beauty
And friendliness that threatened naught of harm.
Yet, gentle as he seemed, she feared at first
To touch him, but anon came up to him
And offered flowers to his soft white lips.

   Glad was the lover's heart and, till the joy
Hoped for should come, he kissed her hand, and then –
Hardly, oh, hardly, could postpone the rest!
And now he frolicked, prancing on the greensward;
Then on the yellow sand laid his white flank;
And gradually she lost her fear, and he
Offered his breast for her virgin caresses,
His horns for her to wind with chains of flowers,
Until the princess dared to mount his back,
Her pet bull's back, unwitting whom she rode.
Then – slowly, slowly down the broad dry beach –
First in the shallow waves the great god set
His spurious hooves, then sauntered further out
Till in the open sea he bore his prize.
Fear filled her heart, as, gazing back, she saw
The fast receding sands. Her right hand grasped
A horn, the other leant upon his back;
Her fluttering tunic floated in the breeze.

Now, safe in Crete, Jove shed the bull's disguise
And stood revealed before Europa's eyes.
Meanwhile her father, baffled, bade his son

Cadmus, set out to find the stolen girl
And threatened exile should he fail – in one
Same act such warmth of love, such wickedness!

The poet continues with the adventures of Cadmus, which are not
important to the history of Crete.

The next quotations focus on Minos, who was born out of the union
between Zeus and Europa. First we give the story of Minos, Theseus and *Miscellanea*
the Minotaur as it is told by Diodorus Siculus. The Minotaur is the monster that was born of Pasiphae's union with a beautiful bull (that story is
told later in connection with Daedalus).

Diodorus Siculus, *Library of History*, Book IV, 60.1 - 61.8

60. It remains for us now to speak of the Minotaur which was slain by
Theseus, in order that we may complete our account of the deeds of
Theseus. But we must revert to earlier times and set forth the facts
which are interwoven with this performance, in order that the whole
narrative may be clear.

Tectamus, the son of Dorus, the son of Hellen, the son of Deucalion,
sailed to Crete with Aeolians and Pelasgians and became king of the
island, and marrying the daughter of Cretheus he begat Asterius. And
during the time when he was king in Crete Zeus, as they say, carried off
Europê from Phoenicia, and carrying her across to Crete upon the back
of a bull, he lay with her there and begat three sons, Minos, Rhadamanthys, and Sarpedon. After this Asterius, the king of Crete, took Europê to
wife; and since he was without children by her he adopted the sons of
Zeus and left them at his death to succeed to the kingdom. As for these
children, Rhadamanthys gave the Cretans their laws, and Minos, succeeding to the throne and marrying Itonê, the daughter of Lyctius, begat
Lycastus, who in turn succeeded to the supreme power and marrying Idê,
the daughter of Corybas, begat the second Minos, who, as some writers
record was the son of Zeus. This Minos was the first Greek to create a
powerful naval force and to become master of the sea. And marrying
Pasiphaê, the daughter of Helius and Cretê, he begat Deucalion and
Catreus and Androgeos and Ariadnê and had other, natural, children
more in number than these. As for the sons of Minos, Androgeos came
to Athens at the time of the Panathenaic festival, while Aegeus was king,
and defeating all the contestants in the games he became a close friend of
the sons of Pallas. Thereupon Aegeus, viewing with suspicion the friend-

ship which Androgeos had formed, since he feared that Minos might lend his aid to the sons of Pallas and take from him the supreme power, plotted against the life of Androgeos. Consequently, when the latter was on his way to Thebes in order to attend a festival there, Aegeus caused him to be treacherously slain by certain natives of the region in the neighbourhood of Oenoê in Attica.

61. Minos, when he learned of the fate which had befallen his son, came to Athens and demanded satisfaction for the murder of Androgeos. And when no one paid any attention to him, he declared war against the Athenians and uttered imprecations to Zeus, calling down drought and famine through-out the state of the Athenians. And when drought quickly prevailed about Attica and Greece and the crops were destroyed, the heads of the communities gathered together and inquired of the god what steps they could take to rid themselves of their present evils. The god made answer to them that they should go to Aeacus, the son of Zeus and Aeginê, the daughter of Asopus, and ask him to offer up prayers on their behalf. And when they had done as they had been commended, Aeacus finished offering the prayers and thereupon, among the rest of the Greeks, the drought was broken, but among the Athenians alone it continued; wherefore the Athenians were compelled to make inquiry of the god how they might be rid of their present evils. Thereupon the god made answer that they could do so if they would render to Minos such satisfaction for the murder of Androgeos as he might demand. The Athenians obeyed the order of god, and Minos commanded them that they should give seven youths and as many maidens every nine years to the Minotaur for him to devour, for as long a time as the monster should live. And when the Athenians gave them, the inhabitants of Attica were rid of their evils and Minos ceased warring on Athens.

At the expiration of nine years Minos came again to Attica accompanied by a great fleet and demanded and received the fourteen young people. Now Theseus [Aegeus' son] was one of those who were to set forth, an Aegeus made the agreement with the captain of the vessel that, if Theseus should overcome the Minotaur, they should sail back with their sails white, but if he died, they should be black, just as they had been accustomed to do on the previous occasion. When they had landed in Crete, Ariadnê, the daughter of Minos, became enamoured of Theseus, who was unusually handsome, and Theseus, after conversing with her and securing her assistance both slew the Minotaur and got safely away, since he had learned from her the way out of the Labyrinth. In making his way back to his native land he carried off Ariadnê and sailed out unobserved during the night, after which he put in at the island which at that time was called Dia, but is now called Naxos.

At this same time, the myths relate, Dionysus showed himself on the island, and because of the beauty of Ariadnê he took the maiden away from Theseus and kept her as his lawful wife, loving her exceedingly. Indeed, after her death he considered her worthy of immortal honours because of the affection he had for her, and placed among the stars of heaven the 'Crown of Ariadnê.' But Theseus, they say, being vexed exceedingly because the maiden had been taken from him, and forgetting because of his grief the command of Aegeus, came to port in Attica with the black sails. And Aegeus, we are told, witnessing the return of the ship and thinking that his son was dead, performed an act which was at the same time heroic and a calamity; for he ascended the acropolis and then, because he was disgusted with life by reason of his excessive grief, cast himself down the height. After Aegeus had died, Theseus, succeeding to the kingship, ruled over the masses in accordance with the laws and performed many deeds which contributed to the aggrandisement of his native land.

Miscellanea

Diodorus Siculus also relates the story of Daedalus and Icarus, followed by the death of Minos.

Diodorus Siculus, *Library of History*, Book IV, 75.6 - 77, 79.1 - 80.4

75.6. But now that we have examined these matters we shall endeavour to set forth what relates to Daedalus, the Minotaur, and the expedition of Minos into Sicily against King Cocalus.

76. Daedalus was an Athenian by birth and was known as one of the clan named Erechthids, since he was the son of Metion, the son of Eupalamus, the son of Erechtheus. In natural ability he towered far above all other men and cultivated the building art, the making of statues, and the working of stone. He was also the inventor of many devices which contributed to the advancement of his art and built works in many regions of the inhabited world which arouse the wonder of men. In the carving of his statues he so far excelled all other men that later generations invented the story about him that the statues of his making were quite like their living models; they could see, they said, and walk and, in a word, preserved so well the characteristics of the entire body that the beholder thought that the image made by him was a being endowed with

life. And since he was the first to represent the open eye and to fashion the legs separated in a stride and the arms and hands as extended, it was a natural thing that he should have received the admiration of mankind; for the artists before his time had carved their statues with the eyes closed and the arms and hands hanging and attached to the sides.

But though Daedalus was an object of admiration because of his technical skill, yet he had to flee from his native land, since he had been condemned for murder for the following reason. Talos, a son of the sister of Daedalus, was receiving his education in the home of Daedalus, while he was still a lad in years. But being more gifted than his teacher he invented the potter's wheel, and then, when once he had come by chance upon a jawbone of a snake and with it had sawn through a small piece of wood, he tried to imitate the jaggedness of the serpent's teeth. Consequently he fashioned a saw out of iron, by means of which he would saw the lumber which he used in his work, and for this accomplishment he gained the reputation of having discovered a device which would be of great service to the art of building. He like-wise discovered also the tool for describing a circle and certain other cunningly contrived devices whereby he gained for himself great fame. But Daedalus, becoming jealous of the youth and feeling that his fame was going to rise far above that of his teacher, treacherously slew the youth. And being detected in the act of burying him, he was asked what he was burying, whereupon he replied, 'I am inhuming a snake.' Here a man may well wonder at the strange happening, that the same animal that led to the thought of devising the saw should also have been the means through which the murder came to be discovered. And Daedalus, having been accused and adjudged guilty of murder by the court of the Areopagites, at first fled to one of the demes of Attica, the inhabitants of which, we are told, were named after him Daedalidae.

77. Afterwards Daedalus made his escape out of Attica to Crete, where, being admired because of the fame of his art, he became a friend of Minos who was king there. Now according to the myth which has been handed down to us Pasiphaê, the wife of Minos, became enamoured of the bull, and Daedalus, by fashioning a contrivance in the shape of a cow, assisted Pasiphaê to gratify her passion. In explanation of this the myths offer the following account: Before this time it had been the custom of Minos annually to dedicate to Poseidon the fairest bull born in his herds and to sacrifice it to the god; but at the time in question there was born a bull of extraordinary beauty and he sacrificed another from among those

which were inferior, whereupon Poseidon, becoming angry at Minos, caused his wife Pasiphaê to become enamoured of the bull. And by means of the ingenuity of Daedalus Pasiphaê had intercourse with the bull and gave birth to the Minotaur, famed in the myth. This creature, they say, was of double form, the upper parts of the body as far as the shoulders being those of a bull and the remaining parts those of a man. As a place in which to keep this monstrous thing Daedalus, the story goes, built a labyrinth, the passage-ways of which were so winding that those unfamiliar with them had difficulty in making their way out; in this labyrinth the Minotaur was maintained and here it devoured the seven youths and seven maidens which were sent to it from Athens, as we have already related.

But Daedalus, they say, on learning that Minos had made threats against him because he had fashioned the cow, became fearful of the anger of the king and departed from Crete, Pasiphaê helping him and providing a vessel for his escape. With him fled also his son Icarus and they put in at a certain island which lay in the open sea. But when Icarus was disembarking onto the island in a reckless manner, he fell into the sea and perished, and in memory of him the sea was named the Icarian and the island was called Icaria. Daedalus, however, sailing away from this island, landed in Sicily near the territory over which Cocalus reigned as king, who courteously received Daedalus and because of his genius and his renown made him close friend.

But certain writers of myths have the following account: Daedalus remained a while longer in Crete, being kept hidden by Pasiphaê, and king Minos, desiring to wreak vengeance upon him and yet being unable to find him, caused all the boats which were on the island to be searched and announced that he would give a great sum of money to the man who should discover Daedalus. Thereupon Daedalus, despairing of making his escape by any boat, fashioned with amazing ingenuity wings which were cleverly designed and marvellously fitted together with wax; and fastening these on his son's body and his own he spread them out for flight, to the astonishment of all, and made his escape over open sea which lies near the island of Crete. As for Icarus, because of the ignorance of youth he made his flight too far aloft and fell into the sea when the wax which held the wings together was melted by the sun, whereas Daedalus, by flying close to the sea and repeatedly wetting the wings, made his way in safety, marvellous to relate, to Sicily. Now as for these matter, even though the myth is a tale of marvel, we none the less have thought it best not to leave it unmentioned...

79. Minos, the king of the Cretans, who was at that time the master of the seas, when he learned that Daedalus had fled to Sicily, decided to make a campaign against that island. After preparing a notable naval force he sailed forth from Crete and landed at a place in the territory of Acragas which was called after him Minoa. Here he disembarked his troops and sending messengers to King Cocalus he demanded Daedalus of him for punishment. But Cocalus invited Minos to a conference, and after promising to meet all his demands he brought him to his home as his guest. And when Minos was bathing Cocalus kept him too long in the hot water and thus slew him; the body he gave back to the Cretans, explaining his death on the ground that he had slipped in the bath and by falling into the hot water had met his end. Thereupon the comrades of Minos buried the body of the king with magnificent ceremonies, and constructing a tomb of two storeys, in the part of it which was hidden underground they placed the bones, and in that which lay open to gaze they made a shrine of Aphroditê. Here Minos received honours over many generations, the inhabitants of the region offering sacrifices there in the belief that the shrine was Aphroditê's; but in more recent times, after the city of the Acragantini had been founded and it became known that the bones had been placed there, it came to pass that the tomb was dismantled and the bones were given back to the Cretans, this being done when Theron was lord over the people of Acragas.

However, the Cretans of Sicily, after the death of Minos, fell into factious strife, since they had no ruler, and, since their ships had been burned by the Sicani serving under Cocalus, they gave up any hope they had had of returning to their native land; and deciding to make their home in Sicily, a part of them established on that island a city to which the gave the name Minoa after their king, and others, after wandering about through the interior of the island, seized a place which was naturally strong and founded a city to which they gave the name Engyum after the spring which flowed forth within the city. And at a later time, after the capture of Troy, when Meriones the Cretan came to shore in Sicily, they welcomed, because of their kinship to them, the Cretans who landed with him and shared with them their citizenship; and using as their base a well-fortified city and having subdued certain of the neighbouring peoples, they secured for themselves a fairly large territory. And growing steadily stronger all the while they built a temple to the Mothers and accorded these goddesses unusual honours, adorning their temple with many votive offerings. The cult of these goddesses, so men say, they moved from their home in Crete, since the Cretans also hold these goddesses in special honour.

80. The acount which the myths preserve of the Mothers runs like this: They nurtured Zeus of old without the knowledge of his father Cronus, in return for which Zeus translated them into the heavens and designated them as a constellation which he named the Bears. And Aratus agrees with this account when he states in his poem on the stars:

> Turned backwards then upon their shoulders are
> The Bears; if true it be that they from Crete
> Into the heavens mounted by the will
> Of mighty Zeus, for that when he was babe
> In fragrant Dicton near th'Idaean mount
> They set him in a cave and nurtured him
> A year, the while Curetes Dictaean
> Practised deceit on Cronus.

There is no reason why we should omit to mention the sanctity of these goddesses and the renown which they enjoy among mankind. They are honoured, indeed, not only by the inhabitants of this city, but certain of the neighbouring peoples also glorify these goddesses with magnificent sacrifices and every other kind of honour. Some cities were indeed commanded by oracles from the Pythian god to honour the goddesses, being assured that in this way the lives of their private citizens would be blessed with good fortune and their cities would flourish. And in the end the renown of the goddesses advanced to such a degree that the inhabitants of this region have continued to honour them with many votive offerings in silver and gold down to the time of the writing of this history…

Diodorus Siculus also describes the dominion of Minos and his family members.

Diodorus Siculus, *Library of History*, Book v, 78 - 80

78. Many generations after the birth of the gods, the Cretans go on to say, not a few heroes were to be found in Crete, the most renowned of whom were Minos and Rhadamanthys and Sarpedon. These men, their myth states, were born of Zeus and Europê, the daughter of Agenor, who, men say, was brought across to Crete upon the back of a bull by the design of the gods. Now Minos, by virtue of his being the eldest, became king of

the island, and he founded on it not a few cities, the most renowned of which were the three, Cnosus in those parts of the island which look toward Asia, Phaestus on the seashore to the south, and Cydonia in the regions to be west facing the Peloponnesus. And Minos established not a few laws for the Cretans, claiming that he had received them from his father Zeus when conversing with him in a certain cave. Furthermore, he came to possess a great naval power, and he subdued the majority of the islands and was the first man among the Greeks to be master of the sea. And after he had gained great renown for his manly spirit and justice, he ended his life in Sicily in the course of his campaign against Cocalus, the details of which we have recounted in connection with our account of Daedalus, because of whom the campaign was made.

79. Of Rhadamanthys the Cretans say that of all men he rendered the most just decisions and inflicted inexorable punishment upon robbers and impious men and all other malefactors. He came also to possess no small number of islands and a large part of the sea coast of Asia, all men delivering themselves into his hands of their free will because of his justice. Upon Erythrus, one of his sons, Rhadamanthys bestowed the kingship over the city which was named after him Erythrae, and to Oenopion, the son of Minos' daughter Ariadnê, he gave Chios, we are told, although some writers of myths state that Oenopion was a son of Dionysus and learned from his father the art of making wine. And to each one of his other generals, the Cretans say, he made a present of an island or a city, Lemnos to Thoas, Cyrnus to Enyeus, Peparethos to Staphylus, Maroneia to Euanthes, Paros to Alcaeus, Delos to Anion, and to Andreus the island which was named after him Andros. Moreover, because of his very great justice, the myth has sprung up that he was appointed to be judge in Hades, were his decisions separate the good from the wicked. And the same honour has also been attained by Minos, because he ruled wholly in accordance with law and paid the greatest heed to justice.

The third brother, Sarpedon, we are told, crossed over into Asia with an army and subdued the regions about Lycia. Euandrus, his son, succeeded him in the kingship in Lycia, and marrying Deïdameia, the daughter of Bellerophon, he begat that Sarpedon who took part in the expedition against Troy, although some writers have called him a son of Zeus. Minos' sons, they say, were Deucalion and Molus, and to Deucalion was born Idomeneus and to Molus was born Meriones. These two joined with Agamemnon in the expedition against Ilium with ninety ships, and when they had returned in safety to their fatherland they died and were accorded a notable burial and immortal honours. And the Cretans point out their tomb at Cnosus, which bears the following inscription:

Behold Idomeneus the Cnosian's tomb,
And by his side am I, Meriones,
The son of Molus.

These two the Cretans hold in special honour as heroes of renown, offer- ing up sacrifices to them and calling upon them to come to their aid in the perils which arise in war.

80. But now that we have examined these matters it remains for us to discuss the peoples who have become intermixed with the Cretans. That the first inhabitants of the island were known as Eteocretans and that they are considered to have sprung from the soil itself, we have stated before; and many generations after them Pelasgians, who were in move- ment by reason of their continuous expeditions and migrations, arrived at Crete and made their home in part of the island. The third people to cross over to the island, we are told, were Dorians, under the leadership of Tectamus the son of Dorus; and the account states that the larger number of these Dorians was gathered from the regions about Olympus, but that a part of them consisted of Achaeans from Laconia, since Dorus had fixed the base of his expedition in the region about Cape Malea. And a fourth people to come to Crete and to become intermixed with the Cretans, we are told, was a heterogeneous collection of barbarians, who in the course of time adopted the language of the native Greeks. But after these events Minos and Rhadamanthys, when they had attained to power, gathered the peoples on the island into one union. And last of all, after the Return of the Heracleidae, Argives and Lacedaemonians sent forth colonies which they established on certain other islands and like- wise took possession of Crete, and on these islands they colonized cer- tain cities; with regard to these cities, however, we shall give a detailed account in connection with the period of time to which they belong. And since the greatest number of writers who have written about Crete dis- agree among themselves, there should be no occasion for surprise if what we report should not agree with every one of them; we have, indeed, followed as our authorities those who give the more probable account and are the most trustworthy, in some matters depending upon Epimenides who has written about the gods, in others upon Dosiades, Sosicrates, and Laosthenidas.

Now we move from the somewhat tedious Diodorus Siculus to the poet Ovid. Ovid mentions Minos in his *Metamorphoses*. Book VIII begins with a description of Minos' siege of the city of Megara (a harbour city between Athens and Corinth) and the romantic feelings which Scylla, daughter of the city's king, Nisus, has for Minos. As for the previous history of the events, it has already been mentioned above by Diodorus Siculus that Minos had begun a journey of revenge against Athens and Attica because of the murder of his son Androgeus. Cephalus, who is mentioned at the beginning, played a part in the preceding 'metamorphosis,' and is mentioned only as a trait d'union.

Ovid, *Metamorphoses*, Book VIII, 1 - 151

SCYLLA AND MINOS

The morning star revealed the shining day,
Night fled, the east wind fell, the rain clouds rose,
A steady south wind speeded the return
Of Cephalus with the Aeginetan force.
Their passage prospered and the fair breeze brought
Them sooner than their hopes to Athens' port.
Minos by now was laying waste the shores
Of Megara, testing his martial strength
Against the city of Alcathous,
Where Nisus reigned, a venerable king
Upon whose head, crowning his locks of white,
There gleamed a purple tress, the talisman
And magic guarantee of his great realm.
    Six times the crescent of the rising moon
Had climbed the sky and still the fate of war
Hung in the balance, and on doubtful wings
Long hovered victory between each side.
There was a royal turret, built above
The singing walls where once Latona's son [Apollo],
So the tale goes, laid down his golden lyre
And still its music lingers in the stones.
Here Nisus' daughter often used to climb
And with a little pebble set the stones
A-singing; that was in the days of peace.

And when war came, she often used to watch
From there the stubborn strife and clash of arms;
And, as the war dragged on, she came to know
The captains' names, their blazons, arms and steeds,
And Cretan quivers. Best of all she knew -
Knew more than well enough – their general,
Europa's son, King Minos. When he wore
His fine plumed casque that hid his face, she thought
Him splendid helmeted; if he put on
His shield of shining bronze, the shining shield
Enhanced his beauty; when with arm drawn back
He hurled his long lithe spear, the girl admired
His strength and skill; and if he drew the string
And set an arrow to his long curved bow,
She swore Apollo, shafts in hand, stood so.
But when, unhelmed, he showed his face and rode
In royal purple on his milk-white steed,
With trappings gay, and reined the foaming bit,
Ah, then she gazed almost beside herself,
Almost out of her mind. Happy, she thought,
The javelin he touched, happy the reins
He gathered in his hands. An impulse came
To make her way, were that allowed, across
The hostile lines, a girl among the foe;
A wild impulse to leap down from the turret
Into the Cretan camp, or open wide
The bronze-barred gates, or any other thing
Minos might wish. And as she sat and watched
The white pavilions of the Island king,
'This tragic war', she thought, 'I cannot tell
Whether it brings my heart more grief or joy;
Grief that Minos, my love, should be my foe;
Yet, save the war, I had not seen his face.
Still, if he held me hostage, he could end
The fighting; I should be his comrade; I
The pledge of peace. If she who gave you birth,
Most beautiful of kings, were like yourself,
Well she deserved to fire a god with love!
Thrice blest were I, if, winging through the air,

I stood within the camp of Knossos' king,
Confessed my love, and asked what he required
For dowry – so be it not my fatherland.
Perish my hope of marriage, if the price
Were treachery! Yet many in defeat
Find profit through a victor's clemency.
The war he wages for his murdered son
Is just; his cause is strong and strong the arms
That back his cause. Yes, our defeat is sure!
And if that doom awaits our city, why
Should his assault unlock those walls of mine
And not my love? Better that he should win
Now, with no slaughter, no delay, no cost
Of his own blood. Then, Minos, I'd not fear
Some blundering oaf might wound you! Oaf – for who
Could have the heart, well knowing what he did,
To aim his spear, his cruel spear, at you?
My start is sound: I stand on my resolve
To give myself and as my dowry give
My country too, and so will end the war.
But more than will is needed. Sentries guard
Every approach; the gates are locked; the keys
My father keeps. My father! Him alone,
Alas, I fear; alone he thwarts my hopes.
Would God I had no father! Everyone
Is his own god, for sure. Fortune rejects
A faint-heart's prayers. Fired with such love as mine
Another girl would blithely have destroyed,
Oh! long ago, whatever crossed her love.
Why should I be less brave? Through fire and sword
I'd dare to go. Yet here there is no need
Of fire or sword: I need my father's tress,
That purple tress, more precious now to me
Than gold; that tress will bring me blessedness,
Will give me power to win my heart's desire.'

    Then night, the surest nurse of troubled souls,
Advanced and with the dark her courage grew.
It was the quiet hour when slumber first
Enfolds men's hearts, tired by the long day's toil.

Into her father's chamber silently
The daughter crept and stole (oh, deed of doom!)
His life-tress and, her wicked booty won,
Crossed through the Cretan lines (so sure her trust
In her deserts) and reached the startled king,
And told her tale. 'Love led me to this deed.
I am King Nisus' daughter, Princess Scylla.
I offer you myself, my home, my country;
I ask for no reward except yourself.
Take for my love's sure proof this purple tress
And know I give you – not my father's tress –
I give his head!' And in her guilty hand
She offered him the tress. But Minos shrank
In horror from the gift, that monstrous gift,
And answered: 'You disgrace of our fair age!
May the gods purge you from their world! May land
And sea be barred to you! My land of Crete,
The isle that cradled Jove, I swear shall never
Feel the contagion of so foul a fiend!'
    Then Minos, justest of lawgivers, imposed
Terms on his captive enemies and bade
His fleet weigh anchor and the rowers man
The bronze-bound ships. And Scylla, when she saw
The vessels launched and knew the king refused
Her crime's reward, her prayers exhausted, turned
To storming fury and with streaming hair
And hands outstretched in passionate rage she cried:
'Whither away so fast, leaving behind
Her who achieved so much, deserves so well,
You who were more to me than father, more
Than fatherland? Whither away, so cruel,
Whose triumph is my crime and my deserts?
The gift I gave, my love for you, my hopes
Built all on you alone, do they not move you?
Where can I turn abandoned? Turn again
Home to my fatherland? It lies in ruins.
Suppose it stands, its gates are closed to me
By my betrayal. Back to my father's arms?
He was my gift to you! My countrymen

Hate me and have good cause. The neighbouring cities
Fear my example. I from all the world
Am banished: Crete alone is open now.
If you forbid me Crete, ungrateful wretch,
And leave me here, you're not Europa's son.
Your mother was the Syrtes desolate sands,
A tigress of Armenia, or Charybdis,
Lashed by the wild south wind. Jove's not your father,
Coaxing his darling in a bull's disguise.
That fable's false. It was a real bull
Begot you. Nisus, father, punish me!
Take your revenge! Ye towers and battlements
That I betrayed rejoice in my distress!
Yes, I have earned your joy! And I deserve
To die. But let my death come at the hand
Of one my wrong has injured. Why should you
Impeach my crime, who triumphed by my crime?
My sin against my father and my country
Take as my service done! Fit mate were you
Of that adulteress who in a cow
Of wood beguiled a savage bull and bore
A monster in her womb! Do my words reach
Your ears or do the winds blow them to waste?
Those winds, ungrateful wretch, that fill your sails!
No wonder your Pasiphae preferred
Her bull to you: you were the fiercer beast.
Oh, my heart breaks! He bids them haste away;
Oars strike the sounding waves; the shore recedes
And I too on the shore. All to no end!
In vain have you forgotten my deserts;
Against your will I'll follow. I shall clutch
Your curving poop and you shall carry me
Across the seas' long swell.' And, as she spoke,
She leapt into the waves (her passion gave
Her strength) and swam after the ship and clung -
Vile shipmate – to the Cretan galleon.
    Her father saw her as he hovered near
(Changed to an osprey now with tawny wings)
And swooped to seize and tear her, as she clung,

With his hooked beak. She loosed her hold in terror,
And, as she fell, the light breeze seemed to bear
Her safe above the sea. It was her wings:
Changed to a feathered bird she rode the air –
A Shearer, named from that shorn tress of hair.

After this 'metamorphosis' the poet continues with the story of the
Minotaur.   *Miscellanea*

Ovid, *Metamorphoses*, Book VIII, 152 - 182

THE MINOTAUR

Minos reached harbour in the isle of Crete
And, disembarking, paid his vows to Jove,
A hundred bulls, and hung the spoils of war
To adorn his palace walls. His dynasty's
Disgrace had grown; the monstrous hybrid beast
Declared the queen's obscene adultery.
To rid his precincts of this shame the king
Planned to confine him shut away within
Blind walls of intricate complexity.
The structure was designed by Daedalus,
That famous architect. Appearances
Were all confused; he led the eye astray
By a mazy multitude of winding ways,
Just as Maeander plays among the meads
Of Phrygia and in its puzzling flow
Glides back and forth and meets itself and sees
Its waters on their way and winds along,
Facing sometimes its source, sometimes the sea.
So Daedalus in countless corridors
Built bafflement, and hardly could himself
Make his way out, so puzzling was the maze.
  Within this labyrinth Minos shut fast
The beast, half bull, half man, and fed him twice
On Attic blood, lot-chosen each nine years,
Until the third choice mastered him. The door,
So difficult, which none of those before

Could find again, by Ariadne's aid
Was found, the thread that traced the way rewound.
Then Theseus, seizing Minos' daughter, spread
His sails for Naxos, where, upon the shore,
That cruel prince abandoned her and she,
Abandoned, in her grief and anger found
Comfort in Bacchus' arms. He took her crown
And set it in the heavens to win her there
A star's eternal glory; and the crown
Flew through the soft light air and, as it flew,
Its gems were turned to gleaming fires, and still
Shaped as a crown their place in heaven they take
Between the Kneeler and him who grasps the Snake.

And then comes the story of Daedalus and Icarus.

Ovid, *Metamorphoses*, Book VIII, 183 - 259

DAEDALUS AND ICARUS

Hating the isle of Crete and the long years
Of exile, Daedalus was pining for
His native land, but seas on every side
Imprisoned him. 'Though land and sea', he thought,
'The king may bar to me, at least the sky
Is open; through the sky I'll set my course.
Minos may own all else; he does not own
The air.' So then to unimagined arts
He set his mind and altered nature's laws.
    Row upon row of feathers he arranged,
The smallest first, then larger ones, to form
A growing graded shape, as rustic pipes
Rise in a gradual slope of lengthening reeds;
Then bound the middle and the base with wax
And flaxen threads, and bent them, so arranged,
Into a gentle curve to imitate
Wings of a real bird. His boy stood by,
Young Icarus, who, blithely unaware
He plays with his own peril, tries to catch

Feathers that float upon the wandering breeze,
Or softens with his thumb the yellow wax,
And by his laughing mischief interrupts
His father's wondrous work. Then, when the last
Sure touch was given, the craftsman poised himself
On his twin wings and hovered in the air,
   Next he prepared his son. 'Take care', he said,
'To fly a middle course, lest if you sink

Too low the waves may weight your feathers; if
Too high, the heat may burn them. Fly half-way
Between the two. And do not watch the stars,
The Great Bear or the Wagoner or Orion,
With his drawn sword, to steer by. Set your course
Where I shall lead.' He fixed the strange new wings
On his son's shoulders and instructed him
How he should fly; and, as he worked and warned,
The old man's cheeks were wet, the father's hands
Trembled. He kissed his son (the last kisses
He'd ever give) and rising on his wings
He flew ahead, anxious for his son's sake,
Just like a bird that from its lofty nest
Launches a tender fledgeling in the air.
Calling his son to follow, schooling him
In that fatal apprenticeship, he flapped
His wings and watched the boy flapping behind.
   An angler fishing with his quivering rod,
A lonely shepherd propped upon his crook,
A ploughman leaning on his plough, looked up
And gazed in awe, and thought they must be gods
That they could fly. Delos and Paros lay
Behind them now; Samos, great Juno's isle,
Was on the left, Lebinthos on the right
And honey-rich Calymne, when the boy
Began to enjoy his thrilling flight and left
His guide to roam the ranges of the heavens,
And soared too high. The scorching sun so close
Softened the fragrant wax that bound his wings;
The wax melted; his waving arms were bare;
Unfledged, they had no purchase on the air!

And calling to his father as he fell,
The boy was swallowed in the blue sea's swell,
The blue sea that for ever bears his name.
His wretched father, now no father, cried
'Oh, Icarus, where are you? Icarus,
Where shall I look, where find you?' On the waves
He saw the feathers. Then he cursed his skill,
And buried his boy's body in a grave,
And still that island keeps the name he gave.

Before we turn to the time of the Trojan War, in which Minos' grandson Idomeneus took part, we quote from the journey of the Argonauts, as written down by the 3rd-century B.C. Greek poet Apollonios Rhodios (like Callimachus he was librarian of the famous Alexandrian Library). This is the story of Jason, who along with a large throng of Greek heroes came to steal the Golden Fleece in Kolchis, on the Black Sea. They were helped by the daughter of the Kolchian king, Medeia, one of the most impressive female figures passed down to us in Greek legend.

After their looting of the Fleece the Argonauts returned to Greece, now accompanied by Medeia. They sailed by way of a rather unusual route, from the Black Sea via the Danube to the Adriatic Sea, and from there along the Po and the Rhone to the Tyrrhenian Sea. From there they almost reached the Greek mainland, but a northerly storm pushed them towards the Libyan coast. There they were shipwrecked in the shallow waters of the Gulf of Syrte.

In the beginning of the quotation, the heroes are being helped by the sea god Triton. The quotation shows by the way how difficult navigation was for ships in a time when the use of compasses was not known yet, and how easily a ship could become a plaything for the winds.

Apollonios Rhodios, *Argonautica*, Book IV, 1617 - 1730
He [Triton] drove the ship forward till they reached the sea, then set her
on course, and at once plunged into the depths. The heroes
cried out as they witnessed this uncanny portent. Here still
there's a Bay of Argo and memorials of their vessel
and altars dedicated to Triton and Poseidon,
since for that day they rested up. But when dawn broke,
they ran on with bellying sails before a good west wind,
keeping that barren coastline to starboard. Next morning early

they sighted the promontory and the deep sea gulf
that lay beyond the curve of the jutting headland.
At once, as the west wind dropped, the sirocco began to blow
from the southwest, and their hearts rejoiced to hear it.
But when the sun went down, and that shepherd's star
returned that brings respite to all weary ploughmen,
then, after darkness fell, the sirocco died down,
so they struck the sails and lowered the lofty mast,
bent to their smooth-worn oars, and rowed doggedly on
all night long, and next day besides, and after that day another
full night. Remote Kárpathos, craggy and beetling,
welcomed them. From here they planned to make the crossing
over to Krété, the outermost of all Aigaian islands.
But Talos, the man of bronze, by breaking off gigantic
rocks from the massy headland, stopped them from making fast their
mooring ropes ashore, there in Dikté's sheltered haven.
This Talos was a survivor, of Bronze Age stock, folk descended
from ash trees, living now in the age of the demigods;
Zeus gave him to Európé to be the island's watchman,
and on brazen feet, thrice daily, to pace round Krété.
Now the rest of his body and limbs indeed were fashioned
of bronze, and infrangible; but below his ankle tendon
there ran a vein, full of blood, and the delicate membrane
covering it determined the bounds between life and death.
So they, though worn out with fatigue, at once in terror
bent to their oars, backed the ship off from shore,
and in sore distress would have voyaged far from Krété,
afflicted by thirst and exhaustion both, had not Medeia
cried out to them as they began their withdrawal: 'Listen:
I believe that I alone can win the mastery for you
over this man, whoever he is, even if his whole body
be fashioned of bronze – unless he should prove immortal.
So hold the vessel at large, out of range of his stone-throwing,
until he submits to me, concedes my mastery.'
So she spoke, and they, having got out of missile range,
rested there on their oars, waiting to see what device
she'd contrive against expectation. Covering both cheeks
with a fold of her purple mantle, she ascended
the after deck, and Jason, clasping her hand in his,

led her along the catwalk between the thwarts.
There with her spells she invoked, and placated, the death spirits,
those eaters of life, swift hellhounds, that all around us
circle the air, to pounce upon living creatures.
Thrice now in supplication she besought them with spells,
thrice with prayers, then hardened her will with malice,
and with alien hostile gaze hexed bronze Talos's vision,
teeth grinding in hate-filled wrath against him, while her vehement
fury assailed him with deadly hallucinations.

Zeus, Father, indeed great wonder stirs my spirit
that not only through wounds or disease should annihilation
meet us: some enemies, too, can crush us from a distance!

So Talos, bronze though he was, conceded the mastery
to Medeia's far-reaching magic. While he was hefting
massive rocks to stop them reaching safe anchorage,
he scraped his ankle against a stony spur. The *ichor*
gushed out like melted lead. Not for long after
did he still stand planted there on that jutted headland,
but like some gigantic pine, high up in the mountains,
that the woodmen with their keen axes have left half-severed
when they trudge back home from the forest, and first it's shaken
by gales of wind at nightfall, then finally, later,
comes crashing down, snapped at the stump: so Talos awhile,
though swaying, held himself upright on unwearying feet,
but weakening at last, fell prone, with an enormous crash.
So that night indeed they bivouacked on Krété,
these heroes; but afterwards, at the first flush of dawn,
when they'd erected a shrine to Minoan Athena
and taken on water, they quickly went aboard
to row out as soon as might be past Cape Salmónis.
But as they were running steady across the great Sea of Krété
night suddenly fell, a terror they call the Shroud of Darkness.
This deadly night was too thick for starlight or moonbeams
to pierce, it came as a black void out of heaven,
or some other blackness, up from the nether depths.
For themselves, they had no notion whether it was in Hades
or on the sea that they were drifting: but still they entrusted

their safe return to the sea, not knowing were it bore them.
Then Jason, hands outstretched, called loudly upon Phoibos
appealing for rescue, while down his agonized cheeks
tears ran. Gifts he promised past counting, he'd bring them
in bulk to the god's shrines – Ortygia, Pytho, Amyklai.

Son of Leto, quickly you heard him, lightly you descended
from heaven to the Melantian rocks, that lie there
out in the deep, and springing on one of their twin peaks
in your right hand you brandished high your golden
bow, and all around it gave off a dazzling light.

So now there was revealed to them one of the Spóradés,
a small island over against the tiny islet Hippoúris,
and here they cast anchor and landed. Very quickly the dawn
came up, bringing light, and they built Apollo a splendid
shrine in a shady grove, and a pebbled altar,
and because of the far-beamed radiance they invoked him as Phoibos
the Radiant, and that rocky island they named Anáphé,
'Revelation,' since in their distress Apollo revealed it to them.
They sacrificed such things as men on a desolate beach
could provide for sacrifice; but when they poured libations
of water on blazing faggots, then Medeia's
Phaiakian handmaids, seeing them, could no longer
hold back the laughter that rose within them, so frequent
the sacrifices of oxen they'd seen in Alkínoös's halls.
The heroes scoffed back at them with indecent language,
reveling in the joke, flared up, flung scurrilous insults,
exchanged mockery, all in fun. Because of the heroes' sport,
on that island women still contend against the menfolk
in such raillery, when with their offerings they propitiate
Apollo the Radiant, the guardian of Anáphé.

A generation later (around 1200 B.C., according to most ancient historians; the years most often mentioned are 1184 and 1218 B.C.) the Trojan War broke out. In an evocative passage in his *Iliad* Homer (8th century B.C.) sums up which heroes took part in the war. Idomeneus from Crete is also there. Here we quote parts of Homer's list of heroes. The 'Danaans' mentioned in the text is another name for the Akhaians.

Homer, *Iliad*, Book II, 484 - 516, 527 - 602, 631 - 652

Tell me now, you Muses who have your homes on Olympos.
For you, who are goddesses, are there, and you know all things,
and we have heard only the rumour of it and know nothing.
Who then of those were the chief men and the lords of the Danaans?
I could not tell over the multitude of them nor name them,
not if I had ten tongues and ten mouths, not if I had
a voice never to be broken and a heart of bronze within me,
not unless the Muses of Olympia, daughters
of Zeus of the aegis, remembered all those who came beneath Ilion.
I will tell the lords of the ships, and the ships numbers.

    Leïtos and Peneleos were leaders of the Boiotians,
with Arkesilaos and Prothoenor and Klonios;
they who lived in Hyria and in rocky Aulis,
in the hill-bends of Eteonos, and Schoinos, and Skolos,
Thespeia and Graia, and in spacious Mykalessos;
they who dwelt about Harma and Eilesion and Erythrai,
they who held Eleon and Hyle and Peteon,
with Okalea and Medeon, the strong-founded citadel,
Kopai, and Eutresis, and Thisbe of the dove-cotes;
they who held Koroneia, and the meadows of Haliartos,
they who held Plataia, and they who dwelt about Glisa,
they who held the lower Thebes, the strong-founded citadel,
and Onchestos the sacred, the shining grove of Poseidon;
they who held Arne of the great vineyards, and Mideia,
with Nisa the sacrosanct and uttermost Anthedon.
Of these there were fifty ships in all, and on board
each of these a hundred and twenty sons of the Boiotians.

    But they who lived in Aspledon and Orchomenos of the Minyai,
Askalaphos led these, and Ialmenos, children of Ares,
whom Astyoche bore to him in the house of Aktor
Azeus' son, a modest maiden; she went into the chamber
with strong Ares, who was laid in bed with her secretly.
With these two there were marshalled thirty hollow vessels…

    Swift Aias son of Oïleus led the men of Lokris,
the lesser Aias, not great in size like the son of Telamon,
but far slighter. He was a small man armoured in linen,
yet with the throwing spear surpassed all Achaians and Hellenes.
These were the dwellers in Kynos and Opoeis and Kalliaros,

and in Bessa, and Skarphe, and lovely Augeiai,
in Thronion and Tarphe and beside the waters of Boagrios.
Following along with him were forty black ships
of the Lokrians, who dwell across from sacred Euboia.

They who held Euboia, the Abantes, whose wind was fury,
Chalkis, and Eretria, the great vineyards of Histiaia,
and seaborne Kerinthos and the steep stronghold of Dion,
they who held Karystos and they who dwelt about Styra,
of these the leader was Elephenor, scion of Ares,
son of Chalkodon and lord of the great-hearted Abantes.
And the running Abantes followed with him, their hair grown
long at the back, spearmen furious with the out-reached ash spear
to rip the corselets girt about the chests of their enemies.
Following along with him were forty black ships.

But the men who held Athens, the strong-founded citadel,
the deme of great-hearted Erechtheus, whom once Athene
Zeus' daughter tended after the grain-giving fields had borne him,
and established him to be in Athens in her own rich temple;
there as the circling years go by the sons of the Athenians
make propitiation with rams and bulls sacrificed;
of these men the leader was Peteos' son Menestheus.
Never on earth before had there been a man born like him
for the arrangement in order of horses and shielded fighters.
Nestor alone could challenge him, since he was far older.
Following along with him were fifty black ships.

Out of Salamis Aias brought twelve ships and placed them
next to where the Athenian battalions were drawn up.

They who held Argos and Tiryns of the huge walls,
Hermione and Asine lying down the deep gulf,
Troizen and Eïonai, and Epidauros of the vineyards,
they who held Aigina and Mases, sons of the Achaians,
of these the leader was Diomedes of the great war cry
with Sthenelos, own son to the high-renowned Kapaneus,
and with them as a third went Euryalos, a man godlike,
son of Mekisteus the king, and scion of Talaos;
but the leader of all was Diomedes of the great war cry.
Following along with these were eighty black ships.

But the men who held Mykenai, the strong founded citadel,
Korinth the luxurious, and strong-founded Kleonai;

they who dwelt in Orneai and lovely Araithyrea,
and Sikyon, where of old Adrestos had held the kingship;
they who held Hyperesia and steep Gonoëssa,
they who held Pellene and they who dwelt about Aigion,
all about the sea-shore and about the wide headland of Helike,
of their hundred ships the leader was powerful Agamemnon,
Atreus' son, with whom followed far the best and bravest
people; and among them he himself stood armoured in shining
bronze, glorying, conspicuous among the great fighters,
since he was greatest among them all, and led the most people.

They who held the swarming hollow of Lakedaimon,
Pharis, and Sparta, and Messe of the dove-cotes,
they who dwelt in Bryseiai and lovely Augeiai,
they who held Amyklai and the seaward city of Helos,
they who held Laas, and they who dwelt about Oitylos,
of these his brother Menelaos of the great war cry
was leader, with sixty ships marshalled apart from the others.
He himself went among them in the confidence of his valour,
driving them battleward, since above all his heart was eager
to avenge Helen's longing to escape and her lamentations.

They who dwelt about Pylos and lovely Arene,
and Thryon, the Alpheios crossing, and strong-built Aipy;
they who lived in Kyparisseeis and Amphigeneia,
Pteleos and Helos and Dorion, where the Muses
encountering Thamyris the Thracian stopped him from singing
as he came from Oichalia and Oichalian Eurytos;
for he boasted that he would surpass, if the very Muses,
daughters of Zeus who holds the aegis, were singing against him,
and these in their anger struck him maimed, and the voice of wonder
they took away, and made him a singer without memory;
of these the leader was the Gerenian horseman, Nestor,
in whose command were marshalled ninety hollow vessels...

But Odysseus led the high-hearted men of Kephallenia,
those who held Ithaka and leaf-trembling Neriton,
those who dwelt about Krokyleia and rigged Aigilips,
those who held Zakynthos and those who dwelt about Samos,
those who held the mainland and the places next to the crossing.
All these men were led by Odysseus, like Zeus in counsel.
Following with him were twelve ships with bows red painted.

Thoas son of Andraimon was leader of the Aitolians,
those who dwelt in Pleuron and Olenos and Pylene,
Kalydon of the rocks and Chalkis beside the sea-shore,
since no longer were the sons of high-hearted Oineus living,
nor Oineus himself, and fair-haired Meleagros had perished.
So all the lordship of the Aitolians was given to Thoas.
Following along with him were forty black ships
    Idomeneus the spear-famed was leader of the Kretans,
those who held Knosos and Gortyna of the great walls,
Lyktos and Miletos and silver-shining Lykastos,
and Phaistos and Rhytion, all towns well established,
and others who dwelt beside them in Krete of the hundred cities.
Of all these Idomeneus the spear-famed was leader,
with Meriones, a match for the murderous Lord of Battles.
Following along with these were eighty black ships.

The list goes on. Of the combined fleet which totalled c. 1200 ships, the Cretan contribution of 80 ships together with the 80 of Diomedes were the third largest contingency. Only Agamemnon and Nestor brought more ships in.

Another famous passage, this time from Homer's *Odyssey*, is where Odysseus disguises himself as a Cretan prince and tells Penelope about his 'meeting' with Odysseus. The term 'native Cretans' is a translation of the term 'eteo-Cretans,' which others leave untranslated.

Homer, *Odyssey*, Book XIX, 195 - 219
    There is a land called Crete …
ringed by the wine-dark sea with rolling whitecaps –
handsome country, fertile, thronged with people
well past counting – boasting ninety cities,
language mixing with language side-by-side.
First come the Achaeans, then the native Cretans,
hardy, gallant in action, then Cydonian clansmen,
Dorians living in three tribes, and proud Pelasgians last.
Central to all their cities is magnificent Cnossos,
the site where Minos ruled and each ninth year
conferred with almighty Zeus himself. Minos,
father of my father, Deucalion, that bold heart.
Besides myself Deucalion sired Prince Idomeneus,

who set sail for Troy in his beaked ships of war,
escorting Atreus' sons. My own name is Aethon.
I am the younger-born;
my older brother's a better man than I am.
Now, it was there in Cnossos that I saw him...
Odysseus – and we traded gifts of friendship.
A heavy gale had landed him on our coast,
driven him way off course, rounding Malea's cape
when he was bound for Troy. He anchored in Amnisus,
hard by the goddess' cave of childbirth and labor,
that rough harbor – barely riding out the storm.
He came into town at once, asking for Idomeneus,
claiming to be my brother's close, respected friend.

Finally, another famous passage from Homer's *Iliad*. This is the description of the shield which Hefaistos forged for Achilleus when Achilleus decided to take part in the battle against Troy after the death of his comrade Patroklos. The description gives fascinating insights into what may have been the world of the Akhaians. At the end a dance floor is described, and every visitor to the palace of Knossós will think of the Theatral Area (perhaps a dance floor) which spreads itself out there, to the north of the palace. The passage begins with the visit which Thetis, the immortal mother of Achilleus, makes to the smith of the gods, the crippled Hefaistos. Before the quotation starts, the poet has mentioned a conversation between Zeus and Hera.

Homer, *Iliad*, Book XVIII, 368 - 616

Now as these two [Zeus and Hera] were saying things like this to each
   other,
Thetis of the silver feet came to the house of Hephaistos,
imperishable, starry, and shining among the immortals,
built in bronze for himself by the god of the dragging footsteps.
She found him sweating as he turned here and there to his bellows
busily, since he was working on twenty tripods
which were to stand against the wall of his strong-founded dwelling.
And he had set golden wheels underneath the base of each one
so that of their own motion they could wheel into the immortal
gathering, and return to his house: a wonder to look at.
These were so far finished, but the elaborate ear handles

were not yet on. He was forging these, and beating the chains out.
As he was at work on this in his craftsmanship and his cunning
meanwhile the goddess Thetis the silver-footed drew near him.
Charis of the shining veil saw her as she came forward,
she, the lovely goddess the renowned strong-armed one had married.
She came, and caught her hand and called her by name and spoke to her:
'Why is it, Thetis of the light robes, you have come to our house now?
We honour you and love you; but you have not come much before this.
But come in with me, so I may put entertainment before you.'

　　She spoke, and, shining among divinities, led the way forward
and made Thetis sit down in a chair that was wrought elaborately
and splendid with silver nails, and under it was a footstool.
She called to Hephaistos the renowned smith and spoke a word to him:
'Hephaistos, come this way; here is Thetis, who has need of you.'

　　Hearing her the renowned smith of the strong arms answered her:
'Then there is a goddess we honour and respect in our house.
She saved me when I suffered much at the time of my great fall
through the will of my own brazen-faced mother, who wanted
to hide me, for being lame. Then my soul would have taken much suffering
had not Eurynome and Thetis caught me and held me,
Eurynome, daughter of Ocean, whose stream bends back in a circle.
With them I worked nine years as a smith, and wrought many intricate
things; pins that bend back, curved clasps, cups, neclaces, working
there in the hollow of the cave, and the stream of Ocean around us
went on forever with its foam and its murmur. No other
among the gods or among mortal men knew about us
except Eurynome and Thetis. They knew, since they saved me.
Now she has come into our house; so I must by all means
do everything to give recompense to lovely-haired Thetis
for my life. Therefore set out before her fair entertainment
while I am putting away my bellows and all my instruments.'

　　He spoke, and took the huge blower off from the block of the anvil
limping; and yet his shrunken legs moved lightly beneath him.
He set the bellows away from the fire, and gathered and put away
all the tools with which he worked in a silver strongbox.
Then with a sponge he wiped clean his forehead, and both hands,
and his massive neck and hairy chest, and put on a tunic,
and took up a heavy stick in his hand, and went to the doorway
limping. And in support of their master moved his attendants.

These are golden, and in appearance like living young women.
There is intelligence in their hearts, and there is speech in them
and strength, and from the immortal gods they have learned how to do
    things.
These stirred nimbly in support of their master, and moving
near to where Thetis sat in her shining chair, Hephaistos
caught her by the hand and called her by name and spoke a word to her:
'Why is it, Thetis of the light robes, you have come to our house now?
We honour you and love you; but you have not come much before this.
Speak forth what is in your mind. My heart is urgent to do it
if I can, and if it is a thing that can be accomplished.'
    Then in turn Thetis answered him, letting the tears fall:
'Hephaistos, is there among all the goddesses on Olympos
one who in her heart has endured so many grim sorrows
as the griefs Zeus, son of Kronos, has given me beyond others?
Of all the other sisters of the sea he gave me to a mortal,
to Peleus, Aiakos' son, and I had to endure mortal marriage
though much against my will. And now he, broken by mournful
old age, lies away in his halls. Yet I have other troubles.
For since he has given me a son to bear and to raise up
conspicuous among heroes, and he shot up like a young tree,
I nurtured him, like a tree grown in the pride of the orchard.
I sent him away in the curved ships to the land of Ilion
to fight with the Trojans; but I shall never again receive him
won home again to his country and into the house of Peleus.
Yet while I see him live and he looks on the sunlight, he has
sorrows, and though I go to him I can do nothing to help him.
And the girl the sons of the Achaians chose out for his honour
powerful Agamemnon took her away again out of his hands.
For her his heart has been wasting in sorrow; but meanwhile the Trojans
pinned the Achaians against their grounded ships, and would not
let them win outside, and the elders of the Argives entreated
my son, and named the many glorious gifts they would give him.
But at that time he refused himself to fight the death from them;
nevertheless he put his own armour upon Patroklos
and sent him into the fighting, and gave many men to go with him.
All day they fought about the Skaian Gates, and on that day
they would have stormed the city, if only Phoibos Apollo
had not killed the fighting son of Menoitios there in the first ranks

after he had wrought much damage, and given the glory to Hektor.
Therefore now I come to your knees; so might you be willing
to give me for my short-lived son a shield and a helmet
and two beautiful greaves fitted with clasps for the ankles
and a corselet. What he had was lost with his steadfast companion
when the Trojans killed him. Now my son lies on the ground, heart `
   sorrowing.'

   Hearing her the renowned smith of the strong arms answered her: *Miscellanea*
'Do not fear. Let not these things be a thought in your mind.
And I wish that I could hide him away from death and its sorrow
at that time when his hard fate comes upon him, as surely
as there shall be fine armour for him, such as another
man out of many men shall wonder at, when he looks on it.'
   So he spoke, and left her there, and went to his bellows.
He turned these toward the fire and gave them their orders for working.
And the bellows, all twenty of them, blew on the crucibles,
from all directions blasting forth wind to blow the flames high
now as he hurried to be at this place and now at another,
wherever Hephaistos might wish them to blow, and the work went forward.
He cast on the fire bronze which is weariless, and tin with it
and valuable gold, and silver, and thereafter set forth
upon its standard the great anvil, and gripped in one hand
the ponderous hammer, while in the other he grasped the pincers.
   First of all he forged a shield that was huge and heavy,
elaborating it about, and threw around it a shining
triple rim that glittered, and the shield strap was cast of silver.
There were five folds composing the shield itself, and upon it
he elaborated many things in his skill and craftsmanship.
   He made the earth upon it, and the sky, and the sea's water,
and the tireless sun, and the moon waxing into her fullness,
and on it all the constellations that festoon the heavens,
the Pleiades and the Hyades and the strength of Orion
and the Bear, whom men give also the name of the Wagon,
who turns about in a fixed place and looks at Orion
and she alone is never plunged in the wash of the Ocean.
   On it he wrought in all their beauty two cities of mortal
men. And there were marriages in one, and festivals.
They were leading the brides along the city from their maiden chambers
under the flaring of torches, and the loud bride song was arising.

The young men followed the circles of the dance, and among them
the flutes and lyres kept up their clamour as in the meantime
the women standing each at the door of her court admired them.
The people were assembled in the market place, where a quarrel
had arisen, and two men were disputing over the blood price
for a man who had been killed. One man promised full restitution
in a public statement, but the other refused and would accept nothing.
Both then made for an arbitrator, to have a decision;
and people were speaking up on either side, to help both men.
But the heralds kept the people in hand, as meanwhile the elders
were in session on benches of polished stone in the sacred circle
and held in their hands the staves of the heralds who lift their voices.
The two men rushed before these, and took turns speaking their cases,
and between them lay on the ground two talents of gold, to be given
to that judge who in this case spoke the straightest opinion.
    But around the other city were lying two forces of armed men
shining in their war gear. For one side counsel was divided
whether to storm and sack, or share between both sides the property
and all the possessions the lovely citadel held hard within it.
But the city's people were not giving way, and armed for an ambush.
Their beloved wives and their little children stood on the rampart
to hold it, and with them the men with age upon them, but meanwhile
the others went out. And Ares led them, and Pallas Athene.
These were gold, both, and golden raiment upon them, and they were
beautiful and huge in their armour, being divinities,
and conspicuous from afar, but the people around them were smaller.
These, when they were come to the place that was set for their ambush,
in a river, where there was a watering place for all animals,
there they sat down in place shrouding themselves in the bright bronze.
But apart from these were sitting two men to watch for the rest of them
and waiting until they could see the sheep and the shambling cattle,
who appeared presently, and two herdsmen went along with them
playing happily on pipes, and took no thought of the treachery.
Those others saw them, and made a rush, and quickly thereafter
cut off on both sides the herds of cattle and the beautiful
flocks of shining sheep, and killed the shepherds upon them.
But the other army, as soon as they heard the uproar arising
from the cattle, as they sat in their councils, suddenly mounted
behind their light-foot horses, and went after, and soon overtook them.

These stood their ground and fought a battle by the banks of the river,
and they were making casts at each other with their spears bronze-headed;
and Hate was there with Confusion among them, and Death the destructive;
she was holding a live man with a new wound, and another
one unhurt, and dragged a dead man by the feet through the carnage.
The clothing upon her shoulders showed strong red with the men's blood.
All closed together like living men and fought with each other
and dragged away from each other the corpses of those who had fallen.   *Miscellanea*

   He made upon it a soft field, the pride of the tilled land,
wide and triple-ploughed, with many ploughmen upon it
who wheeled their teams at the turn and drove them in either direction.
And as these making their turn would reach the end strip of the field,
a man would come up to them at this point and hand them a flagon
of honey-sweet wine, and they would turn again to the furrows
in their haste to come again to the end-strip of the deep field.
The earth darkened behind them and looked like earth that has been
   ploughed
though it was gold. Such was the wonder of the shield's forging.

   He made on it the precinct of a king, where the labourers
were reaping, with the sharp reaping hooks in their hands. Of the cut
   swathes
some fell along the lines of reaping, one after another,
while the sheaf-binders caught up others and tied them with bind-ropes.
There were three sheaf-binders who stood by, and behind them
were children picking up the cut swathes, and filled their arms with them
and carried and gave them always; and by them the king in silence
and holding his staff stood near the line of the reapers, happily.
And apart and under a tree the heralds made a feast ready
and trimmed a great ox they had slaughtered. Meanwhile the women
scattered, for the workmen to eat, abundant white barley.

   He made on it a great vineyard heavy with clusters,
lovely and in gold, but the grapes upon it were darkened
and the vines themselves stood out through poles of silver. About them
he made a field-ditch of dark metal, and drove all around this
a fence of tin; and there was only one path to the vineyard,
and along it ran the grape-bearers for the vineyard's stripping.
Young girls and young men, in all their light-hearted innocence,
carried the kind, sweet fruit away in their woven baskets,
and in their midst a youth with a singing lyre played charmingly

upon it for them, and sang the beautiful song for Linos
in a light voice, and they followed him, and with singing and whistling
and light dance-steps of their feet kept time to the music.

He made upon it a herd of horn-straight oxen. The cattle
were wrought of gold and of tin, and thronged in speed and with lowing
out of the dung of the farmyard to a pasturing place by a sounding
river, and beside the moving field of a reed bed.
The herdsmen were of gold who went along with the cattle,
four of them, and nine dogs shifting their feet followed them.
But among the foremost of the cattle two formidable lions
had caught hold of a bellowing bull, and he with loud lowings
was dragged away, as the dogs and the young men went in pursuit of him.
But the two lions, breaking open the hide of the great ox,
gulped the black blood and the inward guts, as meanwhile the herdsmen
were in the act of setting and urging the quick dogs on them.
But they, before they could get their teeth in, turned back from the lions,
but would come and take their stand very close, and bayed, and kept clear.

And the renowned smith of the strong arms made on it a meadow
large and in a lovely valley for the glimmering sheepflocks,
with dwelling places upon it, and covered shelters, and sheepfolds.

And the renowned smith of the strong arms made elaborate on it
a dancing floor, like that which once in the wide spaces of Knosos
Daidalos built for Ariadne of the lovely tresses.
And there were young men on it and young girls, sought for their beauty
with gifts of oxen, dancing, and holding hands at the wrist. These
wore, the maidens long light robes, but the men wore tunics
of finespun work and shining softly, touched with olive oil.
And the girls wore fair garlands on their heads, while the young men
carried golden knives that hung from sword-belts of silver.
At whiles on their understanding feet they would run very lightly,
as when a potter crouching makes trial of his wheel, holding
it close in his hands, to see if it will run smooth. At another
time they would form rows, and run, rows crossing each other.
And around the lovely chorus of dancers stood a great multitude
happily watching, while among the dancers two acrobats
led the measures of song and dance revolving among them.

He made on it the great strength of the Ocean River
which ran around the uttermost rim of the shield's strong structure.

Then after he had wrought this shield, which was huge and heavy,

he wrought for him a corselet brighter than fire in its shining,
and wrought him a helmet, massive and fitting close to his temples,
lovely and intricate work, and laid a gold top-ridge along it,
and out of pliable tin wrought him leg-armour. Thereafter
when the renowned smith of the strong arms had finished the armour
he lifted it and laid it before the mother of Achilleus.
And she like a hawk came sweeping down from the snows of Olympos
and carried with her the shining armour, the gift of Hephaistos.   *Miscellanea*

III. The downfall: Atlantis

Around 1500 B.C. the volcano on the island of Thíra erupted and partly collapsed. The resulting tidal wave and ash- and pumice showers were probably the most important causes of the disappearance of the Minoan civilization (see also the introductory notes to Chapter 9). It is quite possible that the Minoan civilization in Crete and the collapse of the volcano are reflected in the well-known story of Atlantis. We quote here from the only known sources: passages from two dialogues written down by the famous Greek philosopher Plato (c. 400 B.C.): the *Timaeus* and the *Kritias*. In both cases Plato lets the story be told by the same participant in the dialogue, a certain Kritias. Kritias had heard the story from one of his ancestors who in his turn had recorded it from the mouth of a relative of the 6th century B.C. Athenian lawgiver Solon. Solon himself had heard it during a visit to the Egyptian city of Saïs. According to later writers the story was a chronicle written on one of the walls of the temple of the goddess Neith, probably in a combination of writing and illustration. Would this chronicle have referred to the collapse of the volcano on Thíra? In any case we can imagine Solon standing before the temple wall while a priest explained to him what was written and depicted there.

A lot has been written about Atlantis and where it must have been located. Crete is just one of the candidates. Because this book is not a scholarly study, we will not enter into an extensive discussion about Atlantis. But a few remarks about the texts may be helpful. In the first place Plato, and probably Solon before him, had a didactic purpose in repeating the story. That, in combination with the necessary translation, could easily have led to certain interpretations which deviate from the original text (see also the beginning of the second quotation given here). In the first quotation, an 'Atlantic Ocean' is mentioned. In our view, this would be a 4th century B.C. interpretation of a 6th century B.C. Greek translation of an Egyptian term which traces back to the 15th century B.C. Now the Egyptians of the 6th century and earlier did not yet know of the Atlantic Ocean. So it was probably the 'Great Green,' the expression the Egyptians used to refer to the sea to the north of their land, which was meant here. This was the only major sea the Egyptians knew through their own experience. The 'Great Green' was closed off on the northern side by Crete and the Greek islands, and these were known to the Egyptians. The 'straits' mentioned in the text are then not those of Gibraltar but rather some other narrows close to Crete, for instance those between Rhodes and Crete. The 'Pillars of Heracles' could refer to the Egyptian name for Crete, Keftiu, which means 'pillar.' 'Tyrrhenia' could be Tuscany in Italy, but could also refer to Asia Minor, because the 'Thyrsenoi' (one of the Sea Peoples) lived there in the 12th century. The 'shoal of mud' mentioned could have been caused by the ash and pumice that landed in the sea to the east of Crete and which made it unnavigable for a long time.

The first quotation comes from the *Timaeus*. A priest from Saïs is speaking to Solon.

Plato, *Timaeus*, 24d - 25d

Many great and wonderful deeds are recorded of your state [namely Solon's state, Athens] in our histories. But one of them exceeds all the rest in greatness and valor. For these histories tell of a mighty power which unprovoked made an expedition against the whole of Europe and Asia, and to which your city put an end. This power came forth out of the Atlantic Ocean, for in those days the Atlantic was navigable, and there was an island situated in front of the straits which are by you called the Pillars of Heracles. The island was larger than Libya and Asia put together, and was the way to other islands, and from these you might pass to the whole of the opposite continent which surrounded the true ocean, for this sea which is within the Straits of Heracles is only a harbor, having a narrow entrance, but that other is a real sea, and the land surrounding it on every side may be most truly called a boundless continent. Now in this island of Atlantis there was a great and wonderful empire which had rule over the whole island and several others, and over parts of the continent, and, furthermore, the men of Atlantis had subjected the parts of Libya within the columns of Heracles as far as Egypt, and of Europe as far as Tyrrhenia. This vast Power, gathered into one, endeavored to subdue at a blow our country [namely Egypt] and yours [Athens] and the whole of the region within the straits, and then, Solon, your country shone forth, in the excellence of her virtue and strength, among all mankind. She was pre-eminent in courage and military skill, and was the leader of the Hellenes. And when the rest fell off from her, being compelled to stand alone, after having undergone the very extremity of danger, she defeated and triumphed over the invaders, and preserved from slavery those who were not yet subjugated, and generously liberated all the rest of us who dwell within the Pillars. But afterward there occurred violent earthquakes and floods, and in a single day and night of misfortune all your warlike men in a body sank into the earth, and the island of Atlantis in like manner disappeared in the depths of the sea. For which reason the sea in those parts is impassable and impenetrable, because there is a shoal of mud in the way, and this was caused by the subsidence of the island.

This is all that is mentioned in the *Timaeus* about Atlantis and its destruction. There is a more extensive description of Atlantis in the *Kritias*. Just before the quotation starts, Kritias has given a description of Athens in the time of Atlantis. He then continues with a description of Atlantis itself. One remark: in classical Greece a *stadion* (stadium, plural *stadia*) was usually equivalent to nearly 200 meters. But as explained, Solon could also have used the expression *stadion* as a Greek word for an Egyptian length measurement. So the lengths mentioned in the quotation need not be taken as real, Greek *stadia*.

Plato, *Kritias*, 113a - 121c

But before I begin my narrative, I must make a brief explanation, or you may be surprised to hear of so many barbarians with Hellenic names. So I will give you the reason for this. Solon had a fancy to turn the tale to account in his own poetry; so he asked questions about the significance of the names and discovered that the original Egyptian authors of the narrative had translated them into their own speech. In his turn, as he learned the sense of a name, he translated it back again, in his manuscript, into our own language. His actual papers were once in my father's hands, and are in my own, to this day, and I studied them thoroughly in my boyhood. So if you hear names like those of our own countrymen, you must not be surprised; I have given you the explanation. Well, then, the story – and a long story it is – began much in this fashion. As we said before, when we were speaking of the 'lots,' [at the beginning of Kritias' description of Athens] the gods divided the whole earth into lots, some larger, some smaller, and established their temples and sacrifices in them. Poseidon, then, thus receiving as his lot the isle of Atlantis, settled his sons by a mortal woman in a district of it which must now be described.

By the sea, in the center of the island, there was a plain, said to have been the most beauteous of all such plains and very fertile, and, again, near the center of this plain, at a distance of some fifty stadia, a mountain which was nowhere of any great altitude. In this mountain lived one of the original earthborn men of that region, named Evenor, with his wife Leucippe. The pair had an only daughter, Clito, who was just husband-high when her mother and father both died. Poseidon desired this damsel, had to do with her, and fortified the hill where she had her abode by a fence of alternate rings of sea and land, smaller and greater, one within another. He fashioned two such round wheels, as we may call them, of earth and three of sea from the very center of the island, at uniform distances, thus making the spot inaccessible to man, for there were as yet no ships and no seafaring. The island left at their center he adorned with his own hand – a light enough task for a god – causing two fountains to flow from underground springs, one warm, the other cold, and the soil to send up abundance of food plants of all kinds. He then begot five twin births of male offspring and divided the whole isle of Atlantis into ten parts. On the earliest-born of the first pair he bestowed their mother's dwelling place with the lot of land surrounding it, the best and largest of all, and appointed him king over his brethren. The rest he made princes, granting each of them the sovereignty over a large population and the lordship of wide lands. Further, he gave names to them all. Their king, the eldest, received a name from which the ocean, as well as the whole island, got its designation; it is called Atlantic, because the name of the first king of old times was Atlas. His younger twin brother, to whose share fell the extremity of the island off the Pillars of Heracles, fronting the region now known as Gadira, from the name of his territory, was called in Greek Eumelus, but in the language his own country Gadirus, and no doubt his name was the origin of that of the district. One of the second pair was called Ampheres, the other Evaemon, the elder of the third Mneseus and his junior Autochthon, the elder of the fourth Elasippus, the younger Mestor; Azaes was the name of the elder of the fifth pair, that of his brother Diaprepes. All these and their descendants for many generations reigned as princes of numerous islands of the ocean besides their own, and were also, as has been already said, suzerains of the population of the hither or inner side of the straits, as far as Egypt and Tyrrhenia.

Now from Atlas sprang a prolific and illustrious house which retained the throne for many generations, the eldest being always king and transmitting the succession to his eldest descendant. They possessed wealth such as had never been amassed by any royal line before them and could not be easily matched by any after, and were equipped with all resources required for their city and dominions at large. Though their empire brought them a great external revenue, it was the island itself which furnished the main provision for all purposes of life. In the first place it yielded all products of the miner's industry, solid and fusible alike, including one which is now only a name but was then something more, orichalch, which was excavated in various parts of the island, and had then a higher value than any metal except gold. It also bore in its forests a generous supply of all timbers serviceable to the carpenter and builder and maintained a sufficiency of animals wild and domesticated; even elephants were plentiful. There was ample pasture for this the largest and most voracious of brutes, no less than for all the other creatures of marsh, lake and river, mountain and plain. Besides all this, the soil bore all aromatic substances still to be found on earth, roots, stalks, canes, gums exuded by flowers and fruits, and they throve on it. Then, as for cultivated fruits, the dry sort which is meant to be our food supply and those others we use as solid nutriment – we call the various kinds pulse – as well as the woodland kind which gives us meat and drink and oil together, the fruit of trees that ministers to our pleasure and merriment and is so hard to preserve, and that we serve as welcome dessert to a jaded man to charm away his satiety – all these were produced by that sacred island, which then lay open to the sun, in marvelous beauty and inexhaustible profusion. So the kings employed all these gifts of the soil to construct and beautify their temples, royal residences, harbors, docks, and domain in general on the following plan.

They first bridged the rings of sea round their original home, thus making themselves a road from and to their palace. This palace they originally built at the outset in the dwelling place of the god and their ancestors, and each monarch, as he inherited it in his turn, added beauties to its existing beauties, always doing his utmost to surpass his predecessor, until they had made the residence a marvel for the size and splendor of its buildings. They began on the seaside by cutting a canal to the outermost ring, fifty stadia long, three hundred feet broad, and a hundred feet deep; the 'ring' could now be entered from the sea by this canal like a port, as the opening they had made would admit the largest of vessels. Further, at these bridges they made openings in the rings of land which separated those of water, just sufficient to admit the passage of a single trireme, and covered the openings in so that the voyage through them became subterranean, for the banks of the rings of earth were considerably elevated above the sea level. The breadth of the largest ring of water, that to which the canal from the sea had been made, was three stadia and a half, and that of the contiguous ring of land the same. Of the second pair, the ring of water had a breadth of two stadia and that of land was once more equal in breadth to the water outside it; the land which immediately surrounded the central islet was in breadth one stadium; the islet on which the palace stood had a diameter of five stadia. So they enclosed this islet with the rings and bridge, which had a breadth of a hundred feet, completely by a stone wall, building towers and gates on the bridges at either end of each passage for the sea water. The stone, black, white, and red, they quarried beneath the whole central islet and outer and inner rings, thus, by the same process, excavating a pair of interior basins for shipping with a roofing of native rock. Some of their buildings were of a single color; in other cases they entertained themselves by intermingling the stones to produce variegated surfaces of an inherently agreeable character. The whole circuit of the outermost wall they covered with a coat, a ceruse [ointment], as one might say, of copper, the inner with melted tin and the wall of the actual acropolis with orichalch, which gleamed like fire.

Within the acropolis was the palace with the following design. In the very center, surrounded by a golden railing, which it was forbidden to enter, was an untrodden sanctuary sacred to Clito and Poseidon, the very place where the race of the ten princes had been first conceived and begotten; here, too, the seasonable offerings were made yearly to each of them from all the ten lots. Poseidon himself had a temple, a stadium long and half a stadium broad, with a proportionate height, but something un-Hellenic in its aspect. The whole exterior of this temple was coated with silver, except the figures on the pediments; these were covered with gold. Within, the roof was of ivory throughout, ornamented with gold, silver, and orichalch, and all the rest, walls, columns, pavement, were covered with orichalch. It contained golden statues of the god standing in a chariot drawn by six winged horses, and on such a scale that his head touched the roof, and of a hundred Nereids round him riding on dolphins, for that was then believed to be the number of the Nereids. It also contained many other statues dedicated by private persons. Outside the temple there stood golden statues of all the wives of those who had been of the number of the ten kings and of themselves, and many other great statues, dedicated by kings and private persons of the country itself and the foreign nations over whom they were suzerain. There was an altar of size and workmanship to match the edifice; the palace, too, was no less worthy of the grandeur of the empire and the magnificence of its temples.

Uses were found for the waters of the two springs, the cold and the warm. The supply from both was copious and the natural flavor and virtues of their waters remarkable. So they were surrounded by buildings and plantations of appropriate trees as well as with a number of basins, some open to the air and others, which were used as warm baths in winter, covered. Of these there were several sets, for the kings, for private citizens, and for women, and yet others for horses and other beasts of burden, each set with its own appropriate equipment. The waste from them was conducted to the grove of Poseidon, where the trees were of every kind and, thanks to the excellence of the soil, of incredible size and beauty, and then let into the outer rings of water by conduits at the bridges. Here, besides numerous temples to different gods, they had constructed a variety of gardens and gymnasiums. Some of the latter were for men; there were others on each of the two islands formed by the rings, specially for horses. In particular, they had a space reserved as a racecourse in the center of the larger of these islands; its breadth was a stadium and the whole length of the circumference was left free for the contests. Round this racecourse on both sides were barracks for the main body of the bodyguards; a number of the more trusty were stationed in the smaller ring, nearer the citadel; to the most eminently trustworthy of all, quarters were assigned within the citadel about the persons of the kings. The dockyards were filled with triremes and their appropriate equipment, all in excellent order. So much, then, for the appointments of the royal residence. When one had passed the three outer harbors, a wall ran all round, starting at the sea, at a uniform distance of fifty stadia from the greatest ring and its harbor, returning on itself at the mouth of the canal from the sea. This wall was completely filled by a multitude of closely set houses, and the large harbor and canal were constantly crowded by merchant vessels and their passengers arriving from all quarters, whose vast numbers occasioned incessant shouting, clamor, and general uproar, day and night.

I have now given you a pretty faithful report of what I once learned of the town and the old palace, and must do my best to recall the general character of the territory and its organization. To begin with, the district as a whole, so I have heard, was of great elevation and its coast precipitous, but all round the city was a plain, enclosing it and itself enclosed in turn by mountain ranges which came right down to the sea. The plain itself was smooth, level, and of a generally oblong shape; it stretched for three thousand stadia in one direction, and, at its center, for two thousand inland from the coast. All through the island this level district faced the south and was thus screened from the cold northerly winds. In those times it was famous for its encircling mountains, which were more numerous, huge, and beautiful than any that exist today. These mountains contained numerous villages with a wealthy population, besides rivers, lakes, and meadows which provided plentiful sustenance for all sorts of animals, wild or domestic, and timber of different kinds in quantities amply sufficient for manufactures of every type.

Well, this plain, in consequence partly of its original structure, partly of the long-continued exertions of a succession of kings, had assumed an aspect which I shall now describe. From the first, it was naturally quadrangular, oblong, and nearly rectangular; departures from that shape had been corrected by the carrying of a fosse round it. As to the depth, breadth, and length of this fosse, it sounds incredible that any work of human hands should be so vast by comparison with other achievements of the kind, but I have to tell the tale as I heard it. It had been dug to the depth of a hundred feet, had everywhere a stadium in breadth, and, as it was carried completely round the plain, its length came to ten thousand stadia. It received the watercourses which came down from the mountains, made the tour of the plain, meeting the city in both directions, and was thence allowed to discharge into the sea. Beyond the city, straight canals of some hundred feet in width, terminated once more at the fosse on the seaside, were drawn across the plain, with a distance of a hundred stadia between every two. They were used for the floating of timber down to the town from the mountains and the conveyance by boat of natural produce generally, oblique channels of cross-communication being cut from these canals to one another and the city. There were actually two harvests in the year; in the winter the husbandmen trusted to the sky for their irrigation, in the summer they looked to the earth, and released the waters of the canals. As to their numbers, each allotment of land was under an injunction to furnish one leader of a military detachment, the area of the allotment was ten stadia by ten, and the total number of these allotments mounted to sixty thousand. The number of units supplied by the mountains and the territory at large was said to be enormous, and all were regularly assigned to the different allotments and leaders according to their districts or villages. Each leader was then enjoined to furnish the army with the following contribution: one-sixth part of a war chariot, up to the full complement of ten thousand such chariots; two chargers with their riders; a pair of horses without car but supplied with a dragoon with light shield and a driver for the pair, to stand behind the combatant; two hoplites, a pair of archers, and the same number of slingers; three light-armed throwers of stones and the same number of javelin men; four marines, up to the full complement of twelve hundred vessels. This was the war equipment of the royal city; in the other nine there were various arrangements which would take much time to describe.

The distribution of power and prerogative was, and had from the first, been this. Each of the ten kings was, in his own territory and government, supreme over persons and, for the most part, over the laws, and could chastise and put to death at his pleasure. But their authority over and intercourse with one another was regulated by the commands of Poseidon, as they were informed by the law and by an inscription left by the earliest kings on a column of orichalch preserved in the sanctuary of Poseidon in the center of the island. Here, in fact, they were accustomed to assemble at alternate intervals of four and five years, thus showing equal respect for even number and odd; in these sessions, they deliberated on their common affairs, made inquiry whether any of them were transgressing the law, and pronounced judgment. When they were to give judgment, they first exchanged pledges in this fashion. In the sanctuary of Poseidon consecrated bulls roamed at large. So the ten came unattended and made prayer to the god that they might capture the victim of his preference. Then they gave chase with wooden clubs and cords only, but no implement of iron; what bull soever they took they brought him to the column and slew him over it, wetting the inscription with his blood. Now there was written on the column, besides the laws, an oath calling down grievous curses on the disobedient. So when they had offered sacrifice after their own ritual and were devoting all the bull's members, they would mingle a bowl of wine, casting in one clot of the blood for each man; the rest of the blood they cast into the fire, first cleansing the column. Then they drew the wine from the bowl in golden beakers, made a libation over the fire, and swore on oath that they would give judgment according to the laws upon the column, would chastise any who had heretofore transgressed, and hereafter transgress none of these ordinances wittingly, neither giving nor obeying commandment save according to the laws of their father. When each had taken this vow for himself and his house after him, he drank and dedicated his beaker in the god's sanctuary, and so betook himself to the banquet and necessary business. When dark fell and the fire of the offerings was burned down, all vested themselves in fair robes of deep blue, and seated themselves so by the embers of their sacrifice, on the bare earth, and by night, quenching all fire in the sanctuary. Thus they gave and received judgment, if any charged any with transgression. Judgment given, when the morning came, they wrote the judgments on a plate of gold and dedicated it and their robes for a memorial. Now there were many more special laws concerning the rights of the several kings, but the chief of these were that they should bear no arms against another and that if any should essay to overthrow the royal house of any city, all should come to its help – but ever in accord with the rule of their ancestors – they should take counsel in common for war and all other affairs, and the chief command should be given to the house of Atlas. Also, the king should have no power over the life of any of his kinsmen, save with the approval of more than half of the ten.

Now this mighty and wondrous power, which then was in that region, the god arrayed and brought against this our own region, the cause, as the tale goes, being this. For many generations, while the god's strain in them was still vigorous, they gave obedience to the laws and affection to the divine whereto they were akin. They were indeed truehearted and greathearted, bearing themselves to one another and to their various fortunes with judgment and humbleness. They thought scorn of all things save virtue and counted their present prosperity a little thing. So they found the weight of their gold and other possessions a light load. Wealth made them not drunken with wantonness; their mastery of themselves was not lost, nor their steps made uncertain. They perceived with the clear vision of the sober that even these things all receive increase from virtue and mutual love, whereas where the first are sought and held in honor, they decay themselves and the others perish with them. So by reason of such thoughts and the divine strain that persisted in them, their wealth in the things of which we have told was still further increased. But when the god's part in them began to wax faint by constant crossing with much mortality, and the human temper to predominate, then they could no longer carry their fortunes, but began to behave themselves unseemly. To the seeing eye they now began to seem foul, for they were losing the fairest bloom from their most precious treasure, but to such as could not see the true happy life, to appear at last fair and blessed indeed, now that they were taking the infection of wicked coveting and pride of power. Zeus, the god of gods, who governs his kingdom by law, having the eye by which such things are seen, beheld their goodly house in its grievous plight and was minded to lay a judgment on them, that the discipline might bring them back to tune. So he gathered all the gods in his most honorable residence, even that that stands at the world's center and over- looks all that has part in becoming, and when he had gathered them there, he said …

Miscellanea

The dialogue suddenly breaks off here. The rest has not been preserved.

Sources and acknowledgements; select bibliography

SOURCES AND ACKNOWLEDGEMENTS

Apollonios Rhodios, *The Argonautika: The Story of Jason and the Quest for the Golden Fleece*, tr. by Peter Green, Berkeley and Los Angeles, California (University of California Press), 1997 (quoted as 'Apollonios Rhodios, *Argonautica*'). © Peter Green. Quotations reprinted by permission of the Publisher. All rights reserved

Callimachus, 'Hymn to Zeus', in: *Hymns and Epigrams*, tr. by A.W. Mair, Loeb Classical Library vol. 129, Cambridge, Mass. (Harvard University Press), 1921 (quoted as 'Callimachus, *Hymn to Zeus*'). Quotations reprinted by permission of the publishers and the Trustees of the Loeb Classical Library. The Loeb Classical Library ™ is a registered trademark of the President and Fellows of Harvard College

Diodorus Siculus, *The Library of History, vol. III*, tr. by C. H. Oldfather, Loeb Classical Library vol. L340, Cambridge, Mass. (Harvard University Press), 1939 (quoted as 'Diodorus Siculus, *Library of History*'). Quotations reprinted by permission of the publishers and the Trustees of the Loeb Classical Library. The Loeb Classical Library ™ is a registered trademark of the President and Fellows of Harvard College

Hesiod, *Works and Days and Theogony*, tr. by Stanley Lombardo, Indianapolis, Indiana, 1993 (quoted as 'Hesiod, *Theogony*'). © Hacket Publishing Company. Quotations reprinted by permission of the Publisher. All rights reserved

[Homer], *Iliad of Homer, the*, tr. by Richmond Lattimore, Chicago and London (University of Chicago Press), 1951 (here quoted from the paperback edition of 1961, as 'Homer, *Iliad*'). © The University of Chicago. Quotations reprinted by permission of the Publisher. All rights reserved

Homer, *The Odyssey*, tr. by Robert Fagles, Harmondsworth (Penguin), 1997 (quoted as 'Homer, *Odyssey*'). © Robert Fagles. Quotation from 'Book 19: Penelope and her Guest' used by permission of the Viking Penguin, a division of Penguin Putnam Inc.

Lear, Edward, *The Cretan Journal*, ed. by Rowena Fowler, Athens and Dedham (Denise Harvey & Company), 1984 (quoted as 'Lear'). © Denise Harvey & Company. Quotations reprinted by permission of the Publisher. All rights reserved

Ovid, *Metamorphoses*, tr. by A.D. Melville, Oxford and New York (Oxford University Press), 1986 (here quoted from the paperback edition of 1998, as 'Ovid, *Metamorphoses*'). © A. D. Melville

Pashley, Robert, *Travels in Crete*, 2 vols, London, 1837 (quoted as 'Pashley')

Plato, *Critias*, tr. by A. E. Taylor, repr. in Plato, *The Collected Dialogues*, ed. by Edith Hamilton and Huntington Cairns, Bollingen Series 71, Princeton, New Jersey (Princeton University Press), 16th printing, 1996 (quoted as 'Plato, *Kritias*')

Plato, *Timaeus*, tr. by Benjamin Jowett, repr. in Plato, *The Collected Dialogues*, ed. by Edith Hamilton and Huntington Cairns, Bollingen Series 71, Princeton, New Jersey (Princeton University Press), 16th printing, 1996 (quoted as 'Plato, *Timaeus*')

Pococke, Richard, *A Description of the East and some other countries*, vol. 2 part 1: Observations on Palestine or the Holy Land, Syria, Mesopotamia, Cyprus, and Candia, London, 1745 (quoted as 'Pococke')

Spratt, Thomas A. B., *Travels and Researches in Crete*, 2 vols, London, 1865 (quoted as 'Spratt')

SELECT BIBLIOGRAPHY

Much has been written on Crete and its past. The following is a selection of secondary literature frequently consulted by the compiler.

Andrianakis, Michalis, *The Old City of Hania*, n.p., n.d.

Cameron, Pat, *Crete*, (Blue Guide), London, 1993

Castleden, Rodney, *Atlantis Destroyed*, London and New York, 1998

Detorakis, T. E., *History of Crete*, Iraklion, 1994

Encyclopaedia of Islam, the, CD-ROM edition, Leiden, 1999

Fisher, John and Geoff Garvey, *Crete*, (The Rough Guides), 1998

Hopkins, Adam, *Crete: Its Past, Present and People*, London and Boston, 1977

Morris, Jan, *The Venetian Empire: A Sea Voyage*, London, 1980

Psilakis, Nikos, *Monasteries and Byzantine Memories of Crete*, Iraklion, 1994

Schneider, Lambert, *Kreta*, (Dumont Kunst Reiseführer), Cologne, 1998

Wachsmann, Shelley, *Seagoing Ships and Seamanship in the Bronze Age Levant*, London, 1998

Index